Triggering Insights

Be conscious of the following types of details you may tend to gloss over in your dreams. Recording them in your dream dictionary can make meanings more evident:

✔ **What are the key elements?**

- How would you describe the dream structure?
- What were the main scenes and settings in the dream?
- Was there a sense of time or direction?
- How was the dream lit?
- What was your viewpoint?
- What characters were present?
- What were the primary images, objects, symbols, or patterns?
- Did numbers occur in the dream?

✔ **What are the motivations?**

- What actions were taken, and by whom?
- What choices or decisions were made, and by whom?

- What outcomes were reached?
- At what speed was the action occurring?
- What statements were made?
- What was left incomplete?
- What impressions did you have about the dream while dreaming?

✔ **What are the feelings?**

- What feelings did you or other characters have?
- What senses were you using to perceive?

✔ **How is each part about you?**

- What do you have in common with each symbol and character?
- How do the emotions, decisions, and actions parallel something in your own life?

Things to Look for in Dreams

✔ Fear and love

✔ Symbols

✔ New informa[tion]

✔ Change poin[ts]

D1005355

Dream Dictionary For Dummies®

Cheat Sheet

Keeping a Dream Diary

A diary helps you monitor your dreams as well as discover themes or how your dreams have become true or insightful. Make the most of your dreams with these tips:

- ✔ **Personalize your diary:** It can be neat and tidy, a large sketchbook with no lines, a simple spiral-bound book, or even a computer.

- ✔ **Use your diary effectively:** Your diary is a record of what's going on in the hidden dimensions of your life. You can use it for more than just recording dreams:

  - Write about your dream goals and your dream-sabotaging ideas.
  - Examine your sleep pattern and cycles.
  - Collect images from magazines, books, flyers, and so on that trigger dreams and make collages, diagrams, and illustrations with those images.
  - Write or copy inspirational quotes, poetry, and prayers.
  - Write about waking dreams, dream fragments, and single symbols.
  - Write the date of each dream and put a star next to important dreams.
  - Write in the present tense, recording as many details as you can.
  - Document your dream incubation statements.
  - Write about dream images that have carried over from the previous day and what happens in the days after an important dream.

- ✔ **Write even if no dreams come:** Commit to writing something every day to make your diary more effective. Here are some ideas:

  - Write about your emotional state.
  - Invent a dream character, dream locale, and a dream theme.

For Dummies: Bestselling Book Series for Beginners

Dream Dictionary FOR DUMMIES®

by Penney Peirce

BICENTENNIAL
1807
WILEY
2007
BICENTENNIAL

Wiley Publishing, Inc.

Dream Dictionary For Dummies®

Published by
Wiley Publishing, Inc.
111 River St.
Hoboken, NJ 07030-5774
www.wiley.com

WILEY

About the Author

Penney Peirce is a gifted intuitive empath, visionary, and author, as well as a popular lecturer, counselor, and trainer specializing in intuition development and its application to personal life and business, She is an expert in dreamwork and expanded perception, working throughout the U.S., Japan, South Africa, and Europe since 1977 as a coach to business executives, psychologists, scientists, other trainers, and those on a spiritual path. She has been involved with The Center for Applied Intuition (scientists and intuition), The Institute for the Study of Conscious Evolution and The Arlington Institute (futurists), and The Kaiser Institute (intuition and hospital boards and CEOs). Penney is known for sophisticated, useful, intriguing insights into the hidden dynamics of what makes for true success. She weaves together teachings in psychology, philosophy, personality typing, and metaphysics with her experience in writing, advertising, design, and corporate art direction. She is the author of several popular guidebooks: *The Intuitive Way: The Definitive Guide to Increasing Your Awareness*, *Dreams For Dummies*, and *The Present Moment: A Daybook of Clarity and Intuition.*

Penney studied at the University of Cincinnati, the New School for Social Research, Columbia, and California Institute of the Arts. She makes her home near San Francisco. Her website is www.intuitnow.com.

Dedication

To my sister, Paula, who has been my friend and sounding board all my life. Though she doesn't remember her dreams as much as I do, she generously makes time to listen to me rattle on about mine.

Author's Acknowledgments

I've been blessed with family, friends, and clients who are good at both giving and receiving. It's so empowering to have flow, stimulating conversation, and honest feedback. I've been tremendously entertained and educated by the dreams these people have shared with me over the years. Plus, working and just talking with them has taught me a tremendous amount about perception.

I've written two *For Dummies* books now, and have enjoyed both experiences. My editors, Lindsay Lefevere and Jennifer Connolly, are very good at what they do, highly professional, and thankfully, patient and kind, as well! They kept me going as I was writing the dictionary section of this book, during times I was having to practice mindfulness and cheerfulness as a way to maintain my intuitive edge as I delved into yet another word and what was contained in its depths.

Finally, I'd like to thank Rod McDaniel for his unflagging support, inspiring suggestions, and enthusiastic belief in my potential.

Publisher's Acknowledgments

We're proud of this book; please send us your comments through our Dummies online registration form located at www.dummies.com/register/.

Some of the people who helped bring this book to market include the following:

Acquisitions, Editorial, and Media Development

Project Editor: Jennifer Connolly

Acquisitions Editor: Lindsay Lefevere

Copy Editor: Jennifer Connolly

Technical Editor: Marcia Emory, PhD

Editorial Manager: Jennifer Ehrlich

Editorial Supervisor:
Carmen Krikorian

Editorial Assistant:
Erin Calligan Mooney, Joe Niesen,
LeeAnn Harney, David Lutton

Cover Photos: © Getty Images

Cartoons: Rich Tennant
(www.the5thwave.com)

Composition Services

Project Coordinator:
Patrick Redmond

Layout and Graphics: Joyce Haughey,
Melanee Prendergast,
Alissa Walker, Erin Zeltner

Proofreaders: Jessica Kramer,
Susan Moritz, Penny Stuart

Indexer: Potomac Indexing, LLC

Wiley Bicentennial Logo:
Richard J. Pacifico

Publishing and Editorial for Consumer Dummies

Diane Graves Steele, Vice President and Publisher, Consumer Dummies

Joyce Pepple, Acquisitions Director, Consumer Dummies

Kristin A. Cocks, Product Development Director, Consumer Dummies

Michael Spring, Vice President and Publisher, Travel

Kelly Regan, Editorial Director, Travel

Publishing for Technology Dummies

Andy Cummings, Vice President and Publisher, Dummies Technology/
General User

Composition Services

Gerry Fahey, Vice President of Production Services

Debbie Stailey, Director of Composition Services

Contents at a Glance

Table of Contents

Introduction

● ●

*W*elcome to a fascinating journey into your inner worlds. Whether you're already a prolific dreamer or are just peeking into the unknown, you're sure to get results from the insights, techniques, and tips provided in *Dream Dictionary For Dummies.* Not only does this book outline important dream skills, this book also provides a totally unique dictionary — a fascinating read in itself — that lists the meanings of hundreds of dream symbols.

Before you delve into the nuts and bolts of how this book is organized, it will help to understand some important points about dreams so you can use your dream life to discover more about your inner self:

- The dream world is not separate from the waking world; they are extensions of each other and are mutually supportive and cocreative.

- Everything you do in dreams is real; it's just happening in other dimensions of your awareness.

- It's normal for your awareness to constantly shift through all the dimensions; you change focus continually, day and night.

- Dreamwork is a way to discover what your whole self, the you beyond your logical mind, is doing.

About This Book

In this book, you find out how to make sense of your dreams and harness them to increase creativity, solve problems, find life purpose, and obtain accurate personal guidance. Even if you just read the dictionary definitions, you can begin to understand symbology in a much deeper way. Dreams teach us so much about what's possible in life. I want your inner dream life to help expand your idea of how big you are, how much knowledge you have to draw from, how much you can accomplish, and how interconnected you are with everything and everyone. This book is designed to help you synchronize your body, emotions, mind, and soul so that you can experience the divine sanity that underlies your life's unfolding.

In the dictionary portion of this book, you can find a unique form of symbol definition. Each word has been defined on three levels (physical, emotional, and mental-spiritual) so that you can be precise and holistic when interpreting your dreams. Sometimes symbols pertain to all the levels at once. The meanings listed in this book are accurate, useful, and modern.

Throughout this book, you encounter dream diary writing exercises that can prompt dream insights. The key to improving your intuition and success with dreams is to make your normally intangible, unconscious inner world more conscious and real. Writing about your dreams and dream process in a diary is an excellent way to do this. I strongly encourage you to record your dreams every morning. In the evening before sleep, write about your dream intentions. Your dream diary can be a record of your inner growth process. I explain tips for doing these things in Chapter 2.

Just as in any *For Dummies* book, you can jump in anywhere, move backward or forward through the material, and find enormous value. If you want a concise mini-course on dreamwork and dream interpretation, read all the chapters in order — I've designed the flow of the material as a developmental process. If you're in a hurry and want to jump right in and see what last night's dream means, go straight to the dictionary.

Conventions Used in This Book

So you can navigate through this book more easily, I use the following conventions:

- *Italic* is used for emphasis and to highlight terms.

- **Bold** is used to indicate key ideas and dictionary words that are defined.

- Sidebars, in gray boxes, give interesting information that isn't critical to understanding the topic at hand.

Foolish Assumptions

I made some assumptions about you as I was writing, and if true, this book will be especially useful in your quest for deeper meaning:

✔ You may be disillusioned by most dream dictionaries because they seem antiquated and not pertinent to today's levels of sophistication about psychological and spiritual growth.

✔ You may be interested in dreams casually, but not quite understand the real power they hold.

✔ You may be so busy and rushed that you don't think you have time to work with your dreams, even though they fascinate you.

✔ You may remember your dreams but not have a variety of useful tools and frameworks to use in decoding them.

How This Book Is Organized

Dream Dictionary For Dummies is divided into three parts and seven chapters. The material flows like this:

Part 1: Decode Your Dreams

Part I gives you the basics for establishing a solid, reliable dream habit and finding the hidden meanings in your dreams. Chapter 1 gets you started. It gives good reasons to dream, helps you understand the basic dream process, and gives tips for enhancing your ability to dream. Chapter 2 helps you activate the key components of the dream process, prepare for sleep and wake up consciously, and keep a dream diary to track your personal dream process. Chapter 3 helps you know your dream territory and recognize and work with physical dreams, emotional dreams, and mental-spiritual dreams. In Chapter 4, you'll dive into decoding symbols and understanding the multiple levels of dream meaning. Chapter 5 takes you into deeper work with decoding your dreams, helping you make sense of all types of dream experience and giving you a variety of methods for uncovering hidden messages.

Part II: Dictionary of Symbols

Part II gives guidelines on how to use a dream diction-ary, and presents a unique way to understand dream symbols. You'll find each word interpreted on three levels, as it might pertain to the physical world, the emotional world, and the mental-spiritual worlds.

Part III: The Part of Tens

Part III provides a little "dream dessert." Here you'll find ten useful techniques for exploring dream mes-sages and ten of the most common dreams and their meanings.

Icons Used in This Book

There are certain nuances of dreamwork that can increase your effectiveness. This icon alerts you to these time- and trouble-saving ideas.

The history of dreams is replete with fascinating tid-bits of information. Watch for this icon to find some fun details.

This icon clues you in to points you definitely should remember.

Keeping a dream diary is one of the best ways to establish a consistent dream life. This symbol indicates a diary writing exercise.

Where to Go from Here

This little book is a powerful tool containing countless insights into the meaning of your inner and outer life. To begin the journey of discovering these secrets, start with your most immediate interest. No matter where you enter this book, you'll find something that pertains to your life and leads to the next curiosity. Doing the exercises and suggested activities will uncover more clues. Stick with it and enjoy your discoveries!

You can gather some friends for a dream support group. Dream groups jumpstart and accelerate the dream process for members, and discovering so many unique, beautiful dream styles is very validating.

Part I
Decode Your Dreams

The 5th Wave   By Rich Tennant

"Well, certainly your friends always said you could be a Super Bowl winning quarterback—in your dreams."

In this part . . .

*P*art I gives you the basics for establishing a solid, reliable dream habit and finding the hidden meanings in your dreams. In Chapter 1, you find good reasons to dream and understand the basic dream process. You can even discover tips for enhancing your ability to dream. Chapter 2 helps you activate the key components of the dream process, prepare for sleep and wake up consciously, and keep a dream diary to track your personal dream process. Chapter 3 helps you know your dream territory and recognize and work with physical dreams, emotional dreams, and mental-spiritual dreams. In Chapter 4, you dive into decoding symbols and understanding the multiple levels of dream meaning. But you can go deeper into dreamwork in Chapter 5, decoding your dreams, helping you make sense of all types of dream experience, and finding a variety of methods for uncovering hidden messages.

Chapter 1

Opening Your Dream Door

• •

*D*reams really are, in the truest sense, a doorway: to greater self-awareness, knowledge, success, and the possibility of a rich, full life. Sounds great, but how do you open and walk through that door? This chapter is a great place to begin. You'll see that there is an actual pathway, with clearly delineated steps, that can take you from wishful thinking about dreams to a reliable dream habit. You'll find your previously mysterious, invisible inner life can be revealed on a regular basis to assist you in many useful ways.

In this chapter, you'll discover some specific bene-fits of an active dream life, familiarize yourself with the steps in the dream process, and fine tune your understanding of sleep and dream dynamics. This way, you can build motivation and enthusiasm, be aligned with the natural flow of dreams, and get out of your own way by becoming aware of what inhibits dreaming.

Dreaming Fully

You can engage with the dream process better after you have some ideas about what dreaming does. Scientists write dreams off as the haphazard firing of neurons in the brain, but when you work deeply with dreams over time, you begin to understand them quite differently, seeing their spiritual roots. The following sections will help stretch your context for dreaming and inspire you about their vital importance in maintaining a healthy and happy life.

The function of dreams

The best way to begin understanding more about your dream life is to first understand how dreams function:

- **Dreams are restorative.** When you have uninterrupted sleep and go through a series of deepening dream cycles during the night, you touch into and revisit your spiritual core and life purpose. Dreaming helps you stay on track, remember who you really are, how you fit into the whole, and renew yourself with fresh life energy and motivation.

- **Dreams are about creation; the ultimate Dreamer is your soul.** Most cultures where mystical spiritual experience is valued believe that the soul projects (think "movie projector") or "dreams" the personality and entire physical life into being. "Life is but a dream," we so often hear. When you remember that you are the soul, or the Dreamer, and not the dream itself, you have more power to change the "dream" and create a life where your destiny can unfold instead of suffering and pain. You're not stuck! Dreams show you what's possible. All you have to do is dream something different! You are only as limited as your imagination.

✔ **Dreams are about learning to be superconscious — and you're learning 24 hours a day.** You are dreaming not only at night but during your daytime waking reality, too. Your nighttime dream world is as real to your soul as your daytime world. They feed into each other, inform each other, teach each other. You, the soul, are never unconscious! You are always focusing on themes and issues that further your growth, flowing through different realms of your awareness. By interpreting day and night dreams, you can discover what's going on in your innermost life.

What's in it for you?

A productive dream life begins with being fired up and motivated. You won't get started or stick with it unless you understand the benefits that dreaming provides. So I've listed some important ways you can improve your life by working with dreams:

✔ **Entertain yourself and grow your imagination.** Dreams give you many interesting, fun things to talk about with your spouse, friends, and family.

If you do nothing more than fly without an airplane or interact with dragons in your dreams, you'll be far richer than if you'd lived by logic alone. Dreams keep you childlike and open, and help promote a free, joyful spirit. Since anything goes in dreams, it's not much of a stretch to extend the same dynamic imagination to your waking reality. Imagination may be one of the most undervalued skills you have. It determines the quality of your life, since what you can imagine is truly as far as you'll let yourself go. Dreams show you it's not so hard to move beyond your comfort zone.

✓ **Discover what's what in your psyche.** Dreams provide firsthand contact with the fascinating mystery: "Who am I?" They teach you about your psychological process and the subconscious beliefs and fears that interfere with growth and happiness. Your dreams can show you how to be more flexible, tolerant, loving, and lovable.

✓ **Tap your inner wisdom.** Dreams relay accurate, inspired advice from your higher mind, or soul, the part of you that always knows the truth. They may even warn of problems that are brewing, or help you prepare for an upcoming event. Dreams reveal your unlimited creativity and notify you when you're off center and need to realign with your life purpose.

✓ **Be all that you can be.** Dreams expand your sense of personal identity because you realize you're composed of energy, emotions, thoughts, and higher patterns of awareness. You'll start thinking of yourself as more than a physical body and will have access to new realms of experience that empower you to be more, know more, and do more.

✔ **Develop intuition and innovation.** Recalling dreams, interpreting them, and intending them are all acts that require intuition and imagination. The more you work with dreams, the more you'll learn to trust yourself, and you'll realize how naturally intuitive and creative you are.

✔ **Increase real life success.** Dreams help you in real ways — with problem solving, decision making, improving communication, healing yourself and others, even manifesting the help and resources you need. The dream state is a fertile field awaiting the seeds you sow.

✔ **Melt barriers of time and space.** Dreams expand your capacity to know things that are in the past, the future, in other locations, and other dimensions of reality. Dreams that come true, or give you information you couldn't obtain by normal means, can open you to know, not just theorize, that we are all much more vast than we realize.

Understanding the Steps in the Dream Process

To develop a conscious, intentional dream practice and receive the full benefit from your dreams (for more on the benefits of dreaming, see the section

"What's in it for you?" earlier in this chapter), it helps to know the steps in the dream process. Each step is important and each feeds energy to the others. Drop one step out and the whole process falls apart. The following stages are expanded in more detail in subsequent chapters. The more times you repeat the full sequence of the following steps, the stronger and more second nature your dream habit will become:

1. **Intend to remember a dream.** The best way to launch your dream process is to have a strong resolution to know your own mysteries. Then be more specific. You can prepare your awareness to be fertile and receptive, but if you want to dream, you must have a need or curiosity that serves as an energetic magnet. Decide what kind of dream, experiences you want to have. Do you want to visit an exotic place or connect with a relative who's died? Do you want to heal psychological or physical wounds? Perhaps you'd like to go to school or to the inventor's library and learn about future technologies. Maybe you need help solving a problem. Pick something specific or ask for general guidance; then program your subconscious mind before sleep. For example: "I will remember my most important dream in the morning." Or, "Bring me an insight concerning which job offer to accept."

2. **Sleep well; wake up well.** If you're too stressed or wake often during the night, your dream cycles will be disturbed. If you try a few pointers from the lists of dream inhibitors and

dream enhancers later in this chapter, you can learn to get a better night's sleep. When you wake in the morning, take a few moments to gently rise from the depths of sleep, to come back to daily reality slowly, so you can maintain a connection with your dreams. Maintain the subtle feelings and sensations in your body before your mind kicks into gear.

3. **Recognize dream activity.** It's important to develop a habit of turning your attention immediately to your dreams as you awake. Let your first thought of the day be: What have I just been doing? Dreams come in various forms: a cinematic saga, a fragment, a single symbol or word, or even a highlighted experience later in the day after you awake. Speak in present tense about dreams: I'm swinging on a rope, jumping from tree to tree. I sense I might fall. Speaking to yourself in the past tense can distance you from the dream.

4. **Record your dream.** Once you've learned to preserve your live connection with your dreams, you must do something to make the dreams real and physical to your body. This way your body, which is intimately connected with your subconscious mind, knows you meant what you said the night before when you asked to remember your experiences in other dimensions, and it will cooperate. If you do nothing, your body will think you're crying "Wolf!" So tell someone right away, describe the dream into a recorder, or write it in your dream diary!

5. **Decode the message.** Making sense of your dream is perhaps the most daunting step, but also the most fun. There are many techniques for discovering the hidden messages in dreams, and you will find lots of ideas in this book. This is where you will determine what dream zone you've been visiting, where you'll use the dream dictionary and penetrate into your dream symbols. This is where you'll ask yourself: How is this dream image, dream choice, dream action, dream emotion, part of a process I'm going through right now in my waking life? How are the dream elements part of a life lesson I'm learning so I can become more of my true self? Bringing the subliminal into conscious awareness validates the process.

Remember, you are always the best interpreter of your dreams, though asking for insight from others can often be helpful.

6. **Follow through.** If your dream contains guidance, insight, a warning, an answer to a problem, an inspiring image, or an intriguing thought, use the information. Follow through on what you receive, because this is why you dreamed the dream in the first place — so you could discover more about yourself. Using dreamtime insights in daily life reinforces your intention to connect the two halves of your experience, completes the dream cycle, and frees you to move into a new phase of exploration and creativity.

7. **Do it all again.** When establishing a reliable dream habit, your subconscious mind will engage fully and bring you dreams consistently after you repeat this process at least three times. Some people say seven times, just to be sure.

Tuning In to Your Dreamtime Dynamics

Science tells us that everyone dreams for a total of approximately two or three hours per night. Robbed of vital dream activity through sleep deprivation or stress, we become irritable and disoriented, and will balance ourselves by dreaming excessively the first chance we get.

The dreams of children are shorter than those of adults and often contain animals and monsters. Nearly 40 percent of children's dreams are nightmares, which may be part of the normal developmental process of learning to cope.

In the following sections, you explore the stages of the natural sleep/dream cycle you progress through several times each night, and I give you various ways you can improve your sleep/dream cycle.

Know your dream cycles

Every night you rotate through four basic phases of sleep that repeat approximately every 90 minutes. During these cycles, you oscillate between awareness that is close to waking reality and awareness that penetrates deep into the collective, spiritual realms. What's important to understand here is that if your deep sleep cycles are disturbed, you may not be able to renew your vitality and sense of purposefulness easily.

- ✔ **Phase one:** Brainwaves slow from their waking frequency, called *beta*, to the more relaxed *alpha* state, where you may feel you are floating, and pictures may drift through your mind. Your muscles relax, and your pulse, blood pressure, and temperature drop slightly.

- ✔ **Phase two:** Your brainwaves slow more until they reach the level known as *theta*. You are now in a light sleep state characterized by many bursts of brain activity. Most dreams occur at this level, during which the eyes move back and forth rapidly beneath the eyelids. This is known as Rapid Eye Movement, or *REM sleep,* and it lasts from several minutes to an hour.

During REM sleep, your extremities may twitch, but most of your body is paralyzed. Your heart may beat erratically, and breathing can become irregular and shallow. When awakened, you easily remember your dreams. A newborn infant experiences eight to ten hours of REM sleep per day. By age five, a child's sleep pattern has become almost the same as an adult's.

- ✔ **Phases three and four:** In the third and fourth phases, about 20 to 45 minutes after you fall asleep, your brainwaves finally reach the ultra-slow, regular *delta* frequency, which produces a deep, "dead sleep." You progress from 20 percent delta waves in phase three to over 50 percent in phase four. If awakened during either of these stages, you feel fuzzy and lost; so resist waking fully, and drop back to sleep immediately.

Dream breakthroughs

Many people have made discoveries while dreaming. Here are some examples of extraordinary breakthroughs that can inspire you to pay close attention to the deeper meanings of your dreams:

✓ **Friedrich August von Kekule:** A professor of chemistry in Ghent, von Kekule had been searching for the molecular structure of benzene. In 1865, while dozing before his fire, he dreamed of a snake seizing its own tail. He awoke suddenly with the revolutionary idea that certain organic compounds are not open structures, but form closed chains or rings.

✓ **Melvin Calvin:** A 1961 Nobel Laureate in chemistry for his work with photosynthesis, Calvin, while daydreaming in his parked car, recognized the structure of phosphoglyceric acid in a matter of seconds.

✓ **William Blake:** The English artist and poet William Blake, while searching for a less expensive method of engraving his illustrated songs, dreamed his dead younger brother, Robert, appeared to him and revealed a process of copper engraving, which Blake immediately tested, verified, and began using.

✓ **Elias Howe:** Howe, who invented the sewing machine, couldn't figure out how the needle would work. He dreamed he was taken prisoner by natives who danced around him with spears that had holes near their tips. He changed his design to incorporate the dream's idea and it worked!

Enhance your dream ability

Like so many people today, you may be working too many hours, or splitting your time between too many people and activities. You may be living on the surface of yourself, feeling frustrated, disgruntled, and fragmented. By the time bedtime comes, you're probably too keyed up to sleep well. In the morning you may still be too tired to think seriously about the "luxury" of interpreting your dreams. Put some attention on the need to harmonize the flow of your sleep cycle and dream process by eliminating dream inhibitors and focusing on dream enhancers. By doing so, you can nurture yourself and maximize your success in all areas of your life. Familiarize yourself with the following things that either detract from or add to dreaming proficiency:

✔ **Dream inhibitors:** Drugs such as marijuana, cocaine, barbiturates, sleeping pills, tranquilizers, muscle relaxants, many mood-stabilizing drugs, as well as alcohol, tobacco, and stimulants like caffeine and amphetamines — can delay sleep, reduce your amount of REM sleep, and your ability for dream recall. Dream activity also can decrease when you are socially overactive and too stressed. Too much aerobic exercise close to bedtime tends to release adrenaline, which can prevent sleep.

✔ **Dream enhancers:** Dream activity occurs more frequently when you've been engaged in quiet, private activities like meditating, reading, studying, or after a period of new learning. Eating foods like turkey, milk, bananas, or cheese, that contain the amino acid tryptophan, before bed can have a sedating effect. Vitamin B complex, especially B6, has been shown to produce more vivid dreams, as has the herb St. John's Wort. The hormone melatonin seems to help regulate your body clock, and even a small amount has been shown to help induce drowsiness. Ask your physician before you take any kind of supplements, however, and be sure not to exceed the recommended doses. A warm bath before bed can also lead to dreaming, since as you cool down afterward, you tend to get sleepy.

Chapter 2

Increasing Dream Recall

• •

*B*ringing dreams back from the dream world is both a science and an art. If you follow some proven principles and pay attention to your attitude and intuition, you can easily recall your dreams. The key is: The more you remember your dreams, the more you'll remember your dreams! In this chapter, I show you how to prepare to dream and how to develop a reliable dream habit.

Starting the Flow with a Positive Attitude and Open Intuition

In Chapter 1, I outline the steps in the dream process. You can maximize the results from that process by following these tips to keep your attitude positive and your intuition open:

✔ **Keep your attitude positive by being enthusias-tic about the power of dreams.** Start with a posi-tive, expectant attitude. Talk to yourself about what exists: what you *do* enjoy, what you *are* doing, what you *have* now. Prime yourself with curiosity and let it percolate. A soft, receptive, nonjudgmental attitude helps the perfect dream occur. Record your dreams happily and gratefully; this tells your subconscious mind that it did a good job.

✔ **Keep your intuition open by trusting yourself and the process.** Whatever you receive is just right because your soul is running the show! Stay neutral, centered in your body, and in the moment when doing dreamwork. Be true to your own sense of things, find similarities between ideas and themes, and be honest about what's real. Trust first impressions but penetrate into the core with sustained attention.

Dream recall decreases when you're stressed and anxious, yet increases with enthusiasm. Also, dreamwork decreases with depression and increases when you're calm and centered.

Creating a Dream Motive

To facilitate your dream recall, it helps to keep your motivation strong by first clearing any blocks in your subconscious mind. These fear-based ideas can interfere with your receiving the dream insights you need to further your personal growth. First, let's get an idea of some sample blocks; then you can pinpoint your own sabotaging ideas and dissolve them. After that, I'll show you how to build your dream motive through heightened curiosity and the habit of noticing symbolic images.

Clear subconscious blocks

You won't let yourself remember dreams if doing so makes you scared or unhappy. True, it's uncomfortable to face your "dark side," but clearing subconscious fear brings relief, gives you permission to get more out of life, and produces an immediate increase in dream range and recall. Your subconscious might block dreams for a variety of reasons; for example, if you remember your dreams:

- You might have to admit you know more than you let on to others and yourself.

- You might have to experience your anger concerning your father.

- You might discover how preoccupied you are with sex and won't be able to be the "good girl" anymore.

- You might dream that someone you love is going to die, and you don't want to know "bad" things.

- You might have to admit your girlfriend isn't the best partner for you.

To discover and clear your dream blocks, try the following writing exercise:

1. **Quiet your mind.** Make a list of responses to the following statements:

    I do not want dreams to bring me information about _____.

    I do not want dreams to make me have to feel _____.

I do not want dreams to change my life
by _____.

I do not want dreams to overwhelm me
by _____.

2. **Look at the answers and ask yourself:** Why
not? Why not have information about monsters? Why not feel what it's like to fall? Why
not change my life by quitting a job that bores
me? Write about how, if you allowed each
thing, your life might improve.

List some trigger questions

Curiosity is a great motivator! By periodically making
a list of intriguing questions — things you want to
know about — you will prime your subconscious
to use dreams as vehicles for answers. Later we'll
work with incubating a specific dream, but for now
let's just free up your imagination! I've given some
examples in the following list; you can add others
that address your important needs and greatest
curiosities:

✔ What do I need to know about my body to
   improve my health?

✔ What beliefs are interfering with my seeing my
   current life situation clearly?

✔ What is the next growth phase of my career?

✔ How can I connect with my grandparents who
   died?

- ✔ How can I improve my relationship with my spouse?

- ✔ What is causing my child's anxiety and irritability, and what can I do about it?

- ✔ How can I move through my writer's block and jumpstart my creativity?

Notice symbolic images

Another good way to prompt the dream flow is to notice things that seem dreamlike or symbolic during the day. Perhaps you see a vibrant flower with a dragonfly on it, a person fixing a flat tire, or a child holding a large dog in her arms. Any of these could be in an actual dream scene because they contain meaning-loaded symbols. Keep a notebook and jot down images or events that seem intriguing. By building the habit of noticing symbols, you'll increase the tendency to recall your nighttime dream symbols. When you start working more deeply with symbol interpretation in Chapters 4 and 5, you'll be speaking the language of symbols much more fluently. Here are some examples of dreamlike images from daily life:

- ✔ Your car won't start.

- ✔ There is thick fog in the morning.

- ✔ A crow sits on the fence and caws at you.

- ✔ You break a tooth.

- ✔ You find a twenty-dollar bill.

Preparing for Sleep

To grease the wheels of the dream cycle, remember that your daytime reality connects to your night-time reality, and the night to the day, in an ongoing continuum. By making an intentional connection between day and night, then night and day, you'll see the current themes in your life more clearly, and more cohesive information will come through your sleep dreams, daydreams, and waking dreams.

For example, you may be unconsciously involved in a debilitating codependent relationship by day, dream at night that your partner is secretly poisoning you, daydream about a past romantic partner who embodied healthy characteristics, see an animal being inordinately affectionate, and start to sob without realizing why you're so moved. All of this is your soul speaking to you in dream language about loving yourself more.

To be more aware 24 hours a day, I show you how to prepare for sleep in an intentional way, and then how to wake up more consciously.

Review and complete the day

Before you drop into your dream world, take stock of what you accomplished during the day and what you wanted to do when you set out in the morning. This frees your mind to pay attention to what you do in your dreams and helps you dream more intentionally. Some questions to ask:

- ✔ Did I do what I wanted to do today?

- ✔ Am I proud of the way I behaved? Did I treat anyone badly that I'd like to make amends for tomorrow?

- ✔ Was I wasteful? disciplined? playful?

- ✔ What am I grateful for that happened today?

Set your intention to dream

Next, take some quiet time to review your trigger questions, pressing needs, or childlike curiosities. What experiences do you want to have in your dreams? Do you want to visit an old friend, fly without a plane, learn more about plants, solve a career problem, talk to spiritual guides, or help others? Once you have a goal, try the following technique to align your body and mind for dreaming:

1. **Think enthusiastic, imaginative thoughts.** Dreams are *so* wonderful! It's going to be fun to dream tonight. I'm going to pay special attention to (flying)!

2. **As you prepare for sleep, sit on the side of your bed, close your eyes, and talk to yourself about your intentions.** Tell yourself:

I am relaxed and ready. My body knows exactly how to have the perfect dream. My intuition is functioning perfectly to deliver my dream accurately to my mind. My mind knows how to recognize my most important dreams and describe them in detail. My soul knows what I really need to know. I trust all my parts.

Once you've aligned yourself, try this exercise to incubate a specific dream:

1. **Put attention at the back of your neck where your head and neck join.** Nod your head up and down so you can feel the spot exactly.

2. **Imagine a small ball of golden light floating in front of you.**

3. **Think about what you want to achieve in your dreams and formulate a concise sentence describing your goal.** Make it simple and specific. In the morning when I wake up, I will remember my most important dreams. Or, I will fly in my dreams tonight and remember my flying dreams. Or, I will wake with an insight about how I can heal my back pain.

4. **Repeat the sentence several times, and then visualize it.** Put it inside the ball of golden

light. Let the light illuminate and activate the sentence.

5. **Place the ball of golden light, with its dream seed, inside the back of your neck at that magic spot.** Let the soft warm light gently penetrate and dissolve into your reptile brain and carry your message to the place where it can be acted upon. Relax and trust that this will occur as you sleep, and in the morning, you'll wake refreshed with the response you've requested. When you feel at ease, happy, and confident, lie down and go to sleep, smiling.

Dedicate your bedroom to dreaming. Instead of using your bed as an office, think of your bedroom as a personal sleep sanctuary. To quiet your bedroom, remove noisemakers like television, radio, and telephone. Move the bookcases to another room. Meditate in bed, sitting up, before sleep, or use the time to write in your dream diary.

Waking Up Consciously

The next part of working with the continuous circuit of day and night is to complete your nighttime experience by recalling and recording your dreams, then setting clear intentions for the day, which you will review the next night before sleep. To do that, you

must wake up with the least amount of disturbance.
If you're jangled awake by a loud alarm or barking
dogs, your connection to your dreams can easily be
broken. Consider having an alarm go off in another
room, waking to soft music, or having a light turn on
automatically.

If you sleep like a log and wake too groggy to remember
a dream, try a sequence of waking mechanisms that
builds in intensity: A light goes on, music in another
room sounds, and finally an alarm next to your bed
rings. Before sleep, suggest to yourself that you'll
notice each of the signals and wake progressively
with each.

Maintain soft awareness

Leaving extra time for dreamwork in the morning
pays off. Float a moment or two before your "to do"
mind kicks in. That soft, still mental state helps
you stay connected to the frequency of the dream
world, and your dreams often pop up magically.
Here are some recall tips to practice first thing
after waking:

- Say to yourself: What have I just been doing?
  Where have I been?

- Keep the subtle sensations in your body.

- Scan internally for the most predominant images
  floating in your soft awareness.

✔ Describe the images, subtle feelings or emotions, and actions you've taken in the dream in present tense.

✔ Make your dreams conscious and real. Tell someone, describe the dream into a recorder, or write it in your diary. You don't have to interpret the dream right now.

Create your day intentionally

After recording your dreams, turn your attention to the day. Collect yourself; be centered and calm. What's left from yesterday that you want to complete today? You're creating your day the same way you created your dreams. Tonight, before sleep, you'll review and complete your daytime goals. Make a list of your intentions:

✔ What impact do I want to have on other people, and on the world, today?

✔ What kind of experience and attitude do I want to have today?

✔ What do I want to give and receive today?

Recalling Your Dreams by Keeping a Dream Diary

Writing about your dreams helps make them more real to your body, which reinforces the dream habit.

A diary is a great way to monitor your dreams, see what themes you've been focusing on, and how your dreams have come true or been insightful. Here I show you how to make the most of your dream diary.

Personalize your diary

To help build the "fun" factor, so important to motivating yourself to have a rich dream life, make your diary a favorite object. Fill it with stimulating sensory elements, interesting things to pay attention to, and useful organization and design ideas:

- ✔ **Are you neat and tidy?** A small, bound journal with a tasteful design on the cover, smooth paper, and narrow lines might suit you.

- ✔ **Are you colorful, impulsive, and dramatic?** You might like a large sketchbook with pages that fall open easily with no restricting lines. Or maybe you'd prefer a cheap spiral-bound notebook from the drugstore.

- ✔ **Type your dreams in a computer cyber-diary.** Using a cyber-diary is a speedy way for you to edit and add on, but it isn't quite as tactile and sensory as a paper journal, and doesn't stimulate the dream centers as well.

- ✔ **Divide each page in half vertically or horizontally.** Use half to record your dreams, and half to divine the meaning. Or use two-thirds of the page for dreams and a third as a margin for notes.

You can capture your dream in the middle of the night by having your diary or a piece of paper handy along with a pen light.

Use your diary effectively

Think of your dream diary as a record of what's going on in the hidden dimensions of your life. You're a private eye on a stakeout, conducting surveillance. Besides recording your dreams, you can use your diary for other things as well. Try any of these ideas:

- ✔ Write about your dream goals and your dream-sabotaging ideas.

- ✔ Examine your sleep pattern and cycles.

- ✔ Collect images from magazines, books, flyers, and so on, that trigger dreams and make collages, diagrams, and illustrations with those images.

- ✔ Write or copy inspirational quotes, poetry, and prayers.

- ✔ Write about waking dreams, dream fragments, and single symbols.

- ✔ Write the date of each dream and put a star next to important dreams.

- ✔ Write in the present tense, recording as many details as you can.

- ✔ Document your dream incubation statements.

- ✔ Write about dream images that have carried over from the previous day and what happens in the days after an important dream.

Use the back of your diary

Create a section in the back of your diary where you keep ongoing lists. It stimulates your imagination to see so many ideas clustered together, and you may notice repeating themes that will factor into your interpretations. Here are some possible lists:

- ✔ **My many faces:** What myriad roles do you play in your dreams?

- ✔ **My dreamscapes:** Where do you travel and what places do you frequent in your dreams?

- ✔ **My dream teams:** Who do you dream about?

- ✔ **My dream symbols:** What images repeat in your dreams? What images surprise you and why?

- ✔ **My dream themes:** What issues concern or bother you in your dreams? What activities are you repeatedly focusing on in your dreams?

Write even if no dreams come

You'll remember dreams more consistently if you commit to writing something — a dream or pseudo-dream — in your diary every day. Here are some ideas that can make writing in your diary more rewarding:

- ✔ **Write about your emotional state.** If you can't recall a dream after you programmed one, write about the emotional state you woke up in, how your body feels, your first thoughts, or the first person who comes to mind. It's important to give your body the message that you meant what you said the night before. So, make up a dream; your body won't know the difference, and your dream habit will grow stronger.

✔ **Invent a dream character, dream locale, and a dream theme.** Start your story with Once upon a time . . . . Describe the physical landscape. Ask: What does this character need? Let your character ask a question. Exaggerate whenever you can. Describe things using lots of sense-oriented adjectives and adverbs. Who's innocent, who's the bad guy, and who's the good guy? Have the characters learn something. Create a title a five year old would like.

Take your dream diary with you when you travel. Most people report that dreams are more active when they are away from their routine and sleep in new places.

Chapter 3

Identifying Dream Activity

● ●

*A*s you prepare to find the meaning of your dreams, you'll want to know what kinds of dreams are possible. Identifying the categories and focus of your dreams is one of the first steps in dream interpretation. Dreams appear both at night and during the day, and they occur within several distinct realms or zones of awareness, fulfilling various functions. In this chapter, I show you the differences between, and how to work constructively with, the physical, emotional, and mental-spiritual dream zones.

Knowing Your Dream Territory

Dreams cover a lot of territory, bringing you insight about mundane things like solving problems at work and preventing illness, or loftier things like helping you stay on purpose spiritually. Dreams also reveal ways your energy and awareness can be stuck, through repressed, blocked emotions, or locked-in beliefs you've never examined. During the night and day, your dreams speak to you on one or all of the following levels:

- ✓ Your subconscious mind (suppressed fears and ideas that block soul expression) and your super-conscious mind (wisdom and love that free soul expression).

- ✓ Your body and physical life, your emotional life, your fixed beliefs and important new ideas, and your spiritual destiny and life purpose.

- ✓ Your individual growth process, other people and their growth processes, the evolution of your relationships, and society's collective process of evolution.

- ✓ Or they may speak to you on many levels of your-self simultaneously.

Notice waking dreams and daydreams

Your soul dreams your entire waking world into existence, and no Hollywood director can rival its mastery over plot, dialogue, timing, and special effects. When you need a wake-up call or a clue to a new direction, your soul can create an experience — a waking dream — that gets your attention through shock, drama, humor, or amazing coincidence and synchronicity.

A *waking dream* is a real-time standout symbol or experience that seems like a "sign," or a short series of images tied together in an attention-getting way. These experiences have an emphasis that makes you want to pay closer attention. In Chapter 2, I ask you to notice dreamlike images during the day to prime your mind to focus on symbols so you can bring more symbols back from your nighttime dreams, but also so you can begin to interpret waking dreams and daydreams.

There are hidden messages in waking dreams, and they can be interpreted just like nighttime dreams. Here are some examples of what waking dreams might mean:

- ✔ **Waking dream:** You're not sure you should go out with your old lover, and the day before your date, your car's clutch breaks and you can't drive.

  Possible meaning: You're telling yourself that being with this person again could handicap your full self-expression.

- ✔ **Waking dream:** On a driving trip you see three dead owls on the roadside in an hour.

  Possible meaning: You are drawing your attention to the need to pay more attention to the wisdom of your body, mind, and spirit.

- ✔ **Waking dream:** You've been criticized for being insensitive. In the early morning as you're jogging, two spotted fawns cross your path and aren't afraid of you.

Possible meaning: You need to feel more innocent and share your heart energy with others more.

↙ **Waking dream:** Your sink, dishwasher, and toilet back up and overflow.

Possible meaning: You need to clear an emotional block that is clogging your creative flow and life force.

Daydreams may be a little harder to recognize at first, because you tend to be absent-minded or "spaced out" while they're occurring. See if you can catch some of your flights of fancy, subliminal conversations with imaginary characters, or unconscious visions and wishes, and then write about your underlying concerns, desires, and growth themes in your dream diary.

If it takes less than five minutes to fall asleep, you're probably sleep-deprived. The ideal drop-off time is 10-15 minutes, meaning you're tired enough to sleep deeply, but haven't been exhausted all day. Sleep apnea or deprivation can sometimes cause overactive *hypnogomic* visions as you're falling asleep, or *hypnopompic* hallucinations as you're waking up. For example, you may hear a dream's soundtrack, feel things that aren't there, or glimpse vivid dream fragments while you're half awake.

Notice the dream zones

All dream experiences are real at some level. Dreams are always about a process of growth, and they occur in one of the *dream zones* or dimensions of awareness:

- ✔ Physical
- ✔ Emotional
- ✔ Mental-spiritual

When interpreting your dreams, you'll start by identifying what part of your growth process you're working on. Is your dream about a problem in your physical world, like needing to sell your house? Are you focusing on your emotional world and a fear of displeasing someone, or how angry you are about a betrayal? Are you focusing on your mental-spiritual realm, wanting to receive new information and inspired guidance? By knowing the dream zone, you can more easily pinpoint the source of the issues you're trying to understand, dissolve, or create.

Notice movement between zones: Flying, falling, diving, climbing

During both day and night, you move constantly through the dream zones, shifting your awareness up or down in frequency. When you "space out" during the day, for example, you're actually ascending into higher zones, and when you shudder suddenly, you're descending to the physical world in a rush of consciousness. At night, the movement between dream zones might be symbolized by flying, falling, climbing, or diving. Ascending with or without a vehicle is a representation of the mind expanding to a higher zone or dimension. Descending, via an elevator or staircase or by free falling, is a symbol of your mind returning to the "lower, slower" physical reality.

The most important part of dream interpretation is being able to track what your inner awareness is actually doing. The basic movement of your consciousness between zones accounts for many of the symbols you will encounter.

Recognizing and Working with a Physical Dream

Many dreams deal with the functioning of the physical world. Some of the topics of physical zone dreams are:

- **Daily residue:** You watch a scary movie before bed, argue with your mate, or bring a problem home from work, then continue to process it in a dream.

- **Health and healing:** You receive information about a disturbance in your energy flow, or body, so you can avoid a budding health problem. Martha dreamed she entered a rehab center, and the counselor gently took a glass of wine out of her hand. She hadn't realized she was drinking too much.

✔ **Problem solving and decision making:** You
receive guidance so you can proceed in your
life. An interior designer needed an innovative
focal point for a large wall and dreamed of using
ladders in an odd, interesting arrangement.

✔ **Skill development:** You accelerate your learning by practicing in your dreams a new ability
you're trying to learn in waking life. Jenn, a
new professor, worried about being good
enough in front of her large classes and dreamed
repeatedly of public speaking until she was
totally comfortable.

Recognize physical symbols

As you learn to work with symbols in the next chapters,
it will help to recognize images that pertain to physical
processes. Here are some examples of physical zone
symbols:

✔ **State of your body:** Jar, earthenware pot, bowl,
cup, glass, cave, basement, house, room, closet,
train, bus, car, trailer, motorcycle, bicycle, tree,
actual organs, tumors, body parts, aura

✔ **Body processes:** Eating, drinking, chewing,
urinating, defecating, vomiting, washing,
shaving, swelling, growing, flowing, breathing,
stoppages

✔ **Health issues:** Hospital, clinic, doctors, nurses,
surgery, massage or bodywork, energy healing,
acupuncture, bandages, casts, X-rays, injec-
tions, construction, digging, sculpting, jogging,
exercising

Make a physical dream work for you

Try the following writing exercise to track your "daily residue" dreams:

1. **Look through your dream diary for dreams that might have been triggered by something that happened in daily life.** Did the dream provide further insights that you applied? What happened right after you had the dream? Write about these things in your diary.

2. **When you find a connection between a perception in waking reality and a similar dream, write about the underlying theme.** What was it about the original trigger experience that made you focus on it so much that you needed to dream about it? What is your soul telling you?

Recognizing and Working with an Emotional Dream

Every time you express or deny intensity of feeling, you can be sure there is fodder for a powerful emotional dream. Though dreams from the emotional zone can be disturbing, they provide guidance about clearing blocks to superconscious experience. Some topics of emotional zone dreams are:

✔ **Psychological processing:** You root out fears, pain, vulnerabilities, blind spots, and subconscious blockages so you can become conscious of what holds you back, clear it, and be courageous and free. You may dream about fears of being powerless, in pain, unworthy, unsuccessful, out of control, overwhelmed, victimized, rejected, losing loved ones, changing, dying, or facing the void.

✔ **Taboos:** You explore forbidden territory, inhibitions, and suppressed desires, often about sex, crime, or antisocial behavior, as a way to free self-expression. Cheryl, a sensible accountant by day, dreamed of wild sexual trysts with rock stars by night. Joe acted out his secret vengeance thoughts about his self-centered brother.

✔ **Relationship dynamics:** You receive insights about how you relate to others and how you give and receive so you can improve your ability to love. This includes learning to balance your internal yin and yang energy. One woman dreamed she was a helpless passenger in a car driven by another, aggressive woman. Another dreamed she took her obnoxious neighbor a cake instead of reporting him to the police.

✔ **Past life memory:** You travel in time to revisit memories of other lives, or to clear blocked energy where emotion is stuck. You re-experience, in a dream, a previous death, trauma, remorse, deep grief, terror, or a situation where you had too much ego.

✔ **Precognitive warnings:** You receive forewarning of sudden change or upheaval: A loved one is about to die, you are soon to lose your job or partner, or the world is about to experience a shocking event like Pearl Harbor, Kennedy's assassination, or September 11. Or, you are shown an omen to watch for that is a clue to success in a new endeavor.

✔ **Out of body travel:** You collapse time and space and visit a distant sick friend you're worried about, have a visitation from a dead relative with a message for you, or travel with a friend who's actually in India.

Recognize emotional symbols

With a little practice, you can figure out how to immediately sense the "charge" that's often present with emotional zone symbols. Here are some examples of images that pertain to emotional processes:

✔ **State of your emotions:** Water, lake, ocean, river, pool, swamp, flood, tidal wave, swimming, diving, fishing, drowning, boats, rafts, water vehicles, fire, house burning, forest or brush fire, campfire, fire in a fireplace, smoke, explosion, storm, tornado, hurricane, earthquake, volcano, mudslide

✔ **Emotional processes and issues:** Babies, children, fish, snakes, lions, tigers, bears, sharks, dolphins, puppies, hummingbirds, otters, horses, elephants, sex, relationships, celebrities, battle, betrayal, hiding, hoarding, being drained, being chased, exposure, nudity, poison, suffocation, paralysis, prison, weapon, trap, losing or finding important items or money

Make an emotional dream work for you

Use your diary to press into emotional issues and explore deeper feelings with the following exercise:

1. **Write about a relationship dream, a night-mare, and a sex dream, asking yourself about each:** If I accept what's happening in the dream and extend the action further, what happens? If I let the dream take an odd turn, what might happen that I never expected?

2. **Write out three of your wildest fantasies about sex, taboos, the dark side, or death.** It's okay to be politically incorrect! Write about what you learn.

Teenagers and small children need about ten hours of sleep, while those over 65 need about six. For the average adult, eight hours is optimal. Some studies suggest women need up to an hour's extra sleep a night compared to men, and not getting it may be one reason women are more susceptible to depression.

Recognizing and Working with a Mental-Spiritual Dream

Many dreams deal with patterns and processes in your mental and spiritual realms. Some of the topics of mental-spiritual zone dreams are:

- **Mental clutter:** You become aware of fixed mental beliefs, worries, and rigid ideas, as well as information that doesn't belong to you, so you can dissolve it and expand into greater self-expression. Donna dreamed she was to inherit the possessions of the women in her mother's lineage. Instead of great treasures, she received tiny restrictive shoes, primitive sewing implements, and raggedy clothes. She realized she needed to clear a belief system based on limitation that she inherited from her mother.

- **Guidance:** You receive instructions or guidance, often from historical figures, spiritual guides, dead relatives, or animals, to know how to proceed or that you are supported. Susan dreamed she was putting on mascara, but had the mascara with the wand she didn't like. There is another kind she just bought that has a perfect wand. Where is it? From this fragment, she realized she wanted her new business to be the way *she* wanted it to be, not the way others were telling her it *should* be.

- **Teaching others:** You teach others so you can see how wise you really are. Steven, a car mechanic, dreamed he was teaching a large class, gesturing

with a piece of chalk. On the blackboard were
scrawled complex mathematical formulas. He
realized he must know about math and have
teaching ability that he'd never tried to develop.

✔ **Creativity:** You experience creative genius to
remind you of your potential and how much you
love innovation and artistic expression. Dennis
dreamed he was painting the air, and a scene
from reality revealed itself with each brush-
stroke. He realized the paintbrush was his own
perception, and that he could create his reality
as effortlessly as he painted the air.

✔ **Interdimensional communication:** You connect
with loved ones who've died, historical figures,
extraterrestrials, or your *soulgroup* (people who
feel like spiritual family) as a way to remember
your multidimensional nature. Mary dreamed her
dead father brought her a birthday present.
Inside the box were numbers she somehow knew
were the vibrations of her true self.

✔ **Parallel realities:** You explore other worlds and
parallel realities that reveal new aspects of yourself. A housewife had regular dreams about being
part of a mission impossible-style team in which
she was a courageous, undercover operative. She
realized she was smarter and had more power
than she thought.

✔ **Extrasensory perception:** You develop expanded
perception, like clairvoyance, telepathy, time
travel, materialization, teleportation, spiritual
healing, and enlightenment to find a higher viewpoint. Paula dreamed she went inside a sick boy's

body and made him vomit up a stomach full of poppy seeds; the boy, who she didn't know, was a drug addict.

✔ **Spiritual awakening:** You learn to regulate your awareness to open to more enlightenment. Jack dreamed he had to fly through a shallow band of energy with lots of little explosions in it. Jack stretched out flat and held steady so he wouldn't hit the sparks. He passed through easily. He realized he was learning to tune out negative thoughts so he could reach spiritual truth.

✔ **Global-collective visions:** You see trends and events that pertain to the earth and people as a whole over long periods of history and into the future. Rob dreamed he saw an ancient time when the Egyptian pyramids were surrounded by water, and was surprised later to find reports that it may have been true.

Recognize mental-spiritual symbols

Let's look at the symbols that represent mental processes and spiritual growth. Here are some examples:

✔ **State of your mind:** Air, wind, storms; things that fall from the sky like hailstones or satellites; caged birds, low-flying birds like owls, crows, jays, or sparrows; ruler, tape measure, closed box, hourglass, numbers, calendar, spider web, spider; library, university, books, dictionary, elementary school, exams; attic, hat, headband, scarf on head

✔ **Mental processes:** Flying close to earth, airplane, hang glider, sailplane, balloon, jet, elevator, tall buildings, skyscraper, high tension line, ladder, tower, futuristic technologies, geometric patterns, spoken words, written language; crystal, diamond, jewels

✔ **Spiritual growth processes:** Rocket, spaceship, UFO, flying high above earth, white birds, feathers, hummingbird, eagle, hawk, dragonfly; climbing tall ladders, staircases, or mountains; lotus flower, standing snake, spiritual teachers and guides, religious figures, angels, spiral, city, colony, conference; grids of light, sun, planets, galaxies, northern lights, stars, outer space, the void

Make a mental-spiritual dream work for you

Use this dream diary exercise to find insight about your mind's dynamics and discover messages from spirit:

1. **Pick five recent dreams and write about them:** If this dream were talking to me about my mental clutter, what beliefs or worries might I eliminate? If this dream were talking to me about the fixed ideas that are holding me back, what might they be?

2. **List your three most pressing questions:** Imagine that a wise guide, teacher, animal, or historical figure comes and gives you advice. Write out your dialogue as though it is a dream sequence.

Fun dream facts

You may be intrigued by a few of these interesting facts about dreaming:

- To fall asleep we must cool off; body temperature and the brain's sleep-wake cycle are closely linked. The blood flow mechanism that transfers core body heat to the skin works best between 64 and 86 degrees. Later in life, the comfort zone shrinks to between 73 and 77 degrees — one reason older people have more sleep problems.

- The luminous rays from a digital alarm clock can be enough to interfere with the sleep cycle. The light turns off a neural switch in the brain, causing levels of a key sleep chemical to decline within minutes. Scientists have not been able to explain a study showing that a bright light shone on the backs of our knees can reset the brain's sleep-wake clock.

- Men tend to dream more about other men, while women dream equally about men and women. Over two thirds of dreamers report experiencing déjà vu in their dreams, though it's more common in women. All mammals dream, and other animals may also dream. Elephants sleep standing up during non-REM sleep, but lie down for REM sleep.

- You cannot snore and dream simultaneously! Sleep apnea, or strangulated breathing, occurs often as muscles relax deeply in REM sleep and the body then tends to wake suddenly from an adrenalin-fueled need to reopen the airways. This interferes with dreaming.

- Flying dreams are found worldwide and have existed since ancient times, long before the invention of the airplane. Dreams are penetrable; it has been found experimentally that you can communicate with a person who is dreaming.

Chapter 4

Unlocking the Secrets in Symbols

● ●

Symbols are the language of dreams, an intuitive shortcut your soul uses to talk to you. They convey a vast amount of encoded information that always pertains to your own process of living and evolving. Every symbol is somehow about you. In a typical dream scene composed of a group of symbols you can find clues to how you're developing, what you want to create, how you need to heal, or how to make correct choices. In this chapter, I show you different types of symbols and how to interpret them.

Discovering How Symbols Can Come Alive

Everything is a symbol, really, and conveys underlying meaning. What do your clothes, car, furnishings, cologne, business card, phone message, hairstyle, and body say about who you are? The symbols that appear in your dreams are just as indicative of you as those in daily life. Do you dream of outer space or eating French pastries? Are your dreams populated with cats, babies, mobsters, angels, or large insects with shiny eyes? Dreaming about a hummingbird instead of a bald eagle reveals as much about your inner self as your real-life choice of a pickup truck over a sports car. There's a good reason those symbols appear in your daytime and night-time reality when they do; they represent character-istics or aspects of spirit you want to activate in yourself.

To truly understand what a symbol represents, you must *feel into* or merge into the symbol, pretend to be the thing, and speak from its point of view about what it knows. This way, you enter the direct experi-ence of what it is to *be* a daisy, a polar bear, a set of lost keys, or a school bus. And the symbol comes alive. Once you become the symbol, it's easier to see how the image is a part of you and your life process.

Try the following writing exercise to practice merging with, becoming, and speaking as a symbol:

1. **Pick an object from your house:** Choose any-thing, such as a vase, an easy chair, the sheets on your bed, a broom, the welcome mat, a candle, a statue.

2. **In your imagination, step into the object:**
   Line your energy up with it, feel its life, what
   it knows, and where it comes from; tell its
   story, and why it's in your life right now; write
   directly from your intuition in first person/
   present tense, allowing anything to come.

Familiarizing Yourself with Kinds of Meanings

Every symbol has an archetypal definition, a meaning
that describes universal themes common to all people
in all cultures. Additionally, it can have a personal
definition, and mean something unique to you alone.
Kayaking in a fast river might mean a fluid emotional
process archetypally, but because you flipped
over in a boat and almost drowned, to you it means,
"Danger!"

Notice archetypal meanings

Archetypal meanings of symbols often have sweeping
themes that describe spiritual truths and processes,
like the hero's journey into the underworld to face
and conquer fear; the nurturing relationship between
divine mother and divine child; or death, rebirth,
and transformation into a brilliant new spiritual form.
You can find great archetypal insights about symbols
by exploring the classic myths and legends of the
world.

The following exercise will help you identify archetypal meanings:

1. **Make a list of ten dream images, either single items or a snapshot of a scene.**

   For example: Going to the doctor, a bruised apple, swimming across a lake, a black-and-white dog.

2. **For each one, imagine a spiritual teacher or guide is giving you insight about what it means as a soul lesson or spiritual process.**

   For example: Going to the doctor – you're working with spiritual guides to change the way you run energy through your system; bruised apple – you're healing an emotional wound that caused you to not develop or offer your talents to the world; swimming across a lake – you're beginning a sustained spiritual quest; black-and-white dog – you're examining ideas about good and evil, right and wrong, especially as connected to friendship.

Notice personal meanings

The following exercises give you a variety of ways to become more familiar with personal symbols.

Here are several methods for imagining personal symbols:

✔ Make a list of your positive character traits, the things you like about yourself. Next to the words, list images that represent those characteristics.

✔ For example, for *free* you might list horse, eagle, wind; for *industrious* you might list ant, bee, beaver, hammer.

✔ Pick the traits about yourself you'd like to represent to the world. What do you want others to notice about you? Imagine, describe, or draw a logo for yourself.

✔ Imagine, describe, or draw a meditation symbol that represents your essence.

Symbolizing someone else can help you discover personal meanings as well. Try these methods:

✔ **Make a list of ten people you've seen in the media.** Write their first and last names in your diary. Then ask your imagination: If these people had different names that conveyed their essences or important qualities of their personalities, what would they be? Don't be logical. Take the first impressions you get. List the pseudonyms next to their present names.

✔ **Pick three people you know.** For each one, ask: If this person were a tree or an animal, what would he or she be? What kind of music would he be? What kind of car would she be? What is this person's secret fantasy? What does his bedroom look like? If this person were a geometric symbol what would she be?

Experiment with titling your dreams as a way to develop personal meanings from symbols:

1. **Make a list of ten past dreams, or recent situations in your waking life that seem like dreams.**

2. **Use your imagination.** Let the most colorful images and whimsical actions in each dream connect and form a poetic title that captures the spirit of the dream and makes it instantly meaningful to you.

   For example: Sauna jailbreak, colorful lost dogs, vegetable windfall, gummy and tooth-less, healer mom.

Cracking Symbols Open

There are several ways to unlock the meanings in symbols. In the sections that follow, I describe a few methods and give you a chance to practice them.

Find archetypal meanings vertically

Symbols exist between the reality of the body and the reality of spirit. They represent messages from the soul to your mind and personality, and messages from your body and emotions to the mind and soul.

The meaning behind every symbol eventually helps you determine the actions that are most purposeful for you.

You can find the archetypal meanings of a symbol by moving your awareness *vertically* — "up" into the symbol's highest essence, or "down" into the symbol's deepest core. You can distill a universal meaning by asking questions like, What's underneath this meaning? What came before that idea? or What is the highest spiritual experience this symbol provides? Try the following exercise to interpret a symbol vertically:

1. **Pick a dream fragment or a piece of a longer dream.** Focus on the symbol that seems most important and describe it in a short phrase. For example: (Blue Pegasus) is a symbol for the image I see of (a flying blue horse).

2. **Ask yourself: If I could feel what it's like to be blue, without fear or reservation, what sensations and emotions would I experience? If I could feel what it's like to be a flying horse, what sensations and emotions would I experience?** Write about the experiences, in first person/present tense, using as many sensory and emotional words as possible. Try to include vision, hearing, touch, taste, and smell.

3. **Ask yourself: If I were a flying blue horse, aware of all its sensations and emotions, what would I naturally know about myself, the world, and life?** What insights would I have? Write about your answers.

4. **Next, ask: If I had all the sensations, emotions, and knowing of a flying blue horse, what lesson would I be teaching myself?**
   What purpose would I be fulfilling? Write about your answers.

Find personal meanings horizontally

You can find the personal meanings of a symbol by expanding your awareness *horizontally* or sideways across the world. You can uncover associated ideas that are similar to the symbol, that have a meaning specific to you, by asking questions like, What does this symbol remind me of? What memories do I connect with this image? Traveling the horizontal path to a symbol's meaning is a totally subjective journey; symbols hold different meanings depending on how much love and fear are connected with the viewpoint. To discover the personal meanings you have with a symbol, you must trust your subconscious mind.

The method of free association can help flush up a symbol's related meanings from your subconscious. With this horizontal method, you describe the thoughts, impressions, and feelings you receive when you think of the symbol, no matter how silly.

When looking for associations, look also to your opinions and judgments. Your most forthright, candid, and judgmental ideas are often most revealing. Logical assumptions about what symbols stand for are often boring, and only skim the surface. Look for emotional reality, or that special intuitive "hit" that makes you pause a moment. Omit the enticing details that wander tangentially away from the point or you'll get bogged down. The association you find may be an episode from your life. Summarize the story in your diary, then look for a key word that stands out. This word is often tied to the meaning of the original symbol.

The flower petal technique helps you find connections and personal meanings without going off on a tangent of increasingly irrelevant associations:

1. **Close your eyes and imagine a large open flower with many petals.** In the center of the flower, place a symbol you'd like to decode; let's use a snake. Focus on the image and be willing to receive any ideas.

2 **Move your awareness out to the first petal.** Imagine another image, idea, personal memory, or word on that petal, something that's related to snake. The first thing might be poisonous. Note the idea in your dream diary.

3. **Return to the center and connect with the snake symbol again.** Go to the second petal and see what idea or image is there. Maybe this time it's sexuality. Note the idea in your dream diary.

4. **Return to the center and feel the symbol.** Go to the third petal. This time you get ancient wisdom. Continue going back to the center,

then out to a petal, until you've exhausted the meaningful associations. Don't jump from petal to petal or you might start associating the associations with each other. Soon you should have an intriguing list: poisonous, sexuality, ancient wisdom, dangerous, slippery, sensual, "snake in the grass," dragon, cold-blooded, sacred, teeth, sheds skin, constrictor, transformation, kundalini.

5. **Review your collection of words, feelings, memories, and concepts.** As you write, ask yourself: How are these ideas like me or my life right now? How do these ideas relate to each other and fit together to describe a situation in my life?

Often a symbol's personal meaning pertains to a traumatic or confusing event in your past. You can find associations to memories and thematically interrelated experiences by following these steps:

1. **Pick an image from a recent dream and let it appear in your imagination.**

2. **Ask: What does this image remind me of that is present in my life now?** Let yourself receive one or more associations. Write them in your diary.

3. **Ask: What earlier similar experience is tied to these present ones through an association in my subconscious mind?** Let yourself receive one or more associations. Write them in your diary.

4. **Ask: What earlier similar experience is tied to this one through an association in my subconscious mind?** Keep asking until no more come.

5. **Examine the string of connected experiences to find common themes leading into the present.** What core emotions are at the heart of the experiences?

Dream dictionaries of the past

Dream interpretation dictionaries figure prominently in the literature of history. Ancient Egyptians, Mesopotamians, and Greeks used them, as well as Muhammadan scholars. The *Beatty papyrus,* written around 1350 BC and discovered at Thebes, is the oldest dream dictionary existing today. It lists the interpretations of many dream images, as well as incantations and rituals to prevent nightmares. Special dream-interpreting priests were called "Masters of the Secret Things" or "Learned Ones of the Magic Library."

After the printing press made books more widely available to the public in the mid-1600s, a dream dictionary called *Oneirocritica (The Interpretation of Dreams)* by Artemidorus became one of the first best-sellers, comparable only to the Bible in popularity. On the other hand, Sigmund Freud's best work, *The Interpretation of Dreams,* now read by many as a foundation for dreamwork, when published in 1900 sold only 451 copies in two years.

Older dream dictionaries are notorious for listing obscure meanings of symbols that may have made great sense in the more distant past, but don't quite compute today.

Unlock a group of symbols and find the message

Sometimes it helps to pretend you're describing the symbols to a friendly ET-type extraterrestrial who's trying to understand what he's observing on earth. For example, a woman dreamed: *I'm in Europe and have made a huge amount of money, in cash, that I want to bring back into the United States, but I don't want to declare it at customs. I don't want it to show up on the X-ray machine. I'm paranoid and frustrated that I have so much money but may not be able to use it.*

This woman identified three key symbols: a large amount of cash, a foreign country that is the origin of the money, and customs and its X-ray machine. The following list shows you how to unload these symbols to their basest meanings.

- ✔ **What is a large amount of money?** Money is a reward. Money brings opportunity, security, and power. Money is strength and energy. A large amount of money means I can have and do a lot. A large amount of money means I have done something well or been very good.

- ✔ **What is a foreign country?** A foreign country is a place I don't normally live. It's a place where I'm not limited by what everyone thinks of me. A foreign country is exciting and offers unusual opportunities and adventure.

> ✔ **What is customs? What is an X-ray machine?**
> Customs is a guard dog. Customs is the suspicious consciousness at the outside edge of the place I live in. Customs will take things away from me if I have too much. An X-ray machine sees through the outside covering of things to reveal what's underneath.

After this woman could sense the underlying meanings of the individual symbols, she tried merging into them to find out how they might be a part of her current life process. We'll delve into interpreting dreams in more depth in Chapters 5 and 6, but for now, see if you can feel how this woman put the individual symbols together to reveal an issue in her innermost self that she hadn't been aware of previously.

This woman sensed that the foreign country was a new kind of self-expression that was unfamiliar but exciting, a way of having permission to be more of herself and be more successful. The large amount of money felt like a validation of her natural talent and the rewards that could soon be coming to her. Her paranoia about customs felt like an old fear she'd had that everything good would be taken away from her or she'd be criticized if she showed herself fully to the world. So when this woman put all the symbols together, she realized her soul was sending her a message: Move past old limitations, show up for who you really are, be creative in a totally new way, and let your wealth of talent be known.

Chapter 5

Finding Dream Meanings

● ●

*T*his chapter gives you basic principles and techniques for drilling down to find your dreams' core insights. Be sure to check Chapters 4 and 6 for more techniques for exploring dream messages.

Dream Formats

Dreams come in many shapes and sizes, some vague, some detailed, some frightening, some inspiring. They all contain encoded messages aimed at improving your life. Here are some tips for working with dream formats you might encounter:

- ✔ **Vague impression:** Try meditating and receiving any subtle feelings about the impression. Note related thoughts, moods, and sensations in your body. Follow a sensation to a feeling, to a memory or association, to an insight.

- ✔ **Single symbol or dream fragment:** Try merging into the single image and speak as the symbol, or dialogue with it.

- ✔ **Story:** Try breaking the story into scenes, and look for the main lesson or message in each piece by asking trigger questions about the elements and analyzing the symbols. Then put it all back together and see how the whole thing is about your current growth process. Look for insights about where the process wants to go.

✔ **Recurring, incomplete:** With recurring dreams, especially scary ones, there is a subconscious block that needs to be faced. When a dream is interrupted or feels incomplete, try redreaming it in a meditation and take it to a new conclusion.

✔ **Sequential:** When a dream is part of a series where information is revealed over time, treat the separate dreams as scenes in a longer story dream.

✔ **Stream of consciousness:** When the dream contains a long string of images, look for the relationships between the symbols to find a process that relates to your personal growth.

Getting Started: Some Things to Look For

In interpreting a dream, remember that you are first looking for insight about an issue or theme the innermost you is concerned about, working on improving, learning, or creating. You're looking for this wisdom so you can grow and become more of your truest, highest self. In finding that key message, you are likely to receive modifying details that will help you make the necessary changes and fine tune your understanding of the lessons at hand. In addition, you may find insights about other people or society at large, and these will always pertain to your own life, too.

Remember that in dreams, time is malleable, so you may receive information about the past and future as though it is in the present.

In the following sections, I give you a loose framework for looking at key components of dreams that can help you see through the surface to what's happening underneath. Use any or all of them — they are tools for exploration.

Look for fear and love

Dreams deliver messages from your subconscious and your superconscious mind. Looking for fear or love in the dream can give you a clue about your process: Are you trying to clear a blockage or move forward from your soul's clarity?

✔ **Subconscious dream content, related to the past and fear, arises so you can clear the way for more soul expression.** Personal symbology is often connected to these dreams. By looking at contracted fear responses, both in the dream and after, you can discover your subconscious blocks. One woman's dream, which forewarns of the emergence of breast cancer, shows subconscious content: *A snake has gotten inside my body and now it's in my chest and is laying eggs all over. I can't get it out!*

✔ **Superconscious dream content brings guidance from your soul, access to love and wisdom, or understanding of a process shared by all people.** Typically, negative emotion is not present. These dreams feel expansive, loving, open, neutral, and informational. Archetypal symbology is usually related to these dreams. In one man's dream, his soul self is reassuring him that he's entitled to abundance and nourishment: *I'm riding in a car. As I round a curve, a passing truck swerves and vegetables fall onto the road. I stop and pick them up. I'm excitedly stuffing them into my pack — lettuce, carrots, celery, and tomatoes.*

Dreams deliver messages from your subconscious and your superconscious mind. Looking for fear or love in the dream can give you a clue about your process: Are you trying to clear a blockage or move forward from your soul's clarity?

One woman dreamed: *I'm looking over a pilot's shoulder as he guides a commercial jet in for a landing. I'm frightened yet exhilarated when he flies between skyscrapers in a big city, then finally lands safely in a lake.* She determined that she was descending from the mental-spiritual zone into the emotional zone. And when she looked at how the dream fit all the categories, she realized:

✔ **As a physical zone dream:** She needs to develop new skills for navigating more masterfully in her life.

✔ **As an emotional zone dream:** She needs to take risks to move forward in life, and she's anxious about crashing emotionally if she doesn't stay centered.

✔ **As a mental-spiritual zone dream:** She is bringing higher knowledge carefully down past various fixed mental constructs, so it can be applied in her emotional life. She feels she has help from guides and teachers.

In the end, the woman decided her dream was primarily based in the mental-spiritual zone. She had been depressed and needed to refine the quality of her emotions by opening to greater spiritual understanding.

Dreams can deliver messages or instructions verbally or in written form, via a disembodied voice or a few printed words. Mental-spiritual zone dreams originate in realms that are abstract, pattern-oriented, and often devoid of symbols or scenes from daily life.

Look into the symbols

List the main symbols in your dream; then look for the archetypal and personal meanings, as I explained in Chapter 4. Remember, archetypal meanings of symbols take you straight to the core and give insight about universal themes, while personal meanings add insight that has particular relevance to you. Once you understand how each symbol is about a part of you, you can put them together to discover something about your personal growth process.

Look for new information

Dreams routinely bring information that can help you in daily life. One woman dreamed that a friend insisted she drink hibiscus tea, so she actually bought and brewed some and found she liked it. Another woman dreamed of a ray of light shining through the window onto the left side of her abdomen; within weeks, she discovered she had a cyst on her left ovary.

Look at the change points

You can find interesting insights when you examine how your dreams start, shift, and stop. The change points carry clues about your inner dynamics. Ask yourself:

- ✔ At what point do I enter the dream action? *This can tell you something about your main concerns.*

- ✔ What choices do I make in the dream? *This can show where you are passive or aggressive, what you're afraid might happen, or how you unconsciously react to situations.*

- ✔ What causes one scene to shift to another? *You may discover the power you've given to others to control your life, or the unconscious links between beliefs you hold.*

- ✔ What is happening when the dream ends? *This can point out where you typically withdraw from situations or become unconscious, or how you want a situation to turn out.*

Asking Questions That Trigger Insights

Sometimes, you just need to be conscious of details you'd normally gloss over, for meanings to become evident. Start by asking questions about the following main elements:

✔ **What are the key elements?**

- **How would you describe the dream structure?** Did the dream have a beginning, middle, and end? Was it just a fragment? Was it a stream of consciousness, a string of images or episodes that are related to each other in some odd way? This gives you hints about what decoding techniques to use.

- **What were the main scenes and settings in the dream?** Were you inside or outside? Was it urban, rural, or unearthly? How many scenes were there? To notice details, ask yourself how this setting is different from others like it you've seen before. This helps you understand your process — internal, external, worldly, spiritual, stages of growth.

- **Was there a sense of time or direction?** Was it day or night? Were you in the past or the future? Were you facing one of the four directions? This gives insight about information being unconscious, conscious, frozen, or projected, and shows attitudes you're coming from and needing to develop.

- **How was the dream lit?** Were the scenes full of sunlight, in color, or lit by a spotlight? Was it foggy or dark, in sepia, or black-and-white? Were you aware of specific colors? This indicates what you're paying attention to, what's real to you, and the overtones you associate with things.

- **What was your viewpoint?** Were you a participant or playing the role of another person? Were you an observer or commentator? Were you above the action, at eye level, or below? This gives insight about how engaged you are in life and how you use authority.

- **What characters were present?** Were you alone or with other people, animals, or spiritual beings? Were there peripheral characters who never showed up but had an impact on the dream? This tells what aspects of yourself you're developing; shows how you cooperate, give, and receive; and what sort of help you need.

- **What were the primary images, objects, symbols, or patterns?** Was the dream filled with the objects and imagery of normal life? Or was it more otherworldly, abstract, or geometric? Here you can dive directly into symbol decoding.

- **Did numbers occur in the dream?** Did you see three wasps, seven puppies, numerals on a house, or lottery ticket numbers? Did someone tell you his or her phone number or the date or time? More symbol decoding.

✔ **What are the motivations?**

- **What actions were taken, and by whom?** As each action was taken, what goal was pursued? This shows what you're doing in your life and the mistakes you're making or avoiding.

- **What choices or decisions were made, and by whom?** Action proceeds from choices and intentions. What motivated each action in the dream? This shows your soul desires, subconscious fears, and interfering mental structures.

- **What outcomes were reached?** Did actions lead to results? Were you satisfied with the outcomes? Did you resist them or not notice them? This shows what you want to accomplish or think you should accomplish.

- **At what speed was the action occurring?** High speed is a different kind of awareness than slow motion. This shows how you're processing your experience. Slow motion indicates deep understanding physically and emotionally, while lightspeed pertains to direct higher mental-spiritual knowing.

- **What statements were made?** Orders given? Questions asked? By whom? Pay attention to standout declarative statements and questions. Watch for words or phrases you see in print. This indicates key ideas or messages to explore, accept, or dissolve.

- **What was left incomplete?** Were certain actions ineffectual or interrupted? What interrupted the flow? At what point did the action stop? This reveals places you avoid experiencing something.

- **What impressions did you have about the dream while dreaming?** It's common to comment about a dream to yourself while you're dreaming. For instance, "This is a continuation of that other dream I had six months ago." You may have forgotten the previous dream in waking life, but your dream self keeps track. These impressions reveal ongoing deep processes your soul is facilitating.

✔ **What are the feelings?**

- **What feelings did you or other characters have?** Was there an underlying mood running through the dream? Did you experience mild or intense emotion? When exactly? You may want to amplify and exaggerate a mild feeling so you can see what it's really about. This helps you see where your fear and pain lie and how you react or protect yourself.

- **What senses were you using to perceive?** Were you primarily aware through vision? Or did you feel someone touching you, taste food, hear music, or smell flowers? This shows preferred modes of knowing and how deep in your body you're processing something.

✔ **How is each part about you?**

- **What do you have in common with each symbol and character?** Assume there is an aspect of your own emotional makeup, belief system, and behavior that the symbol or character embodies.

• **How do the emotions, decisions, and actions parallel something in your own life?** There are always parallels between the dream and your waking life, perhaps in a different area, about a different subject, or involving different people.

Putting It Together: A Sample Interpretation

While writing one of my books, I dreamed: *I'm walking at night on a city street, slick with rain, in a bad area. I'm following sheets of paper being spit out one by one from a copy machine that act like stepping stones or a bread crumb trail. They keep appearing and I have to pick them up. They're leading me into a dangerous area with many derelicts. Because I'm concentrating on the "paper trail," the derelicts aren't bothering me, but I must not lose focus or look directly at them. Ahead is a hole in a wall at the end of an alley lined with bums; through it is a muddy swampy hellhole area where the bad men come from. I decide I'm not going farther, and I wake up.*

Here's what I made of it, picking the previously listed interpretation tips that stood out to me the most:

✔ **Subconcious or superconscious:** I'm looking at a *subconscious* process because there is darkness and anxiety throughout the dream.

✔ **Dream zones:** The dream fits all the zones. As a *physical zone* dream, it relates to my writing, and how I must keep on, one page at a time, and not get ahead of myself. As an *emotional zone* dream, I see my writing is taking me into deep emotions, fears, and primal experiences that I hadn't expected. As a *mental-spiritual* dream, it's showing me that the book's content (and my life itself) will flow and I'll receive the next piece (experience) just as I need it, and that by staying focused in the moment and on the creative process, I remain stable and safe from distortions or biases caused by fear.

✔ **Dream categories:** Skill development, psychological processing, creativity.

✔ **Dream symbols:** Several images stand out strongly:

> **A city at night, bad part of town:** What is a city at night? It's the dark side of a collective consciousness, a part of the mind filled with desperation. Archetypally, the symbol focuses on collective subconscious fears of being attacked, or perhaps fear of the unknown. As a personal symbol, I may be dredging up memories and associations I have from living in New York City as a young woman in a period of my life fraught with difficulty and rejection.

> **Rain and a muddy-swampy hole:** What is rain, mud, a hole into a swamp? It's a flood of emotion that I can get stuck in and confused by. Archetypally, the symbols focus on emotional paralysis and overwhelm, going into the deepest part of our fear. As personal symbols, they remind me of a vague fear I have of losing direction and freedom through emotional negativity or victimization.

Derelicts: What is a derelict? It's a person who's out of touch with the soul, who feels victimized by life. Archetypally, the hopeless, downtrodden, needy, possibly violent men relate to a negative, suppressed side of our masculine, manifesting energy. Personally, the symbol reminds me of an anxiety I have about poverty swallowing me up. How are the derelicts *me*? They are the starved parts of my own creative-productive self that are overworked, cut off, unappreciated, and unrecognized. They might turn on me, suck me dry, and destroy me and my book if I don't replenish them with play, respect, and warmth.

Copy machine: What is a copy machine? It's a part of my awareness that translates material from other dimensions to my mind and onto the page. Archetypally, it represents the production process. Personally, the symbol reassures me that I have help in my creative endeavor.

Manuscript pages: What are pages? They are formed ideas and manifested communication. Archetypally, the symbol focuses on the finished product of a writing process. Personally, the pages feel like precious jewels and a core part of me.

✓ **The actions, choices, and lessons:** I follow the pages, pay attention, listen to my intuition to stay focused and steady. I learn that if I even *look* at the derelicts, I'll draw their attention and be in danger: a basic principle of how to use the mind? Don't lower my personal vibration? I see I don't need to force the creative process; I am receiving material at a speed I can handle, and I only need to pick up the pages one by one. I learn I'm being guided into deep territory, and the process will keep me safe no matter where I go. Why do I decide NOT to go through the hole into the swamp? Honest response: I don't need to. It might shift me so much it would stop the flow of my creative process; it's not what I'm doing in my life right now.

✔ **Conclusions:** To write the best book, I need to trust the natural flow of creativity and stay in the moment. As my growth process leads me deeper into my core, I will face fears, but I don't need to resist them or they'll get stronger. I must work more with feminine energy and nurture my worker bee self. I can explore beyond my known rational world into the swampy origin place when the possible repercussions won't interfere with a worldly commitment.

Trying Your Hand

Here are a collection of exercises and techniques you can use to work with various types of dreams.

Delve into body, emotion, mind, and soul

Use the following three exercises to listen to your body, emotions, mind, and soul.

Find body messages by following these steps:

1. **Pick a few dreams and write about them as though they are messages to you from your body.**

2. **Ask how the dream might relate to your body's energy level circulation, assimilation, or elimination systems.** Is there a message about your health? Is there an action you should take?

You can sleuth for subconscious emotional blocks by doing the following:

1. **Pick a few dreams and see if there are any images that might have been triggered by fears or blocks in your subconscious mind.**

2. **Make a list of the images, emotions, and actions you took in the dreams.** Write about what the underlying themes are and how these emotions are connected to events in your daily life. Also write about how the themes you discover might be connected with each other.

Find hidden spiritual guidance with these two simple methods:

1. **Pick a few dreams and look for teachings about improving the way you use your mind and heart.** Could a spiritual guide or angel have been working with you to help you become aware of a new principle of consciousness?

2. **Write about what your dreams might mean.** Did they originate from the collective consciousness and were they pertinent socially?

Work with dream fragments

The following two exercises can help you interpret dream fragments.

Find insights by conversing with a dream fragment using the following procedure:

- ✔ Pick a dream fragment and focus on the image or experience. Be your conscious mind asking questions, then be the image/fragment and respond. Record the questions and answers in your diary.

- ✔ Ask the fragment: Who/what are you? What's your special gift? What do you do? What's your function or role in my life?

- ✔ Ask the fragment: Why are you appearing in my dream? What emotions do you want to trigger in me? What message do you have for me? What do you need, or want, me to do?

- ✔ Ask the fragment: Are you the representation of something else, like a kind of energy or belief system? If I integrate the quality you represent, how might I change?

By tracking your feelings about a dream fragment to a best or worst possible scenario, you can find interesting and helpful insights:

1. **Ask yourself:** What feelings or sensations do I have concerning this image? What else comes to mind as I experience the image?

2. **If you reach a fear-based idea, ask:** What would happen if the situation I'm trying to

avoid occurred? If you reach a positive insight, ask: What would happen if the good situation occurred? When you get the answer, ask: And then what would happen? Continue to ask: And then what?, until you arrive at a final outcome. Ask: If this worst or best possible scenario happened, what might I learn?

Make sense of recurring and sequential dreams

Recurring dreams and nightmares typically end midstream without a satisfactory resolution. Sequential dreams seem to be connected in a progression over time. Stream-of-consciousness dreams contain strings of images that form a process. The following exercises will help you work more effectively with these dream categories.

Complete an incomplete or recurring dream by following these simple steps:

1. **Pick a recurring or incomplete dream.**
   Review it in your imagination from the beginning to the point where it abruptly ends. Write about what emotion, feeling, or quandary you're stuck with.

2. **In a meditation, continue the dream as though it is a movie you haven't finished watching.** Don't will it in a certain direction, but let it evolve naturally in your mind, and keep going until you feel the Aha! Then write about what lesson you're learning.

Try this exercise to find wisdom in a dream sequence or stream-of-consciousness flow:

1. **Look for a series of dreams where one picks up where another leaves off (sequential), or dreams that contain a long string of oddly connected images.** Make a list of these dreams or symbol-strings.

2. **For a series of sequential dreams write about the gist of each dream.** Can you sense a progression from one to the next? Is your soul revealing different aspects of an issue to you? Are you showing yourself the next appropriate action in your process? For a stream-of-consciousness dream, look for and write about how the symbols' meanings connect logically to one another in a progression. What process is being described?

3. **Write about how the dreams parallel your waking reality and the themes or life lessons you've been working on.**

Abraham Lincoln, a few days before his assassination, dreamed he heard sobbing and saw his own dead body lying in state in the White House. Just months before the start of World War I, Carl Jung dreamed Europe was engulfed in a great flood in which thousands drowned, and the water turned to blood.

Part II
Dictionary
of Symbols

The 5th Wave   By Rich Tennant

"I think my dream catcher needs some sort of filter. I'm getting a lot of dreams about hot stock investments, low cost airfares, and products that promise to enhance my sexual performance."

In this part . . .

*p*art II gives guidelines on how to use a dream dictionary, and presents a unique way to understand dream symbols. You'll find each word interpreted on three levels, as it might pertain to the physical world, the emotional world, and the mental-spiritual worlds.

Dictionary

• •

A

above/ascend: <u>Physical</u>: If an object or person is above you, you are giving your power or energy away. If you are above, you feel you have greater influence and power. <u>Emotional</u>: You admire or resent someone above you, or feel in control or superior when you are above them. <u>Mental-Spiritual</u>: If something is above you, you need more perspective and und erstanding concerning that idea. It might be an important missing piece of your life purpose. If you are above, you have keen insights about the issue below. Ascending signifies a desire for the big picture, that your attention is on future goals, or your awareness is moving into higher states of consciousness.

accident: Accident dreams aren't necessarily something you can sense before they happen. <u>Physical</u>: If the dream has intuitive "weight" (totally subjective to you), it could indicate a potential problem. You are probably sensing a mistake in the works: an energy flow or process needing revision before you go too far and get in trouble. Slow down and evaluate things. <u>Emotional</u>: You are too emotional, or attached, or a situation is about to go out of control, and you're feeling anxious about what could happen. <u>Mental-Spiritual</u>: You need to pay closer attention to something. You lack key knowledge, or are out of alignment with your purpose. Consider your deepest motives and wisdom.

acorn: <u>Physical</u>: You are looking at your potential, what you can accomplish, how much talent and endurance you have, and how ready you are to act. You are looking at the idea of how much value can be concentrated in a small act, or how the first step of a process influences the outcome. <u>Emotional</u>: You are feeling motives and inner strength, reassuring yourself that you can do what you intend. If there is a stash of acorns, you are hoarding what you consider valuable, or need to conserve resources. <u>Mental-Spiritual</u>: You are touching into your core self, into your life's destiny or blueprint, sensing your purpose and what you are built to do.

actor/actress/acting: <u>Physical</u>: You are looking at your personality, how you live your life, and present yourself to the public. If you are acting, you're examining the roles and qualities you portray to your "audience" in daily life. Look for tips about improving your performance. <u>Emotional</u>: If you're uncomfortable acting, you may feel superficial or forced to please others. If you've forgotten your lines, you may feel anxiety about a real-life situation. A phenomenal performance means you are showing yourself how to be uninhibited and unselfconscious. <u>Mental-Spiritual</u>: You're ready to expand your self-expression, experience more joy, and allow the energy of others, your audience, to help you be your most dynamic self. You are exploring the idea that you can understand anyone by walking in their shoes.

adversary/enemy: <u>Physical</u>: You are facing an aspect of your life or body that you physically fear, a situation you can't control, an illness, or a bad habit like an addiction. <u>Emotional</u>: You're dealing with a repressed part of yourself or may feel threatened by someone or a situation. Whether you fight or flee, and how you feel about the action you take, tells you what you need to do. <u>Mental-Spiritual</u>: You're integrating an important part of yourself that needs to be loved and understood. What seems negative holds a hidden gift or talent.

air: <u>Physical</u>: You need to improve your vitality with more oxygen, by breathing deeply, or improving your circulation. <u>Emotional</u>: Floating on air indicates a need for contentment, while not having enough air means you feel lack of support for your self-expression. <u>Mental-Spiritual</u>: Traveling through the air denotes movement through streams of thought and bodies of knowledge, from the lower realm of individual thought, to the higher, shared collective consciousness where there is freedom from limiting beliefs. Encountering anything in the air represents fixed beliefs based on fear, interferences to clear thought, or specific ideas you should pay attention to.

airplane/airport: Airplanes represent your focus within the mental and spiritual realms. An airport represents a departure point for a transition in your life. <u>Physical</u>: A small plane means you're focusing on a localized reality. Taking off shows a new venture is ready to occur. If a plane can't get off the ground, the venture may be stuck or held back. Landing signifies bringing inspiration, ideas, or energies back to incorporate into your life or body. Missing a plane means you're missing an opportunity. <u>Emotional</u>: A hang glider represents an experience of personal joy and inspiration. The way you feel while riding in or piloting an aircraft shows how you deal with the unknown. Having to fly a plane when you don't know how indicates you're reaching for heights you haven't attained before and are anxious. <u>Mental-Spiritual</u>:

You're focusing on your freedom and power to rise above challenges and obtain higher perspective. A plane crash signals the end of your involvement with a series of beliefs. A jet represents concepts you hold in common with many other people. A rocket indicates you're moving rapidly toward spiritual knowledge. A UFO symbolizes a collective consciousness catalyzed by many souls of similar developmental awareness.

alarm/bell: <u>Physical</u>: If you hear an alarm you are warning yourself to pay attention to your health, habits, inner tensions and pain, or how you act in the world. <u>Emotional</u>: You are bringing an alarming situation to light. Someone is not who they seem to be or something that seems safe might not be. <u>Mental-Spiritual</u>: You are telling yourself to wake up, be aware of inner truth, a message of guidance, and to be more alert to a new period of heightened creativity.

aliens: <u>Physical</u>: You are focusing on how your body could function more elegantly, or on part of your anatomy as represented in the exaggerated features of the alien. Big eyes might mean you're trying to see something more thoroughly and deeply. <u>Emotional</u>: You're focusing on your experience of being an alien, feeling like a stranger in your social setting; there are aspects of yourself you've defined as foreign that need to be familiarized. You need to experience a situation freshly, as if you're from another planet. <u>Mental-Spiritual</u>: You are focused on your own higher awareness, possibly with a technological orientation or multidimensional wisdom. Listen for the message or teachings.

alley: <u>Physical</u>: You are transitioning to a new phase of life, taking a nontraditional route, changing plans as you go, possibly hiding from public view. An alley is a shortcut or escape route on your path through life. Emotional: Alleys — behind houses, narrow, and often containing refuse — represent the subconscious mind and experiences that are slightly negative or dangerous. You feel anxiety about being attacked or heading into a dead-end. Mental-Spiritual: Something is "right up your alley," or perfect for you. You are looking behind the scenes of the normal view, seeing what's revealed in the inner lives of others.

alligator: *(see crocodile)*

ambulance/paramedics: Physical: You are on the verge of a physical problem, or in a situation that needs expert helpers. Emotional: You are having an emotional crisis and urgently need help or want to help someone else. If an ambulance is taking you to the hospital because of a heart attack, for example, you may be experiencing a broken heart. Mental-Spiritual: You are reassuring yourself that there is always help when you need it, that you can relax, trust others, and let yourself receive.

ambush: Physical: You are experiencing an unpleasant surprise or unanticipated challenge, showing yourself how a situation is blocked, or people are working against you. Emotional: You feel overwhelmed by unforeseen circumstances, or betrayed by friends or colleagues. If you are doing the ambushing, you might want to prevent a situation by taking things into your own hands. Ambushes are also unconscious fears surfacing suddenly, or upcoming loss and emotional upheaval. Mental-Spiritual: You are experiencing a sudden breakthrough to higher awareness that you hadn't expected.

amputation: <u>Physical</u>: You are experiencing the radical removal of something from your life that is no longer necessary. Losing a body part points to the need to take care of that area of your body. You are neglecting an ability symbolized by the amputated part. Losing your right arm might mean you need to pay more attention to how you manifest results. You are cut off from a source of vitality. <u>Emotional</u>: You have feelings of separation, loss, helplessness, disempowerment, or even punishment concerning the function or misuse of a part of your body. You are separating yourself from an old wound. <u>Mental-Spiritual</u>: You want to experience wholeness in spite of a loss in your life. You are overcoming fragmentation.

anchor: <u>Physical</u>: Dropping an anchor means you are focusing on one thing and being grounded. Pulling up an anchor means you are ready to begin a new phase of growth and creativity. <u>Emotional</u>: An anchor securing a boat signifies that you feel stable concerning emotional self-expression. Difficulty dropping anchor means that you feel unable to center yourself and calm down, or that you are drifting slightly out of control. <u>Mental-Spiritual</u>: You are showing yourself that there is a way to drop straight through emotional distractions into your core purpose and heart.

angel: <u>Physical</u>: You are refining your physical functioning and energy, or drawing in healing help. You are aligning your efforts in the world with a more divine pattern. <u>Emotional</u>: Angels are the messengers of God to humanity and thus symbolize a bridge between the superconscious and subconscious mind. There is an important message or blessing trying to get through to you that will ease your suffering. <u>Mental-Spiritual</u>: You're focusing on qualities of purity, goodness, faith, protection, and guidance; you are asking for help or developing these qualities in yourself. You are attuning to your soul vibration, remembering who you really are.

animals: <u>Physical</u>: You're focusing on your instinctual nature. You are strengthening the part of yourself represented by the animal; look to the natural traits of the animal for clues. If you are bitten by an animal, it may be important as a "power animal" or protector. <u>Emotional</u>: If the animal is injured or trapped, you need to heal or free a part of yourself. If an animal threatens you, you need to develop that animal's strength or express your own wildness. <u>Mental-Spiritual</u>: Animals are spiritual guides. You are about to develop talents associated with the animal's expertise: the eagle's vision, the wolf's loyalty, the butterfly's transformational ability.

ants: <u>Physical</u>: You are focusing on diligence, hard work, and foresight. You need to work more closely with others, or perhaps you're losing your individuality by conforming to social pressures. Ants inside your body can be toxins that need to be cleansed. <u>Emotional</u>: Something may be bugging you, especially if ants are invading your house. You are irritated or in turmoil. Biting ants symbolize unkind acts and words. <u>Mental-Spiritual</u>: You are experiencing a collective consciousness that operates in harmony for the good of all.

antlers/horns: <u>Physical</u>: You are focusing on aggressive, belligerent, masculine energy. You are sexually aroused or stimulated. <u>Emotional</u>: You are looking at how you defend yourself or "horn in" on others. <u>Mental-Spiritual</u>: Antlers refer to intellectual powers and access, as through sensitive antennae, to ancient wisdom in higher realms. You are working with mature masculine wisdom.

apple: <u>Physical</u>: You're focusing on good fortune and the realization of the fruit of your work. An apple's connection to health may mean you need to pay attention to your nutrition. <u>Emotional</u>: Rotten apples or apple cores mean that your goals have little value or may even be harmful. Beautiful ripe apples mean you are experiencing pleasure and beauty. <u>Mental-Spiritual</u>: Apples represent fullness, wholeness, and knowledge, are a sign of spiritual health, that you have much vitality, wisdom, and richness to offer the world.

architecture/buildings: <u>Physical</u>: You're focusing on your life vision, environment, or the context in which an experience can occur. Houses represent the self, particularly the body. A building's style shows how you think of your foundation, inner structure, postures, or how you appear to others. Parts of a building symbolize parts of your body. <u>Emotional</u>: The condition of a building's architecture, in disrepair, ostentatious, or welcoming, shows how you feel about your personality and lifestyle. <u>Mental-Spiritual</u>: You are focusing on collective beliefs, world views, or the habits of a group. Movement between floors symbolizes rising or falling in status or awareness. Skyscrapers denote mental structures that can lift you into spiritual awareness. A cityscape indicates a complex belief system involving a collective consciousness.

arm: <u>Physical</u>: You're looking at your ability to reach out for what you want and to embrace others and life. Arms show how you send and receive energy, make things happen, and hold what's important to you. If the arm is damaged, you are limited in your ability to create. <u>Emotional</u>: Arms block attacks, defend, and strike others. You are tired from fending off hostility or from holding a heavy load. Perhaps you've been afraid to hug someone and show affection. Mental-Spiritual: You are lifting an ordinary idea up into the light. Reaching to heaven invites revelation and joy.

arrow/bull's-eye: Physical: If you're hit by an arrow, look to that area of your body; tension, pain, or congestion could be building toward a problem. An arrow punctures a blocked area and releases pressure. If you miss the bull's-eye, you need to focus and be in the flow before you act. Emotional: An arrow symbolizes a thought that seeks connection and understanding. A bull's-eye is a goal or "Aha!" If you are shooting, you feel confident about achieving a goal. If you hit a bull's-eye, you feel successful. If you've been shot, you could be wounded by sharp words or the selfish actions of others. Being shot by Cupid's arrow opens you to love and romance. Mental-Spiritual: An important message is trying to make itself known to you. Your soul is trying to make something known through you to the world. Hitting the bull's-eye means you know where to place the insight and how to deliver it.

artery/vein: Physical: An artery shows how your creativity moves into the world, while a vein shows how you receive from the world. You are looking at how much nourishment is reaching your organs and tissues. Blocked arteries can be literal problems, or blocked self-expression. The circulatory system represents your network of contacts and avenues for expression. Emotional: You are seeing how nurtured and expressive you feel. A severed artery or vein means you feel panic about a loss of sustenance or support. Mental-Spiritual: You are looking at how you receive light and energy from your soul and the divine, and how much you give back through gratitude and praise.

artist/artisan: <u>Physical</u>: You are focusing on your creative abilities and life. You need to get in touch with your body, let more energy and ideas flow out of you, or take a break from work and engage your creative, sensual side. A new project wants to be born. <u>Emotional</u>: You are remembering how inspired and creative you are, how joyful and enlivening your creative flow can be. You need to rekindle playfulness, spontaneity, and concentration on craft. <u>Mental-Spiritual</u>: You are in touch with the collective consciousness, from which all creative urges and forms emerge effortlessly. Feel the magic, the smooth flow, the innate beauty in yourself and life.

ashes: <u>Physical</u>: You're focusing on the remains of an old form or structure that has outlived its usefulness. You feel drained and need a fresh supply of fuel. You are dehydrated and slightly toxic. <u>Emotional</u>: You are looking at old values, beliefs, world views, and habits from which you no longer derive benefit. You feel bereft at the loss of something — a relationship, job, motivation, or loved one who has died. A loved one's cremated remains means you are processing feelings about that person or trying to communicate with him or her. <u>Mental-Spiritual</u>: You are letting go of the old, purifying yourself, and moving into a new phase of greater wisdom.

astrology: <u>Physical</u>: You are working with the fundamental energies in your body, aligning with optimal functioning and growth cycles. Important changes are ahead. <u>Emotional</u>: You are seeing your whole personality, accepting all of yourself. Seeking an astrology reading means you're looking for reassurance and understanding. <u>Mental-Spiritual</u>: Astrology signs, planets, and charts represent specific energy patterns and the desire to understand your future. You are seeing the big picture of your life, potentials, life lessons, and action plan.

attic: <u>Physical</u>: You're looking at old behaviors and habits you might want to integrate fully or discard. <u>Emotional</u>: If you are emotional while browsing through mementos, you're ready to face emotional wounds. <u>Mental-Spiritual</u>: An attic stores memories and beliefs from the past, and is associated with the subconscious mind. Playing in the attic means you are imagining realities. Clearing or renovating the attic into a living space means you are opening your mind to inspiration, ready to live more spiritually.

audience: <u>Physical</u>: You're focusing on the people who receive your self-expression. You are looking at how much physical affection or assistance you receive from, or give to, others. You are showing yourself there is a market for your creations. <u>Emotional</u>: Your attitude toward the audience shows how ready you are to show up in your life in a bigger way, or how judged or self-conscious you feel. <u>Mental-Spiritual</u>: You're learning how intimately connected we all are, how others fuel you, and you them. There is no separation and nothing to fear from the outside world.

aunt/uncle: *(see grandparents)*

authority/boss/teacher/parent: <u>Physical</u>: You are working out specific issues with real authority figures in your life. You're contemplating your own authority. <u>Emotional</u>: You're looking at hidden, unresolved issues with your father or mother. The symbol shows how you give your power away or deal with internal and external authority. <u>Mental-Spiritual</u>: You are facing issues of confidence and leadership in yourself, showing yourself how to grow spiritually.

avalanche: <u>Physical</u>: You're experiencing a sudden release. Your life is about to progress rapidly, or your body is about to precipitate a sudden change, like a healing crisis. <u>Emotional</u>: You feel overwhelmed by emotions that have been piling up and denied. You are doing too much and need to stop and let go. Perhaps you're facing a period of emotional upheaval, of feeling buried or swept along by circumstances out of your control. <u>Mental-Spiritual</u>: You are experiencing a break-through and release of old patterns that have kept you frozen and immobile too long.

B

baby: <u>Physical</u>: You're looking at a new idea, potential, or phase of life that's just beginning. You're concerned about an actual pregnancy, or a desire for a child. <u>Emotional</u>: You're clearing your dependent behavior or infantile desires to be babied or pampered. <u>Mental-Spiritual</u>: You're in touch with innocence, unconditional love, vulnerability, and fresh perspective. You are focusing on new information about life purpose.

back/behind: <u>Physical</u>: The back of the body symbolizes your strength to handle life's difficulties. There may be literal back problems, or issues concerning physical support or finances. <u>Emotional</u>: Being behind someone else shows your comfort about following and not receiving recognition. The back also indicates stubbornness. <u>Mental-Spiritual</u>: Anything in back of something else, like a backyard, indicates a private, personal area, something not revealed to the public. You're focusing on something that is just about to become conscious.

ball/circle: <u>Physical</u>: You are focusing on cells or atoms, your energy field, or a specific reality. Throwing a ball indicates communication. Ball sports depict cooperation within a group. <u>Emotional</u>: You're experiencing oneness, peace, and wholeness. Standing inside a circle is protection from evil. You are going in circles, or have come full circle. <u>Mental-Spiritual</u>: Any spherical shape represents the whole world, or the well-rounded self. You are aware of the soul, your destiny, or what exists in the present moment. A ball represents a specific mental focus or state.

balloon: <u>Physical</u>: You're releasing old ideas or toxins from the body. <u>Emotional</u>: You need to celebrate, feel free, or release pent-up feelings. If you're holding the strings, you are afraid to let go. A deflated balloon indicates energy drain or disappointment. <u>Mental-Spiritual</u>: You're contemplating and forming creative ideas, hopes, wishes, fantasies, and prayers.

bank/bankrupt: <u>Physical</u>: You're concerned with physical stability and security. Something you have needs safekeeping. You have great resources at hand. <u>Emotional</u>: You are afraid or rigid. A bank robbery means that what's valuable about you is not respected or safe with others. Bankruptcy indicates emotional exhaustion. <u>Mental-Spiritual</u>: You have a wealth of ideas and talent. There is abundance in the universe to draw from.

basement: <u>Physical</u>: Since a basement contains equipment, like the furnace and water heater, its condition hints at your physical condition. You're exploring issues concerning sexuality. <u>Emotional</u>: You're focusing on your subconscious where repressed ideas, memories, fears, and dangers lurk. <u>Mental-Spiritual</u>:

You're examining the foundations of your life, where you keep what needs to be worked on. Here you access the inner resources you need to maintain your world or handle emergencies.

basket/bowl: <u>Physical</u>: You are focusing on how much you have and need, particularly concerning nutrition and energy. A full basket or bowl represents the harvest of your labors. <u>Emotional</u>: An empty bowl means you feel depleted and need love and nurturance, as these symbols represent the womb. <u>Mental-Spiritual</u>: Bowls and baskets hold abundance and the essence of soul. You may be offering your gifts to others. A begging bowl shows your faith in being provided for.

bathroom/bathing: <u>Physical</u>: You need to purify, renew, or cleanse yourself, care for your body, or eliminate toxins or tension. <u>Emotional</u>: Here you are allowed to focus privately and totally on nurturing and tending to yourself. You are cleansing harmful emotions. An overflowing tub shows emotional flooding and feeling overwhelmed. <u>Mental-Spiritual</u>: Toilets indicate the elimination of old ideas. You are entering a period of spiritual rebirth.

battle/fight: <u>Physical</u>: You are remembering actual past conflicts, or forces and energies in your body are not working harmoniously. It could indicate an attacking illness like cancer. <u>Emotional</u>: You feel threatened and defensive about your ideas and rights. Another person triggers a denied part of yourself. <u>Mental-Spiritual</u>: You are in conflict with yourself, trying to balance personality traits, or your mind is divided.

beach: <u>Physical</u>: You are telling yourself to relax and play, to take a vacation from what's difficult. A life change is imminent. <u>Emotional</u>: You are nurturing yourself, connecting with the rhythms of life and deeper, more universal feelings. You need more space and freedom. <u>Mental-Spiritual</u>: The shore is the boundary between the ego and unconsciousness. You are looking for inspiration; your goals are far-reaching and visionary.

bear: <u>Physical</u>: You're focusing on strength, instinct, a strong mother figure, or the feminine aspect of nature. <u>Emotional</u>: You are dealing with someone who is overbearing, ill-tempered, unpredictable, or playful. You want to withdraw from life. <u>Mental-Spiritual</u>: You need more introspection and patience, to center inside yourself. You are working with a spiritual teacher of great wisdom.

beard/mustache: <u>Physical</u>: You are hiding part of your self-expression. Beards represent male courage, energy, and the power to manifest goals, especially if the beard is pointy or long. You are focusing on the father archetype. <u>Emotional</u>: Specially shaped facial hair shows how you portray yourself to others; a goatee is intellectual or artistic expression, while a beard with no mustache accentuates verbal communication or sensuality. Shaving indicates a willingness to be seen and vulnerable, or fear of losing power. <u>Mental-Spiritual</u>: You are releasing habitual behavior, prejudices, or an old identity.

beaver: <u>Physical</u>: You are focusing on productivity, efficiency, hard work, and staying busy. <u>Emotional</u>: You are damming up the flow of your emotions to feel secure, or avoiding feelings by overworking. <u>Mental-Spiritual</u>: You have a busy social life, easily overcome challenges, have a good design sense, and care for family.

bed/bedroom: <u>Physical</u>: You are focusing on regeneration, love, death, or birth. You need more sleep. <u>Emotional</u>: You need a womblike retreat, more space, or nurturing in your inner life. You want romance, marriage, sex, and a healthy intimate relationship. The bed represents your emotional condition and innermost secrets. <u>Mental-Spiritual</u>: You are trying to connect with your inner realms. Anything under the bed shows what subconsciously threatens your peace.

bees: <u>Physical</u>: You're focusing on fertility, industriousness, creativity, and how you organize your life. As makers of honey, bees symbolize a sweet outcome to projects. You have to cooperate with others to get a job done, or be content with the work you have. <u>Emotional</u>: You've been hurt or have hurt others with gossip or stinging words. Swarming bees reflect feelings of annoyance and bother. Fear of being stung shows you feel you might be injured emotionally. <u>Mental-Spiritual</u>: You're focusing on the harmonious functioning of an organization in which each individual is happy performing its job for the collective good.

bell: *(see alarm)*

below/descend: <u>Physical</u>: You're experiencing a decline in energy or status or a return to what's fundamental. You are dropping into your body fully. <u>Emotional</u>: If you are below someone, it indicates humility, service, yearning, and growth potential as well as feelings of inadequacy or depression. You feel compassion or disdain for what is below you. <u>Mental-Spiritual</u>: You are moving through your subconscious mind on a journey of self-discovery.

bill: <u>Physical</u>: You need to put forth effort to create balance for what you've received, or you need to collect what is owed you. <u>Emotional</u>: You need to be more responsible, generous, and keep your promises. You feel stressed about your image or resources. <u>Mental-Spiritual</u>: Life is handing you the bill for past mistakes, karma, and bad decisions so you can face up to the lessons you need to learn.

birds: Look to the species of bird for meaning nuances. <u>Physical</u>: You want greater lightness and freedom in your body. Singing birds bring good news. <u>Emotional</u>: Birds represent the way you love. Caged birds mean you aren't expressing yourself joyfully or freely enough. Migrating birds are about homesickness. <u>Mental-Spiritual</u>: Birds represent the ability to reach higher realms of awareness. Like angels, birds serve as messengers of the divine, and are symbols of the soul. Look for the messages birds bring.

birth/birthday: <u>Physical</u>: Giving birth symbolizes the beginning of a new project, ability, or stage of life. It relates to the desire for a child or anxiety over pregnancy. Your birthday focuses attention on how you are living your life. <u>Emotional</u>: You feel reborn. You are focusing on feminine, nurturing energy. Birthdays remembered or forgotten by others show how significant you feel as an individual. <u>Mental-Spiritual</u>: You are receiving new ideas, attitudes, plans, wishes, or parts of your destiny, and emerging into new levels of wisdom. Your birthday centers you in your sense of soul and life purpose.

black: <u>Physical</u>: Your body may be unhealthy, blocked, or feeling somewhat comatose. Black portends death or the end of something, as well as gestation. <u>Emotional</u>: You're focusing on your unconscious, the underworld, evil, fear, grief, or negative feelings. You might also feel elegant, formal, strong, and authoritative. <u>Mental-Spiritual</u>: You are aware of the death of old ideas, the mystery, deep space, the void, receptivity, or protection by or absorption into the divine feminine.

blanket: <u>Physical</u>: You need more heat or "fire element" in your body. <u>Emotional</u>: You need to feel protected and safe, hidden, or loved. <u>Mental-Spiritual</u>: You want a period of introspection and self-discovery, where greater self-love can develop.

blind/blindfold: <u>Physical</u>: Open your eyes and use them, connect with reality. <u>Emotional</u>: You aren't aware of something important or don't want to see something. Someone is deceiving you or you are deceiving yourself. <u>Mental-Spiritual</u>: You need to direct attention deeply within to experience a more spiritual or sacred connection with life. Don't be distracted by the superficial.

blood: <u>Physical</u>: You're looking at your vitality and life force as well as danger. Bleeding to death means something is draining your creativity and energy. Menstrual blood symbolizes fertility or cleansing. <u>Emotional</u>: You are focusing on a denied emotional wound, anger, hatred, or fear a loss of part of your life. Bloody violence indicates emotional upheaval. <u>Mental-Spiritual</u>: You are aware of the source of all life, what makes you strong.

blue: <u>Physical</u>: You are too cold, or have a sluggish appetite, metabolism, and circulation. Or you are too keyed up and need calmness. <u>Emotional</u>: You feel sad or depressed. Or you feel clean, precise, serious, masculine, or corporate. <u>Mental-Spiritual</u>: You have, or need, clarity, insight, truth, loyalty, justice, or neutrality. You are detached from an emotion, or overview, a soothing action, or communication based on faith and hope.

boat: Physical: You are focusing on your life's journey, wanting to make a change, or to reach the other side. Emotional: Boats show how you traverse an emotional experience, or help protect you from being overwhelmed by one. Whether a power boat, canoe, or tugboat, you're receiving insight about how you deal with emotional situations. Sinking boats indicate fear of water or an overwhelming emotional encounter you are afraid to experience. Mental-Spiritual: You're embarking on a new spiritual journey. Being becalmed or drifting aimlessly with no paddle shows apathy or lack of purpose.

bomb: *(see explosion)*

bones/skeleton/spine: Physical: You are focusing on your stability, courage to take a stand, inner strength, and the structures you live by. Broken bones represent disrupted energy flow in a particular area of the body. Emotional: You are too hard or emotionally fossilized. You need to release rigidity and resistance. You feel unsupported and weak. Mental-Spiritual: You are getting to the essence of something. Skeletons pertain to death, either literal or metaphorical. You are examining how you receive from your unconscious and transmit energy from your lower self to higher self and vice versa.

book: Physical: You are ready to receive news, or are integrating your life experiences. Emotional: Opening or closing a book symbolizes opening or closing a stage in your life. Mental-Spiritual: You are learning or reviewing your knowledge and wisdom; you are looking for guidance about life issues. Old books represent neglected or forgotten knowledge, an earlier chapter of your life, or even ancient wisdom. You are examining the book of your life — your destiny throughout time.

boss: *(see authority)*

box: <u>Physical</u>: You are focusing on your body, a particular commitment task, or goal. You need order, definition, and less or more structure. <u>Emotional</u>: You are offering a gift to others, or receiving one. An empty box means you have lost something, had something stolen by others, or can't see your own resources. <u>Mental-Spiritual</u>: You are unlocking secrets and mysteries or forming ideas into strategies and goals.

brain: <u>Physical</u>: Pay attention to your head. <u>Emotional</u>: Don't make all your decisions with your head alone, or don't be too hotheaded and impulsive. <u>Mental-Spiritual</u>: You're looking at how you process information and perceive concepts. Make better use of your intellect, pay more attention to facts and details.

brakes: <u>Physical</u>: Using brakes to stop a vehicle implies you should immediately stop or withdraw from a situation before there are disastrous consequences. You are going too fast, not taking care of your body's needs. <u>Emotional</u>: When the brakes don't work, you feel out of control about a situation, too much ahead of yourself, and helpless. <u>Mental-Spiritual</u>: You are focusing on how to regulate the flow of your self-expression.

bread: <u>Physical</u>: You are focusing on nutrition and a need for greater simplicity. <u>Emotional</u>: Bread is basic nurturing and sustenance. Bread crumbs show lack of abundance, or a process leading to greater abundance. Burned toast shows nurturing that was unappreciated and wasted. <u>Mental-Spiritual</u>: Bread is sacred, the "food of life," representing patience, humility, and other godly qualities. Fresh-baked bread shows luck coming. Offering bread to others demonstrates compassion and an open heart.

break: <u>Physical</u>: Breaking things means you need to change an area of your life, like breaking away from a relationship or job. <u>Emotional</u>: You need to break through a barrier into an area of yourself that's been repressed, or release an emotional attachment. <u>Mental-Spiritual</u>: Broken objects signify shattered ideas, hopes, or goals. It can also mean you have broken through limiting thought structures to a higher dimension.

breasts: *(see heart)*

bridge: <u>Physical</u>: Bridges indicate literal travel and life transitions. The condition of the bridge shows the type of journey it will be and your way of entering new territory. Bridges also represent relationships. <u>Emotional</u>: You're making an emotional transition and looking at ways to avoid feeling overwhelmed by emotion or the unknown. You are finding helpful connections between yourself and things you fear. <u>Mental-Spiritual</u>: You are linking life experiences or realms ,like conscious and unconscious, and dealing with unresolved contradictions and paradoxes.

brown: <u>Physical</u>: You're focusing on toxins, waste, or excrement, indicating you need better elimination. <u>Emotional</u>: You feel depressed, negative, or sluggish, or you want more comfort. <u>Mental-Spiritual</u>: Brown suggests thought processes involving greater stability, and the animalistic nature. Or, your mind is muddied with distorted thinking and other people's ideas.

bubble: <u>Physical</u>: You are releasing something from your physical system, or are experiencing indigestion with gas or bloating. <u>Emotional</u>: You want to feel lighter, more childlike, effervescent, celebratory, fun, and spontaneous. You are releasing worries, difficulties, or negative emotions. <u>Mental-Spiritual</u>: Bubbles symbolize wishes or unrealistic expectations, as in "bursting one's bubble." They also show true hopes and ascendant thoughts.

buffalo: <u>Physical</u>: You are focusing on abundance and plenty, or survival. New opportunities are coming your way. <u>Emotional</u>: You're being too obstinate. A buffalo herd symbolizes peace and increase, as well as family loyalty and safety in groups. <u>Mental-Spiritual</u>: You are focusing on how much you honor what you've been given, and whether you show gratitude for your life.

buildings: *(see architecture)*

bull's-eye: *(see arrow)*

burning: <u>Physical</u>: You are purifying, or something is disintegrating so you can move on unencumbered. <u>Emotional</u>: You are releasing anger, criticalness, or intense emotions. You feel passionate. You are living through a trial by fire or a loss beyond your control. <u>Mental-Spiritual</u>: You are focusing on bright new ideas and spiritual purity.

butterfly/caterpillar: <u>Physical</u>: You are transforming yourself in a fundamental way, growing in stages. You need more freedom. <u>Emotional</u>: You are reminding yourself to lighten up, be more tender and gentle. A flitting butterfly suggests social or romantic activity, possible infidelity or superficial involvement with others, yet with a happy attitude. <u>Mental-Spiritual</u>: You are focusing on becoming your most beautiful self. Butterflies represent the soul's essence.

buy/bargain: <u>Physical</u>: You are expanding and fortifying yourself with the tools and opportunities you need in life. <u>Emotional</u>: You feel you don't have enough love or support and are easing anxiety with new possessions. Finding a bargain means you feel lucky, or you are not valuing yourself enough. <u>Mental-Spiritual</u>: Buying indicates the acceptance of an idea or situation. You're focusing on a fair exchange of value, or that you need to receive as much as you give.

C

cactus: <u>Physical</u>: You feel crowded; someone is invading your space. You need better boundaries and more privacy. <u>Emotional</u>: You are defensive, too prickly, and isolated emotionally. You need to be flexible, and express more emotion instead of feeling so dry. <u>Mental-Spiritual</u>: You have adapted yourself to a difficult situation or need to apply a tougher attitude. The resources you need are stored within.

calendar/datebook: <u>Physical</u>: You are planning on creating or doing something that has an end date. <u>Emotional</u>: You are worried about a deadline or having enough time to do everything you need to. <u>Mental-Spiritual</u>: You are learning to be more grounded in time. You're looking at how you use your time and plan your life, how organized and prepared you are. Crossing off days on a calendar means you're marking time until an event happens.

camel: <u>Physical</u>: You are preparing for a journey. You need to conserve resources and energy. You can handle big problems and responsibilities with patience and perseverance. <u>Emotional</u>: You are carrying too many burdens. You need to express and release emotions you've been holding too tightly, or practice forgiveness. <u>Mental-Spiritual</u>: You're capable of going the distance and finding resources within when things in the outside world look bleak or hopeless. Something good is coming to you from a long distance.

camera: <u>Physical</u>: You need to pay attention to what you're doing and notice how others see you. <u>Emotional</u>: You are fixated on a particular reality, resisting change, or you are lost in nostalgia for the past. <u>Mental-Spiritual</u>: You want to stop the action, gain more information, or capture hidden meanings in a situation. You are involved with your world view, attitudes, or credo. Taking snapshots represents daily perceptions, observations, or decisions. Old photos point to something you need to remember from another time.

cancer: <u>Physical</u>: You don't necessarily have this disease, though it could be a warning. A condition in your life may be out of control, consuming your energy and vital resources. <u>Emotional</u>: An emotional issue has been denied too long or an emotional habit is out of control. You feel your life is wasting away. You feel too negative, critical, or hopeless. <u>Mental-Spiritual</u>: You are obsessing about an idea. You need to examine how fully you're living your life, how to uncork your creativity.

captivity: <u>Physical</u>: You need to stop running around and focus. Something needs attention. <u>Emotional</u>: You may feel trapped by circumstances, as though you are a victim with no choices. You may feel you're being punished. Don't give your power away to others. Mental-Spiritual: You've forgotten about free will, that it is okay to say "no." You are remembering that your soul will restrict you when you need to face important issues.

car: Physical: You're focusing on your daily life and life direction or on your body and personality. Mechanical problems indicate blocks in your body or forward movement. Being stuck or backing up means you feel this way about your progress. The condition of the vehicle gives an idea of your health condition. Emotional: Driving indicates you're in control. Riding in the passenger seat or back seat means you are deferring to another's influence or are feeling out of control. Mental-Spiritual: How you drive shows your ability to navigate through life, your ambition, confidence, and ability to make decisions. Your car gives clues to your identity. A stolen car is a loss of identity. Being hit by a car means you are in conflict with another person or way of doing things.

cards: Physical: Playing cards indicates you are using, or need to use, luck and the skills of strategy and timing in a current project or phase of your life. The number and suit of the cards provide clues to the meaning. Emotional: You feel you are gambling in some way, or that success is a matter of luck. Mental-Spiritual: Clubs mean taking action and getting down to business. Spades mean sadness, disappointment, or the presence of an obstacle. Hearts symbolize love, positive emotion, and relationships. Diamonds relate to your concepts of material and inner abundance and resources.

castle: <u>Physical</u>: You are hoping for great success, or preparing to fortify yourself for an endeavor you see as difficult but rewarding. <u>Emotional</u>: You need to protect yourself from attacks, even from your own internal critic. Castles represent a warring, defensive nature. If the drawbridge is down, you're receptive, ready to face the forces of the outside world. There is also a connotation of fairy tale rescues where you are either the hero or damsel in distress. <u>Mental-Spiritual</u>: You need to examine the idea that the world is hostile, that you need power over others, or isolation by being above it all.

cat: <u>Physical</u>: You are focusing on qualities of independence, power, self-sufficiency, mystery, magic, feminine energy or the anima, sexuality, grace, and cunning. When beautiful, a cat means you will meet a charming new person. <u>Emotional</u>: You feel others are fickle and uncaring, seductive, ominous, "catty," or aggressive. A black cat means you're hesitant; you use your intuition. Kittens symbolize unchanged, bothersome, astral plane beings. <u>Mental-Spiritual</u>: A cat's nine lives symbolize good luck and longevity.

cataclysm/catastrophe: <u>Physical</u>: Natural disasters and upheavals symbolize sudden shifts or releases of energy in your body or in the world. <u>Emotional</u>: There is emotional instability, and you're facing an upsetting experience that could change your reality. You are worried about basic survival issues. <u>Mental-Spiritual</u>: You are about to have a breakthrough into a more enlightened state as you let go and have faith.

caterpillar: *(see butterfly)*

cattle: <u>Physical</u>: You're focusing on good luck, the goddess, maternal nurturing, and fertility. Cattle feeding in a pasture signify an easy flow of income. Herding cattle means you are working harder to maintain your income. <u>Emotional</u>: You are focusing on your individuality, and going along with others too much or too little. You feel you are too passive, docile, or contented with your life. <u>Mental-Spiritual</u>: You are focusing on your intrinsic value and what you are capable of producing.

cave: <u>Physical</u>: A cave symbolizes the womb, childbearing, new life, creativity, or an empty place in you that needs more energy and attentiveness. <u>Emotional</u>: Crawling into a cave is being overwhelmed by a present situation. Living in a cave means you feel deprived, isolated, or need sustained privacy to regroup and renew. <u>Mental-Spiritual</u>: You are focusing on your deep inner self, the place of ancient wisdom, contemplation, rites of passage, initiation, the earth, and your feminine side. Coming out of a cave is the emergence of a new self and desire to be involved.

ceiling: <u>Physical</u>: You're looking at the limits you or others place on your progress. A ceiling means protection, if it's also a roof. <u>Emotional</u>: You are focusing on safety and self-expression. A leaky ceiling means an intrusion of unwanted emotions or other people's values that affect you negatively. High ceilings give you room to expand, while low ones make you feel stooped and stunted. <u>Mental-Spiritual</u>: You're looking at how you use your thoughts, how open you are to change, how imaginative and resourceful you can be, or how far you have to go to the next floor. A glass ceiling means you can see farther than you can actually go physically right now. Something unknown holds you back. Being on the ceiling looking down gives you the soul's perspective on a situation.

celebrity: *(see fame)*

cellular phone/telephone: <u>Physical</u>: You are focusing on establishing and maintaining connections and on developing telepathy and clairaudience. <u>Emotional</u>: Losing your phone means you've lost touch with your true feelings or inner self, and to the degree you are dependent on it, how capable you are of being alone. If it's ringing constantly, you need more quiet, gestation-meditation time. You are looking at the balance between extraversion and introversion in yourself. <u>Mental-Spiritual</u>: You are working with a soul group or collective consciousness. You're receiving new information, setting up events in the near future.

chase: <u>Physical</u>: If you are being chased, you are avoiding a situation that is potentially dangerous or unwanted. You have an answer someone needs. If you are the pursuer, you are chasing after a goal, trying to right a wrong that's been committed against you, or gain attention from someone who's rejected you. <u>Emotional</u>: Being chased means you feel indebted to someone, or that you're being driven away from involvement with others. It means a rejected part of you needs to be acknowledged and reintegrated into your personality. <u>Mental-Spiritual</u>: You feel pursued by disturbing, fearful ideas that you don't want to experience. The pursuer may have a message for you. The pursuer may be you!

cheat/steal: <u>Physical</u>: You are picking up hints that someone is not being truthful or committed, or you are trying to take the easy way to greater comfort. You have compromised your beliefs or integrity and are wasting time on fruitless endeavors. <u>Emotional</u>: You feel you aren't meeting the expectations of others, and are experiencing insecurity, and lack of trust and self-esteem. You feel envious of someone else's talent or fortunate circumstances. <u>Mental-Spiritual</u>: If you're cheating at a game, you probably aren't being honest with yourself. Cheating on tests, or stealing, indicates you think you lack knowledge, creativity, or a natural talent, that no one will help you so you have to take what you want.

chess: <u>Physical</u>: You have found a worthy opponent or a perfect match in love or in your professional life. You are looking at how you use your resources to accomplish goals. <u>Emotional</u>: You are showing yourself how to be more deliberate and less impulsive concerning your interactions with others. <u>Mental-Spiritual</u>: You need to think through a situation or problem more carefully before making a decision or taking action. You are looking at the greater plan for your life. *(see games)*

chest: *(see heart)*

chicken: <u>Physical</u>: You're focusing on idle chatter and gossip, what people are saying about you, or what you're saying about others. <u>Emotional</u>: You are looking at qualities of cowardliness, erratic, helter-skelter emotion, or lack of willpower. You are acting like a "mother hen," being too concerned about others. Roosters represent cocky, show-off behavior with little regard for others. <u>Mental-Spiritual</u>: Since chickens aren't known for intelligence, you're telling yourself to be more serious and focused. Hens with eggs represent new life and possibilities. Hearing a rooster crow is a wake-up call.

child: <u>Physical</u>: You are activating a new beginning, fresh perspective, latent talent, spontaneity, or trust in yourself. You are eager to learn, need simplicity, or purity. Young people symbolize lost vitality, so you may need rejuvenation. <u>Emotional</u>: You want to return to a life where you had little responsibility and fewer worries. You are pointing to your own immaturity or the need to receive unconditionally. A childhood anxiety or long-buried issue needs to be resolved. You're nurturing your vulnerable self. <u>Mental-Spiritual</u>: Innocent loving children represent the true self or child within. You are recalling old memories, or getting in touch with your playful creativity. Saving a child signifies saving a part of yourself that is in danger of being lost.

chin: <u>Physical</u>: You are "leading with your chin" and not listening to others enough. <u>Emotional</u>: You may need to be more or less assertive or stubborn. <u>Mental-Spiritual</u>: A strong or weak chin signifies how you cut through to the heart of situations, your determination and resolve.

church: <u>Physical</u>: You are looking at your mistakes and how to rectify things in your life. You need to treat your body as a temple. <u>Emotional</u>: You're looking for guidance, to be uplifted and nurtured, to forgive or be forgiven. You need to be appreciated by those you love. <u>Mental-Spiritual</u>: You're focusing on a spiritual context or space, your value system and the things you hold sacred, religious beliefs, or attitudes toward organized religion. You need to pray for yourself or others, or receive grace, spiritual nourishment, or atonement.

circle: *(see ball)*

city: <u>Physical</u>: You need more privacy or more social involvement. You are dealing with community issues involving cooperation and interdependence. <u>Emotional</u>: To be alone in a city means you feel rejected or overwhelmed by others. A city in ruins means you're neglecting social relationships. <u>Mental-Spiritual</u>: A city with tall skyscrapers indicates you're dealing with collective thought and belief structures and world views.

cliff: <u>Physical</u>: You've reached a jumping off point where you are faced with a major life change. <u>Emotional</u>: You are facing your fears, overcoming the need to retreat. <u>Mental-Spiritual</u>: You are at the edge of consciousness and the unknown, a point of heightened understanding and awareness, where you need to surrender and have faith to proceed farther. You have an expanded view.

climb: <u>Physical</u>: You are making steady progress toward a goal, requiring persistence and strength to overcome obstacles. You experience an increase in social, economic, or artistic pursuits. <u>Emotional</u>: How and what you climb shows your courage, fear, and enthusiasm for growth and the expansion of your world view. <u>Mental-Spiritual</u>: You are focusing on the specifics of your intellectual and spiritual growth, your strategy on your path forward in life.

clock/watch: <u>Physical</u>: You are aware that your biological clock is ticking, or that time is passing, and procrastination about achieving life goals needs to be overcome. You need to speed up or slow down. <u>Emotional</u>: You are anxious about being on time, meeting a deadline, or falling behind. <u>Mental-Spiritual</u>: As with any circle, a clock represents wholeness, but also the present moment, all time, and immortality. Note the hour and minute and look for meaning in the numbers.

clothes/costumes: <u>Physical</u>: You're focusing on the façade, or layers you put between yourself and others, how you portray yourself, your role in life, and how you like to feel personally. Changing clothes or costumes suggests a need for change, or adaptation to a new way of being in the world. New clothes mean social or economic improvement. <u>Emotional</u>: Being undressed to various degrees indicates feelings of vulnerability or not fitting in socially. Underwear connotes hidden sexual issues. Too many clothes show layers of protective identities. <u>Mental-Spiritual</u>: You are examining beliefs about how to express yourself, what you need to do to receive approval, and how vulnerable you can be.

clutter: <u>Physical</u>: You need to let go of or discard something. <u>Emotional</u>: You need more clear space so you can calm down and not be worried about so many things. You are afraid of being alone. <u>Mental-Spiritual</u>: You need to sort through your beliefs and see how many thoughts actually belong to other people, and get rid of them. There may be parts of the self you've rejected that need to be reclaimed.

cobwebs: <u>Physical</u>: Old spider webs and dusty conditions indicate that an area of your life has been neglected, that you've been ignoring an issue for too long. You need more exercise, better circulation, and detoxification. <u>Emotional</u>: You're apathetic, depressed, or afraid to experience emotions from the past. You need to clear emotional blockages. <u>Mental-Spiritual</u>: You are telling yourself to dust off some aspect of yourself, reexamine old beliefs, and clean house so you can see yourself clearly again.

colors: <u>Physical</u>: A pale tint of a color indicates an early stage of development or weak energy, while a dark shade conveys strength, density, toxicity, or blocked energy flow. <u>Emotional</u>: Muddy, clear, intense, light, or dark color tells you about the qualities of your current emotions. <u>Mental-Spiritual</u>: Bright, clear color indicates a heightened sense of reality, even a precognitive or visionary dream. If an object in your dream has an unusual color, you're seeing an extra overlay of meaning. Complex colors, like olive green (green and brown) or turquoise (green, yellow, and blue) contain qualities of each color.

competition: <u>Physical</u>: You are anticipating a competitive event or are involved in improving your performance under pressure. You need to grow and expand, or rest from an intense competition that's over. <u>Emotional</u>: You're focusing on being more assertive, persevering, and ambitious. Watching a competition from the sidelines means you feel others are passing you by. <u>Mental-Spiritual</u>: If you win a competition, you have the necessary skills to accomplish a goal or solve problems. You are examining the need to win and what winning and losing means.

computer/laptop: <u>Physical</u>: You need to get out more, vary your routine, and be more sensual. If the peripheral components malfunction, you are frustrated that you aren't supported or producing effectively. <u>Emotional</u>: If you lose your laptop, examine how dependent you are on external systems to give life meaning, and how you can develop more emotional richness within as well as real-time relationships with others. If you have a virus or someone is hacking into your computer, your privacy is being invaded or you feel you're at the mercy of another. <u>Mental-Spiritual</u>: You're looking at how you structure your awareness, how your mind works. You are connecting to global knowledge and examining your life record and identity. If the computer crashes, you are overloaded and need to take a break from being so mental. If you expand the memory or speed, or get a bigger monitor, you are jumping into new capacities and self-expression.

counselor: <u>Physical</u>: You need to listen to your body. If the person being counseled is not you, you may identify with that person's issues, or be concerned about his or her psychological health in waking life. <u>Emotional</u>: You are seeking support and direction. Pay attention to what the counselor is saying and doing. You need to look within to explore feelings, gain insight about a particular issue, or understand your motives. <u>Mental-Spiritual</u>: You are receiving guidance from your soul or a higher collective consciousness.

countryside: <u>Physical</u>: If your dream has a country setting, you need to focus on physical activity and more wholesome, natural values and goals. You need more space to find clarity, or a slower pace. <u>Emotional</u>: You are telling yourself to return to the basics and simplify your life. You need to feel more generous and patient. <u>Mental-Spiritual</u>: You are experiencing an expansion of thought beyond separate structures into communion and oneness.

crab: <u>Physical</u>: You are looking at your inability to effectively move forward, how you sidestep or avoid difficulties and unpleasantness. <u>Emotional</u>: You are pretending to be tough or looking at your "crabby" personality. Claws indicate a desire to cause pain to others, or fear of being hurt, as well as a tendency to grasp and cling. <u>Mental-Spiritual</u>: As with all water dwelling animals, the crab represents issues in the unconscious.

crash: <u>Physical</u>: Being in a vehicle that crashes or is about to crash indicates that a situation in your life is out of control. It also means you simply arrive suddenly and dramatically at a new level of achievement. Crashing into the ground from the air means you are descending rapidly from the mental and emotional realms, coming back to your body, or you need to be more grounded. <u>Emotional</u>: Crashing into a similar vehicle means a confrontation with someone else's physical presence (car, motorcycle), emotional values (boats), or belief structures and opinions (planes). <u>Mental-Spiritual</u>: You're going too fast, being impulsive and inflexible, listening to incorrect advice, and need to pay attention, and regulate your mind. You're experiencing a spiritual chiropractic adjustment or opening that will catalyze a new phase of your life.

criminal/outlaw: <u>Physical</u>: You're exploring your animalistic side. <u>Emotional</u>: You feel the rules don't apply to you, that you're above others. You take what you want because you feel no one will help you, that others have more than you. You are experiencing guilt over something you've done, and are anxious over being found out. <u>Mental-Spiritual</u>: If you or someone else is breaking the law, you feel too boxed in by customs, expectations, and authority and want to break through limitations.

crocodile/alligator: <u>Physical</u>: You are focusing on hidden danger, deceit, or evil-minded people. The crocodile represents your own aggressive behavior, or negative, snapping attitudes. Emotional: You feel you could be swallowed up by chaos, greed, gluttony, hidden violence, or dark, stifling emotions. Perhaps you've displayed false emotion and shed ingenuous "crocodile tears." Mental-Spiritual: You are focusing on your deepest subconscious, primal mind, your beliefs in evil and lack of safety in the world, and your survival instincts. You need to look for ways to be more sincere.

crossroads/fork in the road: Physical: You are breaking physical habits and seeking new direction in life. Emotional: You are dealing with anxiety about making the right decision, facing the unknown, or separating from loved ones. Mental-Spiritual: You have a choice to make, and it often involves an intuitive component. You are at a powerful point of integration of diverse ideas.

crowd: Physical: You are looking at your own authority, leadership ability, or questioning your role in society. Emotional: You feel you're being swallowed up by other people's ideas and emotions. Or, you need greater anonymity and privacy. Mental-Spiritual: A crowd indicates that you are participating in a group mind or collective consciousness.

crown: Physical: You have received recognition, or want to, for a job well done, or for your innate abilities. You are acknowledging your own competence and power. You are about to receive greater responsibility. Emotional: You are dealing with your relationship to authority figures. There can be issues of vanity, envy, resentment, and need for attention. Mental-Spiritual: A crown symbolizes spiritual authority, often indicating an initiation. It is a transmitter of knowledge from the collective consciousness to your conscious mind.

crystals/crystal ball: <u>Physical</u>: You need to cleanse your body or listen to the messages your body is bringing you. Seeing a crystal in the body means that area may be blocked and needs to receive and transmit energy more fully. <u>Emotional</u>: You are telling yourself you need greater inner peace and transparency (honesty and vulnerability). <u>Mental-Spiritual</u>: You are accessing higher wisdom and opening your intuition, developing clarity of perception and removing illusions. Look for the visions, take note of the messages.

cut: <u>Physical</u>: If your body is cut, or you cut someone else, you are showing yourself an area that needs to release pent-up energy, pain, and contractedness. Cutting yourself indicates a need to release feelings of turmoil by experiencing physical pain. <u>Emotional</u>: You are focusing on severed relationships, cutting off from feelings or other people, sarcastic remarks, or anger and rage. <u>Mental-Spiritual</u>: You need to cut through to the heart of an issue, be honest, and see clearly with spiritually based insight. Having your hair cut means a loss of vital power or a focusing of your consciousness to be aligned with your personal expression.

dam: <u>Physical</u>: The energy or circulation in your body is blocked. You are hoarding something. <u>Emotional</u>: You are focused on repressed emotions, holding back a flood of tears, panic, or anger. A dam breaking means you're releasing past fears and emotions.

<u>Mental-Spiritual</u>: The dam itself represents the reason you hold back your self-expression, whether that be family or cultural beliefs, an unexamined habit, or stubborn resistance to change caused by fear.

dance: <u>Physical</u>: You need more exuberant, spontaneous movement and exercise. You are focusing on romance, sexual exchange, freedom from constraints, participation in life, pleasure, frivolity, and gracefulness. <u>Emotional</u>: If dancing with others, you are looking at partnership dynamics, fluid cooperation with others, and how well you fit in and interact in your social setting. A dance performance shows how confident, talented, joyful, and comfortable you feel expressing yourself in the world. <u>Mental-Spiritual</u>: You are focusing on psychological and spiritual release and sacred communion with the rhythms of life, especially if you're dancing alone. You are integrating the masculine and feminine sides of your nature.

danger: <u>Physical</u>: You are warning yourself about something you've been overlooking. To escape danger portends success. <u>Emotional</u>: You are anxious about a situation in your waking life and need to use intuition to feel what's really happening below the surface. <u>Mental-Spiritual</u>: Confronting danger means you are overcoming fear and learning from the situation. What is dangerous in the dream is something you haven't integrated into your totality.

datebook: *(see calendar)*

daytime: <u>Physical</u>: When a dream setting is during the day, you are experiencing things clearly. What you need to do is obvious. You know where you're going in life. <u>Emotional</u>: The sunnier the scene, the more the activity represents something beneficial, or something you need to see as a good part of yourself. Mental-Spiritual: You're dealing with material that has already become conscious or you are shedding light on an important fact.

deafness: Physical: You are closing yourself off from new experiences. You don't want to hear something you need to acknowledge. Emotional: You feel secluded or excluded from the world. You are too stubborn, resisting change or other people's realities. You aren't sharing your emotional reality with others. Mental-Spiritual: You need to withdraw from the chaos of the world into a quiet inner sanctum to find your own still, small voice of guidance and truth. You need to develop greater flexibility and openness concerning ideas.

death/dead people: Physical: Dreaming of death is not necessarily a literal omen, and it's untrue that if you die in your dream, your body will also die. You're focusing on the end of a phase in your life or a part of your identity, getting ready for rebirth, renewal, and growth. Dying slowly or seeing a corpse represents a devitalized condition or lifeless routine. Emotional: You are experiencing anxiety about endings. Dreaming of another person's death means you're letting go of the quality or emotion that person represents, or you feel the possible loss of that aspect and want to activate it more in yourself. Mental-Spiritual: Talking to a person who has died is resolving incomplete communications, and it helps activate the qualities the person represents to you. You are active in the higher, more telepathic realms of your awareness, receiving guidance from your soul. Seeing yourself after death reassures you that you are eternal.

deer: <u>Physical</u>: You are focusing on your ability to be agile, graceful, and alert. You need to be more responsive to a situation, notice subtle cues, and be quieter. Deer often represent friends, and what kind of friend you are to others. <u>Emotional</u>: You need to experience gentleness, kindness, compassion, innocence, purity, and willingness to surrender. To see a dead or dying deer, or to kill a deer, warns of a betrayal by a friend, or that you have acted without heart. <u>Mental-Spiritual</u>: Deer are considered divine messengers that help open the heart. Pay attention to where they lead you, and what they say or convey with their eyes.

descend: *(see below)*

desert: <u>Physical</u>: You are dehydrated or lacking in important nutrients. You need alone time away from the overstimulation of society to renew yourself. <u>Emotional</u>: You are feeling isolated, lonely, creatively dry or barren, or poor. Storms in the desert indicate emotional issues surfacing that are connected with feeling unloved and neglected. <u>Mental-Spiritual</u>: You are deepening into your spiritual nature, retreating to a place of simplicity, silence, openness, and freedom where you can find clarity. Wandering through a desert indicates a period where you must reexamine what's truly important and possibly give up things you don't need. Finding an oasis means you're connecting with your divine nature, when and where you least expect it.

desk: <u>Physical</u>: Sitting at a desk represents self-exploration and discovery. You are focusing on your work and the technical issues of your life, taking care of business. <u>Emotional</u>: You are protecting your secrets and personal information. How neat the desk is indicates how overwhelmed you feel by details and mundane tasks. If you're at someone else's desk, you lack confidence in your own abilities or are copying someone else's qualities. <u>Mental-Spiritual</u>: You are activating new knowledge and ideas, evaluating problems and opportunities. The kind of desk hints at your sense of personal authority. Desks also represent a place or focus for bringing your creativity to life.

diamond: <u>Physical</u>: You are focusing on being the best you can be, cleaning up your act, and being totally healthy. Owning and wearing diamonds means you attain honor and recognition. Receiving a diamond from someone means you're forming a committed relationship. <u>Emotional</u>: Finding diamonds means you're about to have good luck, while stealing them means you aspire to a higher station in life than you feel worthy of or qualified to have. Losing a diamond means you aren't valuing part of yourself enough. A fake diamond means you or others are pretending to be something you're not, or you feel undervalued. <u>Mental-Spiritual</u>: You're finding clarity in matters that have been clouding you. You are focusing on your own highest, clearest soul consciousness, or clear light. You're looking at core truth, unending love, and what is permanent and enduring.

dig/dirt: <u>Physical</u>: Dirt represents fertility; you are planting the seeds of a new phase of growth. You need to clean out your body or house or simply be more grounded. <u>Emotional</u>: You want to bury, hide, or deny something. You feel unclean or guilty that you've been acting in an unwholesome or devious way. <u>Mental-Spiritual</u>: You are trying to understand yourself better, looking for root causes, hidden secrets, buried treasure, and basic motives. You are reaching down into the subconscious to unearth answers, information, or talent.

diploma: <u>Physical</u>: You have achieved a level of success and expertise and are acknowledged by others. <u>Emotional</u>: You are worried about succeeding at a task or job, or don't feel qualified to handle a situation. You have completed a difficult time of emotional clearing. <u>Mental-Spiritual</u>: You have successfully completed a life lesson or phase of growth and feel natural self-esteem. *(see graduation)*

disease: <u>Physical</u>: Dreaming of illness isn't necessarily literal or precognitive. You may be holding tension and stress in your body, or your energy may be blocked. You need to change a self-defeating lifestyle choice. <u>Emotional</u>: Getting a disease can reflect a fear of the outside world, or distrust of your own body and self. If you contract a disease from another person, you feel that person's influence in your life is detrimental. If the disease has a stigma, as with sexually transmitted diseases, you have anxiety about your morality. <u>Mental-Spiritual</u>: You are looking at your lack of faith, and where you don't feel the divine, loving presence in yourself and in life.

dive: <u>Physical</u>: You are trying to get to the bottom of a current situation. If you're standing on a diving board, you're preparing for a serious temptation or ordeal that's coming in the near future, summoning your courage. <u>Emotional</u>: You are facing and experiencing deep emotional wounds or are seeking to intensify your passion and empathy. <u>Mental-Spiritual</u>: You are delving into your subconscious as well as the greater unknown.

divorce: <u>Physical</u>: This may be a reflection of a real-life experience, or you feel you are being denied a rightful position or an opportunity to work with people you admire. <u>Emotional</u>: You are experiencing stress over a relationship that you're afraid will end or are feeling vulnerable and abandoned. You are caught in the blame game. <u>Mental-Spiritual</u>: You feel alienated from yourself and your truth, and need to reconnect with your purpose. You need to experience how loved and loving you are, that your self-worth is not dependent on approval from others. *(see ex)*

dock: <u>Physical</u>: You are grounding your creative urges. Seeing a dock from a ship means a positive turn of events and new action. <u>Emotional</u>: You are finding security amidst emotional confusion or overwhelming feelings. Sitting alone on a dock means you feel wistful, sad, or dreamy. <u>Mental-Spiritual</u>: You are bringing spiritual insight and visions through your emotion and motivation into fruition in the world, making your dreams real.

doctor/nurse/healer: <u>Physical</u>: You need to attend to your body's condition. Healing has already occurred, is about to occur, or there is a need for healing. If you have an operation in a hospital, you are adjusting the way energy flows through your subtle energy bodies and physical body. You wish for a cure for a problem you're having. <u>Emotional</u>: You need more nurturing, to feel cared for and safe. You feel too deeply probed by someone or are probing into yourself. <u>Mental-Spiritual</u>: You have subliminal insights about the cause of illness in yourself or someone else. You are focusing on the healing authority of your own soul and other knowledgeable souls, making fundamental shifts in the flow of your awareness.

dog: <u>Physical</u>: You are focusing on friendships, new relationships, family values, or masculine energy. You are working like a dog, or dog-tired, and need some rest. <u>Emotional</u>: You are looking at issues of trustworthiness, loyalty, protection, and dogged tenacity, both in yourself and others. Happy dogs and puppies symbolize simple joy in life. Aggressive dogs indicate similar tendencies in you that need appropriate outlets or that you feel defensive about being invaded. <u>Mental-Spiritual</u>: As guardians of the underworld, dogs connect you to the unconscious and often bring important messages. They also teach about openheartedness and positive attitude.

dolphin/whale: <u>Physical</u>: You are focusing on a fluid, easy way of moving through the world, working with your inner senses, especially telepathy and personal vibration. <u>Emotional</u>: You need to trust your friends and colleagues, develop a joyful attitude, and beautiful harmonious feelings. You want protection moving into unknown territory or need to feel more trust when exploring emotions. You are developing heightened sensitivity and good communication in relationships. <u>Mental-Spiritual</u>: You are seeking high-level intelligent guidance, or your soul is sending a message to you. Since dolphins and whales are conductors of souls and keepers of ancient wisdom, it's important to listen to what they say. If you're riding a dolphin or whale, you are experiencing optimism, communion, and love for humankind. Dolphins symbolize spiritual excitement while whales link to profound calmness and peace.

door/doorway: <u>Physical</u>: Stepping through a door symbolizes a new endeavor, or moving from one phase of life to another. A closed door is an unavailable opportunity, or you must exert effort to open it. A choice of many doors shows a juncture at which a choice must be made. Revolving doors suggest you're moving in circles, going nowhere. <u>Emotional</u>: If doors are locked or obstructed, you are making life difficult for yourself through resistance, or there are repressed, hidden emotions you're avoiding. You need to find the key that allows entry without force. If you can't find the door out of someplace, you're feeling trapped by life circumstances. A door slammed in your face represents opportunities that are denied you, possibly because you feel unwanted. Mental-Spiritual: You are bridging two states of awareness. A small door symbolizes the desire for inner exploration and self-discovery.

dove: Physical: You are seeking greater harmony, love, and commitment in relationships, as well as an end to disagreements. Emotional: You need inner peace, a happy domestic and social life, or look forward to the return of an old friend. Mental-Spiritual: Doves bring the olive branch of understanding and also represent the Holy Spirit or a connecting link between heaven and humankind. Released from the hands, the dove flies with joy toward the divine. You are seeking communion.

dragon: Physical: You are focusing on protecting or uncovering buried secrets and talents, your heroic nature, and on balancing your internal masculine and feminine energies. Dragons in western culture represent fire and earth. A fire-breathing dragon in a cave means you are freeing your wildness and protective nature. In eastern culture, dragons represent air and water and are good luck. A flying or swimming dragon indicates you are freeing your emotional, mental, and spiritual life. Emotional: Slaying a western dragon means you are overcoming your fears. Riding an eastern dragon means good fortune and wisdom is coming your way. Mental-Spiritual: You are looking at what is hidden deep within the soul, at your true powers and riches.

drawer: <u>Physical</u>: You are looking at parts of yourself that have been stored away or hidden, that you now are ready to use. An open drawer signifies a new opportunity, and if full, you'll have plenty of resources and help. An empty drawer is an invitation to create. <u>Emotional</u>: You are showing yourself your internal state, whether it is disorderly and chaotic or neatly organized with psychological order. A locked drawer suggests obstacles in your path or resistance from someone. <u>Mental-Spiritual</u>: You are reviewing opportunities, resources, and old ideas. If you clean out your drawers, you are making space for a new, more inspired awareness and updated accomplishments.

drift/float: <u>Physical</u>: You need to strengthen personal discipline and reaffirm your goals, or you need some downtime to relax. <u>Emotional</u>: You have lost your motivation, are distracted, or feel unfocused. You are between projects or phases of your life, feeling anxiety about what to do next. <u>Mental-Spiritual</u>: The motion of drifting and floating represents activity in the spiritual realm. You need to let go and simply "be" wherever you are and realign with your higher purpose, letting new direction arise spontaneously.

driving: <u>Physical</u>: You are focusing on taking charge of your life direction and journey. If you can't see the road ahead, you lack a sense of purpose and goals. Driving into oncoming traffic means you are challenging others and making progress difficult for yourself. <u>Emotional</u>: If someone else is driving, you feel passive, powerless, or at the mercy of external influences. If you're speeding or tailgating, you are being too selfish, and out of harmony with others. <u>Mental-Spiritual</u>: You are experiencing the process of manifesting your life. Driving in reverse means you are caught in illusion, ignoring important facts.

drown: <u>Physical</u>: Your body is bloated and retaining water, or you need to flush out toxins with more water. <u>Emotional</u>: You feel unable to keep your head above water. You are overwhelmed by your life and subliminal emotions, or those of others. You feel frightened of being swallowed up by unconscious forces. You are dealing with difficult issues concerning your mother or your birth experience. Seeing someone drown suggests you're too involved in something beyond your control or you've lost your identity. <u>Mental-Spiritual</u>: You are allowing yourself to be reborn, to surrender to the unknown, and access deep wisdom and feminine energy.

drum: <u>Physical</u>: If you are playing the drums, you are living life on your own terms. <u>Emotional</u>: The kind of drums you play or hear shows the emotional state, and thus the overall tone of your life: it might be jazzy and exciting, militant, wild, or like jungle drums. <u>Mental-Spiritual</u>: To hear a drum symbolizes the rhythm of life, your heartbeat, and the need to keep a steady pace in the pursuit of your goals. There might also be a message in the drumbeat, or someone is calling for help.

DVD: <u>Physical</u>: Watching a DVD indicates you need to activate your visual imagination and relax for awhile. Returning a DVD to the store means you're finished with an experience, ready to begin a new endeavor. <u>Emotional</u>: Moving back and forth through a DVD means you have regrets or remorse and wish you could go back and do something over again, or you are trying to remember something important. <u>Mental-Spiritual</u>: You're looking for new ideas about what's possible in your life, or you're examining everything you've done so far, as though in a life review.

E

eagle/hawk: <u>Physical</u>: You are focusing on your own natural authority, nobility, power, courage, fierceness, and pride. You are looking at long-range goals and ambitions, perhaps connected to attaining wealth and influence. <u>Emotional</u>: You are learning to control your emotions and focus attention more neutrally, though you may be aggressive and somewhat ruthless. <u>Mental-Spiritual</u>: You're stretching your mind into the spiritual realms, looking for clear perception, keen discrimination, and larger perspective. These high-flying birds act as messengers from the sun, or soul, from other souls in the highest dimensions, so look for messages and lessons.

ears: *(see deafness)*

earth: <u>Physical</u>: You are working on being fully focused in your body, being practical, and finishing things so you have tangible results. You need to be more loyal, committed, stable, or careful. Issues of fertility are on your mind. <u>Emotional</u>: Under the earth's surface, for example, in caves, tunnels, basements, cellars, and graves, lurk the contents of your subconscious mind, which are often frightening. You are facing your long-buried monsters. <u>Mental-Spiritual</u>: The earth seen as a globe indicates wholeness, the mother principle, and global awareness. The earth also contains buried treasure and ancient wisdom. You're deepening your awareness.

earthquake: <u>Physical</u>: You're experiencing, or are about to experience, a shake-up of your world that threatens your stability and foundations. If you escape from the quake, you overcome the challenges.

<u>Emotional</u>: You are caught in feelings of anxiety, insecurity, and helplessness. You can't depend on people you thought were reliable. You are letting go of controlling behavior and old fears. <u>Mental-Spiritual</u>: You're focusing on a total change in the way you view your life — and even reality itself — and on the development of new attitudes and mindsets.

east: <u>Physical</u>: You're focusing on a new beginning, renewal, or birth. You need to dedicate yourself to an area of your life, like your goals, career, family, or personal growth. You are looking for opportunities and adventure. <u>Emotional</u>: You are impulsive and ahead of yourself, overenthusiastic and blind to something. <u>Mental-Spiritual</u>: You're looking for fresh perspective, insight, new intellectual knowledge, and control.

eat/food: <u>Physical</u>: You need a consistent diet of healthy foods, or less or more food. You are seeking gratification based on physical pleasures. Eating with others means harmonious cooperation, personal gain, and joyful undertakings. If someone is taking food away from you, you have trouble with jealous people. <u>Emotional</u>: The food you're eating shows a part of yourself you've been denying that needs to be integrated. You are worrying about something that's "eating at you." If you're eating alone, you feel loss, loneliness, rejection, or depression. You crave companionship and the comfort of being loved. <u>Mental-Spiritual</u>: Eating represents taking in new ideas or trying to find spiritual fulfillment.

eavesdrop: <u>Physical</u>: Others are taking advantage of you, or vice versa. You need to pay closer attention in your waking life to what you're being told. <u>Emotional</u>: You feel left out of the loop, that you

must gain advantage by secretive means. You feel insecure because you don't know enough. <u>Mental-Spiritual</u>:
You're looking for insight and information you think
other people have, when what you really need to know
is inside yourself. Be more open to hearing the guidance and criticism of others. *(see gossip)*

egg: <u>Physical</u>: Develop your inner resources, break out
of your shell. You are ready for a new phase of life, and
you're focusing on your creative potential. <u>Emotional</u>:
You feel nurturing and patient, or need this from
others. Cracked, broken eggs mean you feel drained,
unappreciated, vulnerable, fragile, or like a failure.
<u>Mental-Spiritual</u>: You have many unhatched ideas, or
ideas that need to gestate longer. You are focusing on
wholeness and spiritual potential. Broken eggs mean
you've spilled your ideas before they were fully
cooked.

elbow: <u>Physical</u>: You need to make more space for
yourself or push obstacles aside. <u>Emotional</u>: You feel
you are fending off people who want too much from
you, or you hesitate to take up your own space for fear
of being judged. <u>Mental-Spiritual</u>: You are focusing on
your ability to translate your heart's desires into form
without interference, granting yourself the right to be
fully extended into the world.

electricity: <u>Physical</u>: You are focusing on the workings
of your nervous system or your charisma and the
power to affect other people, or be affected by other
intense people. A live electrical wire represents the
threat of sudden disruption or destruction of your
plans. <u>Emotional</u>: Your emotions are too high-strung, or
you need a jumpstart of excitement. To be shocked by
electricity means you need to wake up to a potential

danger. <u>Mental-Spiritual</u>: You are taken with new ideas that tend to overwhelm you or push you to the edge of a sudden personality change. You are "rewiring" your internal circuitry, attuning yourself, preparing to run a higher frequency of spiritual energy through your system.

elephant: <u>Physical</u>: You are focusing on laying solid groundwork for prosperity and success through developing a steadfast character, excellent memory and intelligence, gentleness, family values, loyalty, honor, dignity, and the power to perform daunting tasks. <u>Emotional</u>: You feel introverted and in need of greater kindness and sensitivity. If the elephant is wild or untamed, you are looking at rogue or uncontrollable forces and plundering emotions affecting your life. <u>Mental-Spiritual</u>: You are developing your heart to a high degree, merging intelligence with compassion. You are understanding how lucky you are.

elevator/escalator: <u>Physical</u>: You are experiencing many ups and downs in your life, changing status, or you are moving into different parts of your body to heal yourself. A falling elevator represents a rapid descent from higher dimensions back to the body, often just before you awake. <u>Emotional</u>: If you are going down, you are descending into your subconscious to discover what's blocking you, or you're bringing higher motives to bear in your everyday life. If you're in a falling elevator, you feel out of control or need to surrender. If you're stuck between floors, you need to clarify your intentions and see why you're afraid to move. <u>Mental-Spiritual</u>: Elevators and escalators help you move between levels or dimensions of yourself. If you're moving up, you are addressing important issues, finding a more elevated view, and making progress on your spiritual journey with ease.

enemy: *(see adversary)*

escape: <u>Physical</u>: Escape from jail or a confined place signifies your need to move beyond a restrictive situation or attitude. <u>Emotional</u>: You are resisting something you need to face, or you've allowed yourself to become dominated and must take back your authority. <u>Mental-Spiritual</u>: You are taking an escapist attitude, bucking authority, or are dissolving barriers and boxes — mental structures — you've been living within. To escape from injury means you're connecting with your natural freedom and well-being.

explosion/bomb: <u>Physical</u>: You are experiencing a sudden release of energy or toxicity in your body, or a sudden upheaval and change in your life that might involve loss. Something needs to move, and you need to let go. Finding an unexploded or ticking bomb is a sign that something is about to blow open. <u>Emotional</u>: You are experiencing an emotional catharsis, a release of anger and violence. If you are blown up into the air or engulfed in flames, you feel the brunt of a betrayal or abuse from others. <u>Mental-Spiritual</u>: You are experiencing a release of *kundalini* (a vital force that lies dormant, but once awakened, leads to enormous spiritual energy) energy that frees your consciousness to move to higher realms. You are making rapid progress on your spiritual path.

ex: <u>Physical</u>: People you had past relationships with, even old friends, indicate that you're working out lessons that pertained to those relationships. You are integrating a quality he or she represented that you have ex-ed out or neglected in yourself. <u>Emotional</u>:

You have incomplete emotions from the past that are being triggered by a similar situation in your current life. What you learned from a previous relationship needs to be applied to a present one so you don't repeat a mistake. <u>Mental-Spiritual</u>: You are looking at your inner balance of masculine and feminine energy. You are contemplating the positive traits you want in a new relationship. *(see divorce)*

eyes/eyebrows: <u>Physical</u>: If you see your own eyes, you are focusing on accepting yourself fully, or are receiving information about the condition of your physical eyes. If someone is winking, you're being let in on a secret or something is being kept from you. If there is something in your eye, there are obstacles in your path. <u>Emotional</u>: You are opening to experience the love that comes through these windows of the soul. Closed eyes mean you are afraid to see the truth, are avoiding intimacy, or need to introvert to find deeper knowledge. Crossed eyes mean you are confused. Eyebrows show emotions like amazement, disbelief, doubt, concern, or disapproval. <u>Mental-Spiritual</u>: You are focusing on your ability to see clearly, how you receive insight, your own visions, and level of enlightenment. If you have one eye, you are refusing to accept other viewpoints. If you have a third eye, you have a clear inner vision of spiritual truth. Floating, disembodied eyes are spiritual guides connecting with you.

F

face: <u>Physical</u>: Seeing your face means you're focusing on your self-image or the mask you show others, and how much of your real self shines through. You are experiencing confrontations or heightened visibility in waking life. Emotional: Looking out from another person's face indicates an aspect of yourself you need to accept and express. If your face is scarred, flawed, red, or pimply, you are experiencing erupting emotions, embarrassment, self-consciousness, or slights to your reputation. Interacting with a faceless person indicates you've decided to be impersonal and are not facing emotional discomforts. Mental-Spiritual: Facial expressions convey nuances of attitudes you are unconsciously expressing.

falling: Physical: It's not true that you'll die if you don't wake up before you hit bottom. You need to surrender in an area of your life and have faith. You feel you've lost control, or are headed for failure or a fall from grace. Emotional: You are dealing with feelings of insecurity, helplessness, lack of confidence, fear of losing someone, or worry. Falling a long way and landing safely means you can trust your instinct to lead you out of difficulty. Mental-Spiritual: Falling represents the basic downward momentum of consciousness from the higher realms back to the body, and can happen just before you awake.

fame/famous people: Physical: You need attention, recognition, freer self-expression, and interaction with others at a larger scale than you presently have. You're focusing on qualities in the celebrity that you'd like to activate or make peace with in yourself. Look for specific character traits and judgments you hold concerning the person. Emotional: You doubt your ability to please others and be loved, or to be as excellent as you can be when scrutinized too closely. Mental-Spiritual: You need to get clear about what success means to you. You're glimpsing what you are capable of when your soul is fully present.

fat: <u>Physical</u>: You need more personal space and insulation from others, to take up your own space and be yourself without apology. You need to share and release more of your self-expressive energy.
<u>Emotional</u>: You are afraid of getting fat and being rejected by others. You feel guilty about something you did. You feel you can't get enough love, that you need to hoard your reserves because loss is always imminent. <u>Mental-Spiritual</u>: You are focusing on the need for gratitude, how you should use what you've already been given, how big you really are spiritually.

father: <u>Physical</u>: You are examining the way you use power, authority, protectiveness, control, and leadership skills. You need to be more self-reliant. If your father dies in the dream, you need to take a new leadership role in your life. <u>Emotional</u>: You are working out emotional issues you have with your own father.
<u>Mental-Spiritual</u>: The archetypal father, shown by any male authority figure, represents kingly power, provision, impersonal love, the law, tradition, discipline, and structure. You are looking at your ideas of the Creator.

feces: <u>Physical</u>: You need to cleanse your body, change your diet, or take care with your elimination system. You need to rid your life of toxic people, clutter, and situations that have outlived their usefulness. <u>Emotional</u>: There are aspects of yourself you consider dirty and repulsive. You are in denial, or ending a period of denial and self-deception. You have low self-esteem or are caught in too much complaining and negativity. This also pertains to anal retentive behavior. <u>Mental-Spiritual</u>: You are becoming aware of negative habits and getting rid of them, or simply letting go of a period of life or ideas that might serve as fertilizer to others.

feet: <u>Physical</u>: You are looking at how you take a stand, achieve grounding, find support and balance, and begin to move forward. You need to be more practical and sensible, or you are ready for more independence and freedom. <u>Emotional</u>: Being barefoot means you're connecting directly with what's real, not putting on false airs. Having no feet means you feel unprepared for what's coming. <u>Mental-Spiritual</u>: You're focusing on foundational thought structures and your sense of understanding. You're contemplating your human connection with the world and how to be more fully present. If you're washing someone's feet, you are respecting that person's spiritual self.

fence: <u>Physical</u>: You're focusing on a limitation you've put on yourself, a challenge or barrier to forward movement, the need for privacy and boundaries, respect for others' boundaries, or the need to pause and reconsider goals. Climbing or jumping over a fence means you're expanding into new territory where you may meet with opposition at first. <u>Emotional</u>: You feel ostracized or invaded by others. You are dealing with issues of entitlement. <u>Mental-Spiritual</u>: You are "on the fence" about an issue or decision. You're examining your world view and its limits, especially if you climb to the top of a fence.

fight: *(see battle)*

files/folders/file cabinet: <u>Physical</u>: You need to keep your facts and information straight. Whether electronic or paper, you're retrieving data and resources you need to function successfully and be yourself. You need to design better systems for your life and work. <u>Emotional</u>: You feel overwhelmed by detail, afraid of falling behind, or insecure because you lack information you need. If a file cabinet is locked, there is something you don't want revealed to others or something is being kept from you. <u>Mental-Spiritual</u>: You're focusing on bodies of knowledge or memories and whether to keep making them real or to let them go. A file cabinet with open drawers means you welcome new viewpoints and ideas.

fire: <u>Physical</u>: Check the "fire element" in your body, often connected to the heart and liver. You need to purify and burn off toxins, get more oxygen. You are ready for a transition that might require total release of the old. If you put out fires, you'll overcome obstacles and succeed, though getting there may seem endless. A bonfire suggests there is a larger goal you hadn't considered. <u>Emotional</u>: Setting fires, seeing an inferno, being burned, or being caught in a fire all indicate that you're angry, full of suppressed rage that threatens to go out of control, and you're afraid of the destructive consequences. You feel passionate, impulsive, desirous, or zealous. Breathing fire means a vicious verbal attack. A fire in a fireplace denotes contentment, safety, and romance. <u>Mental-Spiritual</u>: You're involved in a process of purification, illumination, spiritual transformation, and waking to your positive powers. A firefly means you're receiving bright ideas and insights from your highest self.

fireworks: <u>Physical</u>: You want to celebrate a personal achievement. You'd like to be the center of attention and show off to others. <u>Emotional</u>: You're ready to release pent-up emotion and feel more jubilant. You need more exhilarating activity. <u>Mental-Spiritual</u>: You are entering a period of colorful, uninhibited self-expression where you'll discover exciting new ideas, talents, and levels of creativity. You've broken through to a new level of awareness.

fish/fishing: <u>Physical</u>: Catching a fish, especially a big one, portends success in a venture. Seeing fish means you need to be more adaptable, flexible, and sensitive. <u>Emotional</u>: You are focusing on specific feelings in your subconscious. Catching a fish means dealing with one deep emotional issue. Trying to hold a fish that wriggles away means you're having trouble forming or maintaining a relationship. A dead or dying fish signifies disappointment or hopelessness. You are insecure, "fishing for compliments." <u>Mental-Spiritual</u>: You are dipping into the collective unconscious for creative ideas, or messages from the superconscious mind. You are actively pursuing a spiritual quest and transformation.

flag: <u>Physical</u>: You're focusing on your identity as part of a large group or the qualities you hold in common with others. A waved flag warns of dangerous conditions ahead, a new group you're about to encounter, or signals the end of a process you've been engaged in. <u>Emotional</u>: You're focused on feelings of pride, loyalty, family, and patriotism, and issues of belonging or being an outcast. <u>Mental-Spiritual</u>: You're looking at the goals and beliefs you hold in common with a group.

float: *(see drift)*

flood: <u>Physical</u>: You are experiencing an overwhelming situation, often with tribulations and serious repercussions. <u>Emotional</u>: You feel out of control and overwhelmed by repressed emotions or other people's emotions. You have lost your boundaries.

<u>Mental-Spiritual</u>: A gentle flood, leaks in the house, or broken pipes indicate that you're in a process of cleaning yourself up, preparing for a new phase of growth. *(see drown)*

floor: <u>Physical</u>: You are focusing on your support system and the foundations of your life. Repairing, replacing, or shining the floor means you're improving the basic conditions of your home and work life. If the floor is slanted or uneven, you have minor impediments to success that must be patiently remedied. <u>Emotional</u>: You may feel "floored" by emotions that cause you to stop or surrender. <u>Mental-Spiritual</u>: A floor represents a division between the conscious and unconscious mind as well as between various levels of your awareness, as with multi-storied buildings. You are shifting your reality if you're moving between floors. The floor you stand on is the reality you're creating.

flower: <u>Physical</u>: You are focusing on the stage of your personal growth process (bud to full flower), your beauty, attractiveness, sexuality, sensuality, and natural self-expression. <u>Emotional</u>: You're activating feelings of peace, gentleness, kindness, pleasure, sweetness, and love. You want to be defenseless. Withered or dead flowers denote disappointment or loss of hope and joy. The flower's color gives clues to the emotion: yellow/joy, white/sadness and purity, red/romantic love, pink/affection, lavender/spiritual connection. Receiving a bouquet means you are loved, appreciated, and admired. <u>Mental-Spiritual</u>: You are tuning in to your soul and heart, and how perfect, beautiful, and unique you are.

flying: <u>Physical</u>: You're focusing on your dreams, goals, and how far you want to go in life. How you fly represents the way you grow and express your creativity. Flying easily, surveying the landscape, means you're on top of a situation, or that you've risen above something that used to be a problem. Running into power lines, trees, mountains, or other obstacles means you're dealing with people, situations, or ideas that block your progress. <u>Emotional</u>: You need more freedom, exhilaration, adventure, and joy. If you feel fear about the inability to control your flight or flying too high, you doubt your power and skill and may dread the possibility of failure. <u>Mental-Spiritual</u>: You're moving up in frequency, expanding your consciousness through the dimensions. You want more spiritual knowledge, the big picture, or a higher perspective on a situation. *(see above)*

fog: <u>Physical</u>: You are invisible to others, not making the impact you want. A situation hides some important factors. You aren't facing reality. Others are obscuring the truth. <u>Emotional</u>: If the scene is shrouded in fog, you feel confused, directionless, and lost. <u>Mental-Spiritual</u>: You can't see clearly and need to explore the unconscious, unknown inner realms for answers. If the fog lifts, pay attention to what you see.

food: *(see eat)*

forest: <u>Physical</u>: You need to retreat, achieve calmness, rebuild vitality, soak up the greenness of nature. A forest fire implies that the density of a period in your life is finally clearing. <u>Emotional</u>: You feel overwhelmed by potential dangers, the unknown, or the uncontrollable, especially if you are lost in a forest or traversing one. <u>Mental-Spiritual</u>: You are focusing on your subconscious, secrets, mysteries, memories, and feminine wisdom. You're using your intuition to find answers.

fork in the road: *(see crossroads)*

fortuneteller/psychic: <u>Physical</u>: Your life is about to change. <u>Emotional</u>: You are anxious about your future. You're looking at a tendency to give your authority to others who you think know more than you. Be sure to weigh the information you receive against your waking common sense to make sure it isn't fear-based. <u>Mental-Spiritual</u>: You have a strong desire to discover the unknown. Soliciting guidance from a spiritually oriented source means a higher part of you is sending an important message.

fox: <u>Physical</u>: Someone is acting dishonestly or secretively, or you are acting in a cunning or wily manner. You need to remain silent, or speak in favor of diplomacy. <u>Emotional</u>: You feel manipulated or victimized by clever, sly people. You are focusing on a woman who is a "vixen," or "foxy," and whom you don't trust. <u>Mental-Spiritual</u>: You need to sharpen your mental awareness and pay more attention to what's going on around you.

frog: <u>Physical</u>: You need renewal, cleansing, or rebirth. You are ready for a major change. <u>Emotional</u>: Because frogs are bringers of rain and messengers of water spirits, they indicate you are clearing your emotions, becoming more sensitive to others, and diving deep into your unconscious to bring truths to the surface. <u>Mental-Spiritual</u>: You are focusing on metamorphosis; the tadpole becomes the frog, the frog becomes the handsome prince. Pay attention to messages from frogs, and trust your growth process.

front: Physical: The front part of anything, like a front porch or the front bumper of a car, interfaces with the public and the world. You're focusing on how others see and know you, and how you portray your personality to others. Emotional: You are examining how strong or vulnerable you feel about being a leader, pioneer, or innovator. You feel too visible or unprepared. Sitting in the front row means you are ready to be involved. Mental-Spiritual: You're focusing on what is consciously known. If you are in front of other people, you're teaching or initiating; if others are in front of you, you're learning or following.

fruit: Physical: You need more fresh, highly nutritional food. You are fertile and ready to have a child. You are ripe, full of talent, and ready to express yourself or move into a new phase. Picking ripe fruit or seeing a bowl of fruit is an omen of prosperity and success to come. Emotional: You feel abundant, sensual, sexual, seductive, luscious, and tempting. Bitter, rotten, or wormy fruit symbolizes untruthfulness, lack of trust, or an area of self-expression that troubles you. Mental-Spiritual: You are focusing on positive values, the appropriate span of time for a successful process, and the abundance within.

funeral: Physical: A situation, relationship, or aspect of yourself has ended or needs to end. You are putting something to rest, closing the lid on the past, letting go, and moving into a new life phase. Emotional: You are releasing old feelings you've been clinging to. Attending the funeral of someone who is still alive means you need to separate from restrictions you feel from that person and be more independent. <u>Mental-Spiritual</u>: You are examining lifeless ideas and world views that have no relevance for you anymore. You're expanding beyond your known world.

furniture: <u>Physical</u>: You are focusing on the habits, relationships, and the "stuff" of your daily and domestic life. If you're rearranging or moving furniture, you are changing your routine, what you depend on, the way you do things, or the flow of your energy. <u>Emotional</u>: Décor indicates your mood. Dark, formal fabrics and furniture mean depression or seriousness, while lighter, contemporary furnishings indicate spontaneity and inventiveness. <u>Mental-Spiritual</u>: Old or worn furniture symbolizes outdated attitudes and old ways of thinking. How you use the furniture shows your mental habits. New furniture means growth and change.

G

games/gambling: <u>Physical</u>: Playing a game suggests you need to relax and stop pressuring yourself. You are looking at your competitive nature and the rules you live by. You're challenging yourself to do better. Winning at gambling means you're likely to have success in an endeavor, but not necessarily gambling. <u>Emotional</u>: You're being impulsive, taking risks in an area of your life, either mild, enlivening ones, or dramatic, potentially dangerous ones, looking for reward. You're overlooking clues about how to be successful, or want to avoid facing uncomfortable things about yourself. <u>Mental-Spiritual</u>: You need to take more chances and believe you're naturally lucky. You are relying on fate, not taking responsibility for your decisions. You are working out a strategy of a new phase of experience.

garage: <u>Physical</u>: You're looking at your motivation, ability, reserves of energy, and the tools and techniques you use to accomplish your goals. You are in a period of inactivity, getting ready for new direction. <u>Emotional</u>: You're focusing on how stable and safe your life is. The condition (messy, organized) represents the way you store and manage your inner resources. If the garage is crammed with stuff, you feel afraid you won't be prepared for the many demands of the world. <u>Mental-Spiritual</u>: You're focusing on planning, strategizing, goal setting, and maintaining resources, things that allow you to progress. Cleaning out the garage means you are releasing old ideas and techniques that don't work anymore.

garbage: <u>Physical</u>: You need to detoxify or cleanse your body. Rooting through trash indicates you still have use for something you haven't paid attention to in a long time. Or, you have to do something you don't want to do. <u>Emotional</u>: You feel rejected, tossed aside, unwanted, expendable, or distasteful. Rooting through a stranger's garbage shows your desire for useful, free surprises, parts of yourself or new creative ideas. <u>Mental-Spiritual</u>: You're ready to discard habits, attitudes, and beliefs that are no longer necessary. You're dealing with ugly, negative thought structures in others that you're seeking to be free from.

garden: <u>Physical</u>: You're focusing on nurturing your body, and on new projects you'll cultivate in the future. Weeding and watering suggest the need for organization, tending, clearing of clutter, and renewal of purpose. Emotional: You need new life, beauty, peace, a sense of abundance, nurturing, even magic. Mental-Spiritual: You're focusing on your inner life, on the ideas, habits, and relationships that are growing on you and becoming important. A lush garden indicates your interest and involvement with life, spiritual growth, and healing.

geese: Physical: You need freedom or travel, to undertake new actions. You need to communicate and express yourself, especially through stories. A goose laying an egg means a pleasant, valuable surprise. Emotional: You feel you have too much or too little security or loyalty concerning family, marriage, or group affiliations. You need greater perseverance. Mental-Spiritual: You are conforming too much to others or exhibiting silly or gossiping behavior. Migrating geese point to the need to pay attention to instinct and intuition, to going home or centering in the self. You are focusing on your spiritual quest, or journeying to other worlds.

geyser: Physical: You are ready for new action and adventure. Emotional: Your emotions have built to an explosive stage, or you have had a violent outburst of repressed anger and emotion and are looking at how to deal with the repercussions. Mental-Spiritual: There is great enthusiasm in your soul, excitement about life, and new ideas are ready to burst forth.

ghost: Physical: This may be a literal visitation from another being or someone who has died. Look for the purpose behind the appearance. Emotional: You are not occupying yourself fully, or you feel disconnected from your life. You're focused on unresolved memories and repressed feelings, or aspects of yourself that you fear. You are afraid of dying. <u>Mental-Spiritual</u>: You're focusing on desires that haven't successfully manifested, or part of yourself that has remained in the background, unexpressed. A message from a ghost is from your own higher self or a spiritual guide.

gift: <u>Physical</u>: You're looking at your inner talents, acknowledging and honoring yourself. Receiving a gift brings good luck in fortune and love. <u>Emotional</u>: You feel you need to be appreciated and rewarded. You need to be more open and share yourself with others. You are trying to find a way to carefully express your feelings so you don't hurt or upset others. <u>Mental-Spiritual</u>: You need to focus on your lovable nature, on expressing gratitude to others or to a higher power for what's good in your life.

giraffe: <u>Physical</u>: You need to stick your neck out or extend yourself to succeed or find the right resources. You can reach beyond what others can see or do. <u>Emotional</u>: You have your head in the clouds and need to focus on personal and practical issues. If the giraffe is trying to eat grass awkwardly, you are in danger from sudden attacks. <u>Mental-Spiritual</u>: You have the ability to see different perspectives or both sides of an issue, or you need a broader view of a situation. You need to keep your feet firmly on the ground while viewing the distance clearly.

glass/glasses: <u>Physical</u>: There are invisible barriers between yourself, your goals, others, and the world. Broken glass means something you thought would last, will end surprisingly or too soon. <u>Emotional</u>: You feel removed, out of touch with others, or misunderstood. Frosted glass signifies greater feelings of insulation, that secrets are present, or you need privacy.

<u>Mental-Spiritual</u>: Seeing through clear glass or glasses indicates revelation, insight, or a clear perspective. Dirty glass or glasses means you have limiting beliefs or blind spots in the way. Losing your glasses means trouble judging things correctly. Breaking glass is about shattering illusions to move through barriers.

gloves: <u>Physical</u>: You or someone you know needs to be handled with care. You need to get a better grip on something. Your creativity or ability to touch others is veiled in some way. Gardening or work gloves indicate you're ready to begin a new phase of productivity. Driving gloves mean you're taking control of your life direction. Gloves that are too large mean you took on more than you can handle. <u>Emotional</u>: You're protecting yourself from harm. Throwing down a glove means you're challenging yourself or someone else. Boxing gloves indicate you're ready to confront an opponent or critic, perhaps an inner one. <u>Mental-Spiritual</u>: Putting on gloves means you are preparing mentally for something that requires concentration and effort. Taking gloves off is a sign of completion and friendliness. Dropping a glove means flirtation.

glue: <u>Physical</u>: You are piecing together aspects of yourself, building a strong, mature personality. You are repairing a situation or relationship that has been fragmented and damaged. <u>Emotional</u>: You're focusing on being committed and loyal, or you are afraid to be stuck in bad relationships and lose your freedom. You feel distrusting. <u>Mental-Spiritual</u>: You're looking for ideas and visions that link parts of your life together and serve a unifying function.

gold: <u>Physical</u>: You are focusing on a treasured part of yourself, something valuable about a situation you should pay attention to, or an inner lesson that will bring success. <u>Emotional</u>: You are working on issues of self-esteem, internal and external abundance, wealth, good luck, and how openhearted you want to be. <u>Mental-Spiritual</u>: You're connecting with high-quality, pure thoughts, wisdom, and spiritual gifts that cannot tarnish. You're in tune to a level of brightness that will attract similar experiences into your life.

gopher: <u>Physical</u>: You need more contact with your body and the earth. You need to get busy and dig in to a project. Someone is invading your territory, leaving holes for you to fall into; look for hidden snafus. <u>Emotional</u>: The pun "gofer" applies here, as you may feel you are doing others' bidding and not what's important to you. <u>Mental-Spiritual</u>: You have strayed too far from common sense. You need silent, retreat time to regain mental clarity.

gorilla: <u>Physical</u>: You need to take stronger, more forceful action, or temper your dominating behavior. You are focusing on your wildness and sexual nature. <u>Emotional</u>: You are dealing with your primitive instincts, impulses, and reactionary feelings. You need to feel more pride in yourself. <u>Mental-Spiritual</u>: You are dipping into your primal self and your body's non-verbal wisdom.

gossip: <u>Physical</u>: Overhearing gossip means you are gullible or receiving information that is shallow or inaccurate. If you are gossiping, you're being counter-productive and are likely to experience negative reper-cussions or humiliation later. <u>Emotional</u>: You're afraid to confront someone or share yourself openly. You feel unfairly judged or disrespected. You feel ashamed of the way you treated someone else. <u>Mental-Spiritual</u>:

Being gossiped about means you're sorting through negative self-concepts looking for your higher truth, or you are deciding how openhearted you want to be. *(see eavesdropping)*

graduation: <u>Physical</u>: You're acknowledging an achievement and your readiness to move on to new challenges and develop new abilities. <u>Emotional</u>: You need to feel more satisfaction and worthiness. <u>Mental-Spiritual</u>: You've reached a new level of spiritual awareness, an initiation has been completed, and you're entering a new period of inner growth. *(see diploma)*

grandparent/aunt/uncle: <u>Physical</u>: Whether you see a living relative or one who has died, you are focusing on love, security, wisdom, and protection. <u>Emotional</u>: Searching for an older relative means you're revisiting childhood memories and emotional needs. <u>Mental-Spiritual</u>: You are receiving important guidance and wisdom concerning family beliefs and mores.

groups: <u>Physical</u>: You need to work with others without losing yourself. You're looking at ways you can belong to and serve your community. <u>Emotional</u>: You are merging various parts of your character and personality, as well as diverse feelings, to find greater understanding and compassion. <u>Mental-Spiritual</u>: You are focusing on collective consciousness, group mind, and societal beliefs.

green: <u>Physical</u>: You need healing, rest, renewal, or time in nature. You are "green," or lack experience, and need to put in your dues and practice more. You want greater prosperity, money, and abundance. <u>Emotional</u>: You need to feel safe, balanced, calm, peaceful, and harmonious. You need to integrate your male and female energy. Dark green is associated with ambition, greed, and jealousy. Yellow-green can indicate sickness, cowardice, or disgust. <u>Mental-Spiritual</u>: You are freshening up your ideas and growing mentally and spiritually. You are integrating polarized ideas or opposing forces within yourself.

gun: <u>Physical</u>: You're focusing on personal power with others, especially exerted from a safe distance, and aggressive, sexual male energy. <u>Emotional</u>: You feel pressured by a male person in your life. You need to protect yourself. Shooting yourself or others by accident or on purpose indicates overactive, destructive, or vengeful emotions, or a need to assert personal control over a situation. <u>Mental-Spiritual</u>: Firing guns often represents "shooting off your mouth." If you are shot, consider which part of your body has been wounded for clues about the meaning.

guru: *(see priest)*

H

hail: *(see snow)*

hair: <u>Physical</u>: You are focusing on health, strength, sexuality, sensitivity to the environment, or vanity. Having your hair cut means you are adjusting your self image and ambitions, are ready for a major life decision, or someone is censoring you. Smelling someone's hair indicates sexual curiosity and a need for sensual stimulation. <u>Emotional</u>: Being covered in hair means you're confronting your animal nature. If your hair stands on end or turns white overnight, you're experiencing a shock or strong stimulus. Loss of hair signifies vulnerability, anxiety about weakness, and fear of failure or aging. If you're "letting your hair down" or the wind is blowing through your hair, you feel free to express uninhibited feelings. Stroking hair connects to sympathy, protectiveness, and fraternal love. <u>Mental-Spiritual</u>: You're focusing on your attitudes, opinions, and insights. White hair denotes wisdom. Knotted or tangled hair shows uncertainty and confusion. Combing your hair means you're organizing your thoughts, getting your facts straight. Long hair means you're drawing on past history before you act. Touching someone's hair means you are trying to connect on a spiritual or intellectual level.

hallway: <u>Physical</u>: You are making a transition from one life phase to another, beginning a journey into the unknown and further self-exploration. <u>Emotional</u>: If the hall is dimly lit, you feel insecure as you move toward the unknown. <u>Mental-Spiritual</u>: You are about to have an important insight. You're entering a new spiritual or mental rite of passage. The movement of the transition itself is important; notice what is contained in the hallway.

hands: <u>Physical</u>: You're looking at how you greet and touch others, grasp or take hold, make and create things, and how you give and receive. You need to lend a helping hand to someone, or ask for help. Holding hands represents your connection to others and how you connect with the world. Shaking hands with someone means you've reached an agreement, a level of trust, or a new beginning. <u>Emotional</u>: Washing your hands means you're worried or guilty, or you're complete and no longer taking responsibility for something. Rough hands mean a brash or abrasive way of dealing with others. Blood on your hands means you've hurt yourself or others and need to heal the situation. Being in handcuffs means you or something else is holding you back, making you focus on your actions. You are too possessive. <u>Mental-Spiritual</u>: Hands and fingers communicate and convey many messages, often of approval and disapproval. Praying hands mean the left and right sides of your body and brain are balanced and you are in harmony, open to the spiritual realm. Clasped or covered hands mean you're contemplating something, or are hesitant to agree.

hat: <u>Physical</u>: You are looking at a role you're playing, your desire for power and recognition, or your responsibilities in life. A feather in your hat shows achievement. A top hat denotes formality, elegance, and aspirations for wealth. <u>Emotional</u>: You are concealing or covering up something. You are hiding your opinions and attitudes from others for fear of judgment. <u>Mental-Spiritual</u>: You're focused on the containment of your knowledge, or a body of knowledge. Taking off a hat inside, when bowing, or placing it over your heart, means you are sharing your true self.

hawk: *(see eagle)*

head: <u>Physical</u>: You're focusing on accomplishments, self-image, and your perception of the world. You're using your head to solve problems. You need to approach something head-on. A headache means you're headed in the wrong direction. <u>Emotional</u>: You are too hotheaded, headstrong, or have lost your head about something. You are repressing your common sense and rational thinking, refusing to see the truth, allowing your emotions to be out of control. <u>Mental-Spiritual</u>: You're focusing on knowledge, understanding, intellect, logic, and conscious awareness. You need to be less heady, mental, and analytical.

healer: *(see doctor)*

heart/chest/breasts: <u>Physical</u>: The heart shows you're focusing on truth, courage, love, romance, and how fully you are living. The chest and breasts indicate a focus on pride, generosity, nurturing capacity, and how unprotected and trusting you are. <u>Emotional</u>: Problems with the heart, like heartaches or heart attacks, indicate imbalances, loss of love, lack of support and acceptance, or great disappointment. You're looking at how you deal with feelings and express emotion. Hearing a heartbeat suggests you need to re-center into safety and feelings of being nurtured. A racing heartbeat indicates you're anxious, upset, and threatened about something. <u>Mental-Spiritual</u>: You are focusing on integrating your soul's wisdom into your life, understanding who you are, how you give unconditional love, and how courageous you are. You want to get to "the heart of the matter," or the core of a situation, before proceeding.

heel: <u>Physical</u>: You're concerned about something following too closely upon your heels, or you need to improve your appearance (down at the heels, well-heeled). <u>Emotional</u>: You may be too stubborn or rooted (digging your heels in), or you feel extremely vulnerable (Achilles' heel). <u>Mental-Spiritual</u>: You are focusing on limitations of thought that might undermine your purpose, and the need for greater practicality of ideas.

hero/hero's journey: <u>Physical</u>: You are asking yourself to stretch your level of competence, be more courageous and confident, and develop an expanded skill set. <u>Emotional</u>: You are examining your need to rescue others or be rescued. <u>Mental-Spiritual</u>: To make the hero's journey you must first be cut off from your roots and misunderstood, then experience the call to adventure to discover your true self, which comes after a difficult rite of passage where you confront temptation, challenges, demons, villains, handicaps, and unresolved fear. Finally, you experience a spiritual awakening and reach your goal. You must then return to those who misunderstood you and enlighten them. This is the process of spiritual growth we all go through as we evolve. You are reminding yourself that you're living through a stage in the hero's journey, and there is an end eventually. Notice what stage you are focusing on.

hide: <u>Physical</u>: Hiding from someone means you're avoiding an aspect of yourself you've not accepted or integrated. You don't want to face a real situation or issue. <u>Emotional</u>: You need security and protection. Hiding from an authority figure implies feelings of guilt. Hiding an object means you feel it's possible to lose part of your credibility, luck, or power to another person and thus you need to protect or hoard it. If someone is hiding from you, you feel frustrated in your desire for intimacy, honesty, or self-expression with others. <u>Mental-Spiritual</u>: You are keeping a secret, withholding information, or denying the truth.

hippopotamus: <u>Physical</u>: You are focusing on your hidden strengths, abundance, influence, and power. You are faced with a large, immovable obstacle. Hippos are a symbol of protection in childbirth.

Emotional: You feel territorial and easily threatened. You are loyal and protective to those less powerful than you. Mental-Spiritual: You are focusing on the subconscious and collective unconscious, on what lies beneath the surface, attuning yourself to ancient knowledge held in common by many beings.

hitchhike: Physical: You want a free ride. You need to develop more self-reliance. Emotional: You need to lessen your dependency on others. Picking up a hitch-hiker means you are carrying others in some way, taking on too much responsibility, with a tendency to become drained. Mental-Spiritual: You are riding on the coattails of others, borrowing their ideas, not doing your own homework. You may be possessed in some way by discarnate beings.

hole: Physical: You are discovering a hidden aspect of yourself or a situation. Falling in a hole means you encounter a subterfuge or feel trapped by something you didn't notice. You have dug yourself into a hole and can't get out without help. Emotional: You feel hollow or empty inside and need fulfillment. You feel open, revealed, and vulnerable. Mental-Spiritual: You are aware of an opening into a new world or dimension of awareness.

hood/veil: Physical: You are hiding behind a false or deceptive identity, or someone is being deceitful with you. Emotional: You are embarrassed to be seen by others. You are protecting your innocence. Mental-Spiritual: There are perceptual differences between you and others that make communicating very difficult. You are open to being seduced or tricked, "having the hood pulled over your eyes."

horns: *(see antlers)*

horse: <u>Physical</u>: You are focusing on the magnificence of your physical body, and on freedom, power, wildness, pride, energy, majesty, courage, and sexuality. The condition of the horse indicates the state of your energy in waking life. You have been "horsing around" and need to get serious. You need to "get off your high horse" and be less arrogant. Galloping or racing horses represent the drive you need to compete and succeed. <u>Emotional</u>: If you are riding a horse that is out of control, you are being carried away by your passions. An armored horse refers to fierceness, aggression, confrontation, or rigidity. Or you are repressing sexual urges. <u>Mental-Spiritual</u>: Horses link to your instinct, intuition, and prophetic ability. White or flying horses (Pegasus) represent purity and good fortune, as well as a strong motivation for spiritual growth. Black or dark horses signify mystery, occult forces, and gambling on the unknown.

hospital: <u>Physical</u>: You need to heal part of yourself, pay attention to your physical health, allow time and space to rest, or ask others for help. <u>Emotional</u>: You feel emotionally drained. You are looking at your need to rescue others or be rescued. <u>Mental-Spiritual</u>: You are correcting misperceptions, attuning to a higher level of awareness. You are healing others in another dimension. *(see doctor)*

hotel: <u>Physical</u>: You need a break from your life, routine, and habits before a new idea or change can occur. You are between stages in your life, preparing for a new identity. <u>Emotional</u>: You feel unsettled or need to temporarily escape from your ordinary life. You need shelter during a confusing time. <u>Mental-Spiritual</u>: You are involved with a collective consciousness, looking at an issue briefly before spending more time with it later. Hotel lobbies represent an environment where ideas are coming and going, and new ideas are being considered.

house: <u>Physical</u>: A house symbolizes your personal self, life situation, current state, and possibly your health. A new house or a bigger house indicates you've entered a new expanded phase. If the house is too small or cluttered, you are finding motivation to begin to change. <u>Emotional</u>: A childhood home represents emotions, attitudes, and behaviors, created when you lived in that residence, that need to be changed now. If the house is empty, you feel insecure and isolated, or you need to develop more independence. A haunted house means unfinished emotional business related to family, dead relatives, or repressed feelings. A burglarized house means you feel vulnerable or violated, or unconscious knowledge is trying to make itself known. <u>Mental-Spiritual</u>: If the house is under construction and not yet complete, or if it needs repair, you are doing inner psychological work, getting ready for a growth spurt. Cleaning house means you're clearing old thoughts, seeking self-improvement. Specific rooms in the house indicate specific aspects of your psyche. *(see architecture)*

hummingbird: <u>Physical</u>: You are searching for the sweetness of life. You may be literally focusing on how to work with flowers or aromatherapy. You are learning to be flexible and adaptable, making the most of new circumstances. Your body is sensitive and intense now, and you are focusing on your fierce appetite for life experience. You need to raise your energy level and have freedom from restriction. <u>Emotional</u>: You are looking for joy, and need to spread love and happiness to others. You need to find the beauty and good inside yourself and others, going deep, beyond the outer layers. <u>Mental-Spiritual</u>: You are focusing on how to live in the present moment and maintain inner still-ness while in action. Small ideas and concepts possess much power. You are trying to shift away from having flighty thoughts and frivolous ideas. Hummingbird is a magical messenger, bringing special messages from high spiritual levels.

hurricane/tornado/storm: <u>Physical</u>: You are experi-encing sudden changes or a clearing of old structures, like changing jobs suddenly or needing to move. <u>Emotional</u>: You feel an emotional upheaval brewing; destructive and powerful emotions, like rage with ensuing chaos and confusion, are beginning to release. <u>Mental-Spiritual</u>: Being in the eye of the storm symbol-izes the still, calm center within yourself where you can find insight and strength amidst chaos. If you are swept up in the storm, you are experiencing intensely confusing thoughts and are consumed by overwhelm-ing conditions.

1

ice/icicles/iceberg: <u>Physical</u>: You are making slow progress, experiencing bleak conditions, or are frozen out by unfriendly colleagues or friends. You aren't making use of your full potential. If you're walking on ice, you are taking risks, sensing potential danger or mishaps in a course of action. <u>Emotional</u>: You feel hopeless, emotionally paralyzed or blocked, or unable to express your feelings due to an unsympathetic envi-ronment. If you fall through ice, you are about to have an emotional breakthrough where suppressed feelings come to the surface. Melting ice indicates an easing of emotional problems and difficult times. Icicles represent sadness and emotional pain that started to release but became blocked again. An iceberg represents a huge emotional obstacle you need to face, or its hidden aspects might destroy you. <u>Mental-Spiritual</u>: Your ideas and creativity are blocked, or you feel numb and brain-dead.

infestation/insects: <u>Physical</u>: Something or someone is bugging you, or making a pest of itself. You are dealing with minor annoyances and small obstacles that must not be ignored. <u>Emotional</u>: You are worrying excessively or feel irritated. If the insects bite or sting, you are afraid of being wounded by sharp words. Infestations, whether by people, animals, insects, bacteria, or clutter, represent feeling invaded, overwhelmed, overrun, and undermined. Strengthen your boundaries. Look to the location of the infestation for the area of life it's affecting. Be more assertive and take up your own space. <u>Mental-Spiritual</u>: You are neglecting important information because of an obsession with one thing. You need to organize your thoughts and sort through your priorities. Insects represent precision and are often divine messengers.

inheritance: *(see treasure)*

internet: <u>Physical</u>: You need to pay attention to your circulatory systems. You are focused on networking, marketing, communicating about yourself, or expanding your self-expression. <u>Emotional</u>: You feel lonely and want increased connection with others. You feel nurtured by being social or you are too dependent on superficial relationships that avoid true intimacy.

You're avoiding responsibilities that make you feel too dull. <u>Mental-Spiritual</u>: You're avoiding contact with your real self. You're hungry to learn and grow intellectually. You are merging into an awareness of global, collective consciousness and spiritual unity.

intruder/thief: <u>Physical</u>: Someone is trying to control or influence you surreptitiously, or to take something valuable from you, like your authority, reputation, credit for something you did, or actual property. You are experiencing unwanted sexual attention or envy. <u>Emotional</u>: You feel victimized and vulnerable, compromised, disrespected, taken advantage of, or manipulated. You feel guilty for invading someone else's territory or having success you don't feel you deserve. <u>Mental-Spiritual</u>: Disturbing thoughts are breaking into your peace of mind. Someone, or your own inner victim, is trying to bring you down with negative thinking.

invisibility: <u>Physical</u>: You are focusing on a loss, a person or opportunity that has become unavailable, a desire to escape responsibilities, or the need for greater recognition. <u>Emotional</u>: You feel unfairly overlooked and misunderstood. You feel embarrassed and want to disappear, or avoid an unpleasant experience. <u>Mental-Spiritual</u>: If an object disappears, you are focusing on its importance in your life and the knowledge you gain by having or not having it. If you become invisible, you are seeking secret knowledge about others and life. You are looking into the true nature of things.

ironing: <u>Physical</u>: You are trying to smooth out the wrinkles in a situation or relationship. You are trying to improve the image you project publicly. <u>Emotional</u>:

You feel anxiety about being too informal and unkempt. You're focusing on domestic comfort and orderliness. <u>Mental-Spiritual</u>: You're looking for a crisp, true, perhaps somewhat formal, world view. You're learning to communicate clearly to others.

island: <u>Physical</u>: You want to escape from a problem, rest, and relax. You need solitude. You have a strong sense of individuality, boundaries, and integrity. If you're stranded on an island, you are at an impasse in your life, wondering where to go next. <u>Emotional</u>: You feel separate and isolated from others and life. You feel deprived. You need to acknowledge the presence and power of emotion or the unconscious in your life. <u>Mental-Spiritual</u>: You are retreating into yourself, focusing on what's deeply true and real.

itch: <u>Physical</u>: Your body is talking to you. You are experiencing a minor irritation or frustration, or are "itching" to do something new. <u>Emotional</u>: You are having strong sexual urges. You feel anxiety about having to do something or start over from scratch. <u>Mental-Spiritual</u>: You are beginning to grasp a new concept, or understand how a new direction will unfold. You are having a strong, allergic reaction to someone or something, indicating there is incompatibility with your life purpose.

J

jaw: <u>Physical</u>: You need more willpower, determination, or forcefulness in some situation. You are too stubborn and need to be a little more "slack-jawed." <u>Emotional</u>: If your jaw is tight, you feel it's not safe to speak your truth, are withholding anger, or feel extremely nervous about an outcome. <u>Mental-Spiritual</u>: If you are in the jaws of an animal, you are threatened by the rash judgments and actions of others, or you have attacked someone unfairly. If your jaw is broken or dislocated, you are not fully aligned with your own beliefs and principles, or you need to develop greater faith and flexibility.

jewels/jewelry: <u>Physical</u>: Your health is improving. You feel strong, protected, and energized physically. Specific jewels are indicative of different kinds of healing and specific qualities you need to activate in yourself. <u>Emotional</u>: Jewelry you own symbolizes particular relationships. You feel good about yourself, pleased with life's possibilities, and can value and cherish others easily. Broken jewelry means your happiness is challenged. You are decorating yourself to impress others with superficial adornments. <u>Mental-Spiritual</u>: You are focusing on your wealth of knowledge, what you hold precious, and your psychological riches and self-worth. You're attuning to your soul qualities and gifts, the light within, and spiritual ideas. Finding or being given jewels signifies rapid spiritual growth.

jigsaw puzzle: <u>Physical</u>: You are focusing on completing a complex project or bringing your body back to full health, looking for all the pieces or ingredients you need. <u>Emotional</u>: You feel fragmented and frustrated by too many details. You feel overwhelmed by the amount of time something is going to take and need to develop more patience. <u>Mental-Spiritual</u>: You are facing a mental challenge or problem you need to solve. You are putting ideas together in different ways so you can see a larger picture or world view.

job: <u>Physical</u>: You are looking at how well your current work suits you and how satisfied you are with your life direction. You're solving problems from your actual work environment. Some task must be accomplished. Being fired from a job means you need to be more engaged with everything you do, or you're ready to end a relationship. <u>Emotional</u>: If you're job hunting, you feel unfulfilled and frustrated. If you fall asleep or are absent from work, you feel you're in a dead-end situation that doesn't nurture you. <u>Mental-Spiritual</u>: Getting a new job or promotion means you're expanding your self-expression and spiritual growth. How excited you are about your job represents how aligned you are with your life work and soul's purpose.

joints: <u>Physical</u>: You're focusing on how you bridge energy and information from one area, or focus, to another, and how you make connections. Having joint problems indicates you're experiencing difficulties in a process coming together as you want. <u>Emotional</u>: You're looking at how rigid or flexible you are emotionally. A broken joint means energy is leaking from a weakness you haven't faced. <u>Mental-Spiritual</u>: You're focusing on how well you give and receive from others, and how well you transmit awareness between the different levels of yourself.

journey: <u>Physical</u>: You're focusing on your life path, transitions between phases of life experience, and developing new personality traits. Along the way, you face challenges, discover new things about yourself and life. A short journey means change. <u>Emotional</u>: Traveling with a companion or interacting with strangers shows how you feel about intimacy and how well you cooperate and co-create. <u>Mental-Spiritual</u>:

Your destination symbolizes a goal you haven't fully realized. The scenery you see gives you insight into current circumstances. You are on a spiritual quest.

judge/jury/trial: <u>Physical</u>: You're focusing on authority, morality, justice, and order. You are actually dealing with legal issues. <u>Emotional</u>: You feel pressure to be perfect. You are examining an aspect of your behavior that's been out of line, you're judging others, or feel others are judging you. You feel guilty about something, and your conscience is urging you to do the right thing. You feel something or someone is unfair. You are threatened with embarrassment from false statements and accusations, or your reputation is at stake due to your actions. <u>Mental-Spiritual</u>: You need to make a decision about something based on your own mores. You are focusing on universal laws and principles.

jump: <u>Physical</u>: Leaping hurdles and jumping over things means you're experiencing success and strong forward motion. Jumping rope shows you can coordinate your actions well. You're jumping at the chance to do something or jumping in with both feet. <u>Emotional</u>: You are impatient, leaping from one thing to another. You are too impulsive or too controlled. You need to take a leap of faith or look before you leap. You are jumping the gun, jumping through hoops to please others, or jumping ship to avoid consequences. If you're afraid to jump, you don't like change or fear you can't complete a task. You're jumping down someone's throat, expressing sudden criticalness. <u>Mental-Spiritual</u>: You are jumping to conclusions, or you're encountering a quantum leap or transformation. You need to let go and surrender to the unknown.

Jumping up indicates joy and readiness to shift levels of awareness into higher realms.

jungle: <u>Physical</u>: You are exploring your instincts, wild side, passions, and untamed nature. You feel entangled in a situation, and you can't find your way out. <u>Emotional</u>: You're afraid of being out of control and messy. You are freeing yourself from inhibitions. You feel lost or trapped by a chaotic, unpredictable, dark situation. Negative feelings are hindering your progress; you must cut through with greater mental clarity. <u>Mental-Spiritual</u>: You're traveling through the deep part of your unconscious or subconscious mind, facing exotic, dangerous creatures that represent creative ideas, new motivations, and untapped abilities.

kangaroo: <u>Physical</u>: You're focusing on enthusiasm, leaping ahead, and making quick progress, as well as endurance, strength, mobility, and freedom to move. You are about to go on an unexpected, exciting journey. <u>Emotional</u>: You need to protect yourself by kicking something out of the way. You are protecting a vulnerable part of yourself, or are focused on an overprotective female figure, or on mothering itself. You're jumping over obstacles, like fears and limitations. <u>Mental-Spiritual</u>: You are jumping from one idea to another, and need to develop greater concentration skills. You need to use more intuition. You've set yourself up as a kangaroo court, being judge and jury, possibly directed at yourself. You are connecting with family in a larger sense, and with ideas like caretaking and sharing.

keys: <u>Physical</u>: You're accessing new opportunities, unlocking secrets, or opening doors to a new phase of creativity. You are looking at issues of power and authority, being able to go where others cannot, and reach goals easily. Handing a key to someone else means relinquishing responsibility to others. <u>Emotional</u>: You are locking away or protecting things, ideas, or parts of yourself. You are excited or nervous, keyed up. Keys that don't fit a lock indicate frustrated desires or feeling shut out of a relationship or opportunity. Losing your keys indicates you aren't ready for a new opportunity, are out of control, or are blocking yourself through doubt. <u>Mental-Spiritual</u>: You're at a turning point, about to find a solution or obtain guidance. If you find a key, you're looking for an answer to a question you didn't know you were asking, decoding information, or searching for new potential within yourself or in relationship to others. You're attuning to methods for attaining wisdom, higher spiritual knowledge, and enlightenment.

kidnap: <u>Physical</u>: An area of your life has taken you hostage by being too emphasized. You need a chance to get away from the entanglements of your daily routine to start fresh. <u>Emotional</u>: You feel victimized, trapped, or carried away by the desires and plans of others. You feel forced to do something against your will, or you are taking advantage of someone. You've given your power away. <u>Mental-Spiritual</u>: The part of yourself that has kidnapped you needs attention and recognition. You're developing a strategy to evolve beyond limiting conditions.

kill: <u>Physical</u>: You are addressing or trying to get rid of an unwanted part of yourself or an issue that's causing great distress. You want to make someone go away.

Killing small animals can refer to abortion. You are stalled, "killing time." <u>Emotional</u>: You are experiencing intense feelings of anger, frustration, even hatred. Killing in self-defense means you're standing up for yourself, developing confidence. Killing someone you know means you're worried that you've hurt the person through actions you've taken. <u>Mental-Spiritual</u>: Your motivation has been killed by some idea or has simply died. You are experiencing ego death and loss of identity. You are removing fixed ideas that interfere with spiritual progress.

kiss: <u>Physical</u>: You are focusing on bonding, sharing, and making connections with others, especially in intimate relationships. You want to be more sexual. <u>Emotional</u>: You need affection, approval, appreciation, romance, love, intimacy, and passion. Watching others kiss means you are participating in others' lives too closely, or are focusing on infidelity, jealousy, or voyeurism. You feel betrayed (kiss of death), rejected (kissed off), or are detaching from something (kissing it goodbye). <u>Mental-Spiritual</u>: You are opening your heart, finding similarities between yourself and others, and learning to experience communion.

kitchen: <u>Physical</u>: You need better quality food and nutrition. You are in a creative process, cooking something up. <u>Emotional</u>: The state of the kitchen reflects how you experience your well-being, abundance, nourishment, and emotional warmth. You're focusing on how nurtured you feel and how you nurture others. <u>Mental-Spiritual</u>: You're focusing on receiving spiritual nourishment. If you are cooking a meal for yourself and/or others, you are actively engaging in the process of healing and opening to love.

kite: <u>Physical</u>: You need to be free, expansive, and break loose from too much practicality. <u>Emotional</u>: You feel out of control, at the whim of circumstances. You feel giddy. <u>Mental-Spiritual</u>: Without care and attention, you could crash or fail suddenly. You need to pay attention to managing your life and maintaining a good balance of activities. You are looking for higher perspective on situations and on yourself.

knee/kneel: <u>Physical</u>: You're focusing on your ability to be adaptable or humble (to kneel). <u>Emotional</u>: You are caught in too much pride, stubbornness, emotional inflexibility, and refusal to change. You feel subservient, submissive, inferior, or dominated. You feel defensive, with "knee-jerk" reactions to situations. <u>Mental-Spiritual</u>: You're focusing on the need to experience awe and reverence. You need to be more fully engaged with life instead of having "knee-deep" involvements.

knife/sword: <u>Physical</u>: You're focusing on male aggression and sexuality, as well as protection and readiness to take decisive action. You're creating by carving something from scratch. You're achieving easily (a knife through butter). <u>Emotional</u>: You feel attacked, betrayed, and emotionally injured (knife in the back). As a phallic symbol, a knife can represent sexual assault. You feel you're at war. You're injuring yourself or want to hurt someone else. <u>Mental-Spiritual</u>: You are developing your intellect and the ability to think clearly, analyze, cut through, or penetrate into your subconscious mind. *(see cut)*

knock: <u>Physical</u>: Something new is about to arrive in your life. You want to start a new endeavor, and need the support or invitation of others to begin. You are pregnant (knocked up). You need to stop doing something (knock it off). <u>Emotional</u>: You want greater intimacy and social connection with others. You feel frustrated, exhausted, like a victim (school of hard knocks, knocking your head against the wall). <u>Mental-Spiritual</u>: Something needs attention. A message, warning, guidance, or neglected part of you is breaking through to your conscious mind. You're criticizing something or someone (knocking it, knocking them down a peg). You're experiencing something amazing and stunning (a knockout). You're feeling superstitious (knock on wood). *(see alarm)*

knot: <u>Physical</u>: Something is restricting you, or you're trying to control something or prevent loss. <u>Emotional</u>: You're experiencing anxiety and worry (being tied in knots). You're making a commitment and focusing on security, as in marriage (tying the knot). <u>Mental-Spiritual</u>: You're working on a complex problem that needs to be solved. You're untangling a confusing situation.

L

ladder: <u>Physical</u>: You are concerned with career aspirations, achievement, increasing material prosperity, or climbing the social ladder to greater status. You are making progress via hard work. Climbing down a ladder means you're avoiding responsibilities. Falling from a ladder means you encounter hardships and setbacks. You are concerned with the health of your spine. <u>Emotional</u>: Holding a ladder for someone else means you are being unselfish and generous, helping to support and stabilize that person's growth, or are receiving such help yourself. A broken ladder or missing rungs indicates fear of failure, challenges, or a handicap due to missing life experiences. <u>Mental-Spiritual</u>: You are climbing to a new level of understanding and spiritual awareness, actively pursuing your spiritual path. You are looking for a different perspective. You need to meditate and pray.

ladybug: <u>Physical</u>: You are about to encounter good luck and fortunate circumstances. <u>Emotional</u>: You feel friendly, helpful, charming, and beautiful, or can see these good traits in others. <u>Mental-Spiritual</u>: You're focusing on feminine energy and receiving blessings or messages from the spiritual realms.

lake: <u>Physical</u>: You're looking at the settings and situations of your life. If you're floating on, swimming in, or boating on a calm lake, you're experiencing peace, freedom from limitations, and ease. <u>Emotional</u>: If the lake is disturbed and wavy, you're going through emotional turmoil, are being overwhelmed or shaken up by situations, and may experience losses. <u>Mental-Spiritual</u>: You're exploring the unknown, wanting to penetrate into the mysteries, especially if you're diving or swimming under water.

lamb: <u>Physical</u>: You're focusing on innocence, purity, and gentleness. You're ready to have children or good, trustworthy friends. <u>Emotional</u>: You feel you've had to sacrifice a precious part of yourself, or you give too much of yourself to others. You need to be more assertive. You're opening your heart to romance. <u>Mental-Spiritual</u>: You're working with humility, sweetness, and letting go of stubborn resistance to make progress spiritually.

laptop: *(see computer)*

laryngitis: <u>Physical</u>: You are focusing on the importance of what you need to say to others. Losing your voice indicates you need to think twice about speaking up right now. <u>Emotional</u>: You feel overpowered by other, more forceful or glib people, as though your contribution isn't worthwhile or you aren't strong enough. You feel misinterpreted. <u>Mental-Spiritual</u>: You need a period of silence and contemplation, to let your truth arise naturally. You need time to carefully craft your message.

late: <u>Physical</u>: Being late for an appointment means you're reminding yourself not to miss opportunities. You're experiencing anxiety over being behind on a project. You don't want to be controlled by outside circumstances. <u>Emotional</u>: You feel ambivalent toward a situation, passive-aggressive toward an authority, are neglecting a responsibility, or would like to avoid a commitment. You feel disrespected or insulted by someone. <u>Mental-Spiritual</u>: You realize you want to learn more, grow more, be more involved in life, make a contribution, and live fully in the present moment.

lava: *(see volcano)*

leak: <u>Physical</u>: You are wasting energy on fruitless endeavors. You're experiencing the slow loss of resources. <u>Emotional</u>: You're giving too much of yourself away to others, without being appreciated. You feel the loss of something. Repressed feelings are slowly emerging from your subconscious. <u>Mental-Spiritual</u>: You're giving your ideas away. New insights are seeping into your consciousness, one bit at a time.

left: <u>Physical</u>: The left side of the body symbolizes receptivity, creativity, going with the flow, and nontraditional ways of doing things. You need to receive the qualities symbolized by someone or something to your left. You need to work more with your inner-directed, feminine/yin energy and pay attention to the women in your life. <u>Emotional</u>: You're activating repressed feelings, artistic sensitivity, and intuition. You feel too passive or negative. <u>Mental-Spiritual</u>: You need to take a break from your intellectual orientation. You're exploring mysteries, what's dangerous, destructive, and irrational. If you're left-handed, the meanings for left and right may be reversed.

legs: <u>Physical</u>: You're looking at how steadfast you are, how you take a stand, step or move forward, and support yourself by making money. You're examining your pace, how fast or slowly you're moving ahead. <u>Emotional</u>: A broken, injured, weak, or deformed leg suggests you're hesitating (or preparing) to take initiative, you feel emotionally vulnerable, or you are stubbornly refusing to change. You lack balance, autonomy, or independence, and rely on various crutches to get by. <u>Mental-Spiritual</u>: Focusing on someone else's legs means you want to adopt their successful ideas and methods. If one leg is shorter than the other, you're emphasizing one idea at the expense of others. *(see feet)*

letter/postcard/e-mail: <u>Physical</u>: Receiving a letter indicates you're focusing on a new opportunity or challenge, or a quality represented by the writer of the letter. Sending a letter means you need to communicate and express yourself more. <u>Emotional</u>: An unconscious aspect of yourself or a repressed emotion is trying to surface and make itself known. <u>Mental-Spiritual</u>: You're receiving guidance from your inner self. An unopened letter or unread e-mail indicates you aren't using your intuition, or are deliberately ignoring certain information. If you receive or send a postcard, look for meaning in the picture side.

library/hard drive: <u>Physical</u>: You are seeking new meaning or new skills. You need to study and evaluate a situation before taking action. <u>Emotional</u>: If the library is disorganized, too much information is coming at you at once, you feel overwhelmed by information and details, and are having trouble sorting through it all. <u>Mental-Spiritual</u>: You're focusing on knowledge you have accumulated over the years, and what is crucial to your success now. You are hungry to learn. You are tapping into the collective consciousness and the *akashic records* (memory banks of the planet) to explore your own and planetary history as well as your life vision. *(see files)*

light/lighthouse: <u>Physical</u>: You are lightening up, letting go of density, clutter, or physical weight. A light bulb turning on means you're ready to face reality. <u>Emotional</u>: You are lightening up your emotions, becoming more humorous, joyful, and untroubled. <u>Mental-Spiritual</u>: Your awareness is moving into clarity, truth, understanding, wisdom, and enlightenment. You've found an answer, seen the way through a problem. Small, pointed lights like candles, flashlights, or light bulbs represent insights or guidance. Broad, diffused light represents an atmosphere of understanding. Lights turning off means you need to face something in your subconscious, or let your mind be quiet. Lighthouses and beacons symbolize an inner source of guidance you must follow to be safe.

lightning: <u>Physical</u>: You are likely to have a stroke of good luck. You must act on something immediately. <u>Emotional</u>: You are experiencing a shocking turn of events. If you are struck by lightning, a transformation or irreversible change is occurring in your life. You feel afraid you're being punished by the wrath of God. <u>Mental-Spiritual</u>: You are opening to sudden awareness, illumination, and purification. Something is being pointed out to you by divine intelligence, possibly a warning.

lion: <u>Physical</u>: You're focusing on courage, power, aggression, fierceness, and protectiveness, especially of those you consider family. As king of beasts, the lion symbolizes strength of character and quiet strength, dignity, dominion, majesty, pride, and leadership skill. A lioness means you're hunting for opportunities and will find what you need. You're looking for honesty in those around you. You are too laid back or lazy. <u>Emotional</u>: You want to control or rule others and have greater influence. You want to be the center of attention, are showing off, or being arrogant. You need to exercise more restraint in your ambitions. Being attacked by a lion indicates a huge obstacle coming, or you are acting in a self-destructive way. <u>Mental-Spiritual</u>: As spiritual guides, lions glow with golden sunlight, leading you safely to your destination. You are becoming a spiritual leader.

lips: <u>Physical</u>: You are focusing on a need to speak and communicate, eat, or kiss someone to find romance, affection, and sex. <u>Emotional</u>: The expression the lips were making indicate feelings you need to experience and understand better: pleased, scornful, approving, aloof, indifferent, seductive. You are hungry emotionally, dealing with feelings of greed, lust, or gluttony.

<u>Mental-Spiritual</u>: You are opening to greater tenderness and intimacy, and thus to a spirit of communion. To buy, see, or wear lipstick suggests you are not being truthful.

lizard: <u>Physical</u>: You are focusing on primal instincts and desires for food, sex, and safety. You want to bask in the sun. You are involved in a process of creativity, renewal, and revitalization. <u>Emotional</u>: You're focusing on someone you consider to be cold-blooded or thick-skinned, or you are too much this way. <u>Mental-Spiritual</u>: You are developing better powers of perceptiveness as well as a quicker response time. The lizard is considered a protective spirit, and brings fertility and tranquility in the home.

loss/lost: <u>Physical</u>: Losing something means you are focusing on lost opportunities, past relationships, or forgotten aspects of yourself. You're warning yourself of a potential real loss. You need to clean out and reorganize your life. <u>Emotional</u>: You're worrying about not having enough and need to release an attachment to what the lost item symbolizes. You feel insecure about the path you're taking. If someone else is lost, you have unresolved issues regarding the person. <u>Mental-Spiritual</u>: If you are lost, you need to experience your center, orient yourself to a new direction, or get rid of confusing situations. You have lost sight of your goals. You are experiencing ego death or loss of identity, a step toward awareness of a spiritual reality.

luggage: <u>Physical</u>: You are holding on to too much and are weighed down by clutter, unfinished business, responsibilities, and possessions. It's time to pack up and move on, take a break, determine what's important to keep, and what you can leave behind.

Emotional: You need to reduce problems, create better emotional boundaries, and alleviate pressure and worries. If someone is carrying your bags, you are about to experience some supportive relationships. Mental-Spiritual: Heavy bags or excess baggage means you need to throw out old ideas and prejudices. A new set of luggage means a new set of priorities and movement into a new reality.

lungs: Physical: You are focusing on taking a breath of fresh air, finding a new start, reorganizing your life. You need renewed creativity, inspiration, and motivation. You are warning yourself about an actual respiratory problem. Emotional: You are involved in a situation or relationship in which you feel stressed and suffocated. You are dealing with issues of grief, sadness, isolation, or suffering. Mental-Spiritual: You are opening to a more expansive world view and a greater connection to the world.

M

magic/magical powers: Physical: You want something to work miraculously, or you want to avoid going through all the normal steps. If you have a magical power, you can make your dreams come true. Performing magic suggests you need to approach problems from a new angle, or an issue or task is trickier than you anticipated. Riding a magic carpet means you're overcoming obstacles and physical limitations. Emotional: Black magic means you feel manipulated or controlled, or are doing this to others. You feel deceived, exposed to evil and treachery. You've attained your goals in an underhanded way. Mental-Spiritual: You are disillusioned or fooling yourself or someone into believing a lie. If you have magical powers, you can serve others in a grand way.

makeup/mask: <u>Physical</u>: You are covering up your true identity, putting on a false face for the public due to shame. You're putting your best face forward. If others are wearing masks, a situation is not as it seems, you have trouble identifying people's true nature, or you struggle with lies, deceit, or jealousy. Putting on makeup reflects concern about appearance and social presentation. <u>Emotional</u>: You lack confidence in yourself. You're trying to please others. Difficulty applying makeup suggests anxiety about an important social event. Smeared makeup shows failed attempts at presentation. <u>Mental-Spiritual</u>: The reality you're dealing with is symbolic of another, deeper reality. You're experimenting with playing new roles. Removing makeup shows a need to see yourself more clearly. *(see face)*

map: <u>Physical</u>: You are beginning a journey, searching for a new path, studying the variables inherent in a change of direction and what the ensuing experience will bring. You're looking for alternate routes to accomplish your goals. <u>Emotional</u>: You feel lost and panic-stricken. <u>Mental-Spiritual</u>: You are soliciting guidance from higher parts of yourself, looking at your destiny and its most natural unfolding.

market: <u>Physical</u>: You want to fill a lack or physical need, or are bored and need a growth spurt. You need the stimulation of new possessions, nurturance of fresh food, and support of new tools and resources. The specific items you're shopping for symbolize your inner needs. <u>Emotional</u>: You want to feel good by having the good things of life. An empty market means you feel a void within, you feel hopeless and depressed, or have missed opportunities. <u>Mental-Spiritual</u>: You're shopping for possibilities, decisions, or variety. You need to exchange with the hustle-bustle world, business, and commercial ventures. You're tuning in to healthy ideas of an industrious, cooperative, prosperous society. If the market is clean, busy, and well-stocked you're ready to experience abundance and greater involvement in the world. *(see buy)*

marriage: <u>Physical</u>: You have a literal desire to marry. You want to join forces with a person or entity, as in a new business partnership. The characteristics of the person you are marrying are the qualities you need to incorporate within yourself. <u>Emotional</u>: You need to harmonize your feminine and masculine energies, or unify other separate aspects of yourself. Marrying your ex means you've learned from past mistakes, or need to learn the lessons now, or a current relationship is parallel to the old one. <u>Mental-Spiritual</u>: You are in a transition period, focusing on greater commitment, harmony, communication skills, diplomacy, generosity, cocreativity, and loyalty.

mathematics: *(see numbers)*

maze: <u>Physical</u>: You feel lost or confused in an area of your life and may need to just pick a direction and see where it goes, knowing there are twists and turns along the way. You are reminding yourself that it's natural to make mistakes. <u>Emotional</u>: You are making a situation harder than it really is, blocking your progress by complaining or protesting. <u>Mental-Spiritual</u>: You are on a spiritual path, a quest for meaning and truth. You need to work intensively with your intuition. You are being blocked by fixed beliefs, fear-based ideas, and lack of faith.

medicine/pill: <u>Physical</u>: You are focusing on healing yourself. Your troubles are temporary. You are looking at the actions you need to take to improve a situation. <u>Emotional</u>: If you suspect the medication is incorrectly prescribed, you distrust your support people and caretakers. Someone is lying to you or trying to manipulate you, or you are operating in an underhanded way. You feel poisoned by an outside influence that you took too personally. <u>Mental-Spiritual</u>: You are adjusting your awareness to a healthier level that is conducive to the expression of your vitality and soul. You are correcting misperceptions that have caused you to make mistakes.

men: <u>Physical</u>: Any male figure represents your animus or the way you use and understand masculine energy. You need to express more, or less, power, compartmentalization, assertiveness, or initiative. <u>Emotional</u>: You are facing unresolved issues with your father or male relatives. <u>Mental-Spiritual</u>: How the men are dressed provides a clue about the area of your life that needs more yang energy. You are focusing on will, logic, and intellect.

mermaid: <u>Physical</u>: You are focusing on your mysterious, secretive female aspect, or anima. You are unable to fully participate in a love relationship, or cannot give your all in a situation. <u>Emotional</u>: You are facing emotional traumas, learning to be comfortable with feelings. You are linking your primitive and conscious nature. For a man, the mermaid can represent fear of seduction and sex, or being drowned by the feminine aspect of his psyche. For a woman, the mermaid can mean doubt about femininity or sexuality. Mermaids are often associated with transgender identity confusion. Mental-Spiritual: You are bringing beauty and wisdom up from your unconscious. You are facing temptations, exploring the depths, overcoming obstacles with superhuman skills and strength, in the inner realms first.

merry-go-round: Physical: You're going in circles, or are stagnating. You are in the beginning stages of romantic love. Emotional: You are expressing anxiety about the transition into adulthood or to greater responsibilities. You want to retreat to childlike joys. You are afraid of remembering and reliving parts of your childhood. Mental-Spiritual: You are aware of the cycles of life and creativity, and are focusing on the restfulness and rejuvenation of playing and flowing easily.

metal: Physical: You are focusing on qualities of neutrality and strength of character. Emotional: You feel someone is too cold, hard, overly technological, or inhuman, or you are being this way. Mental-Spiritual: Since metal is cold and hard yet malleable and can melt, it represents an attitude that is rigid but not brittle, yet capable of conducting great heat or passion. You are focusing on spiritual or superconscious information and truths.

milk: Physical: You are focusing on wholesomeness, domestic bliss, deep inner nourishment, maternal instincts, motherly love, and human kindness. To spill milk means a loss of faith, precious resources, opportunity, and trust. Emotional: You need to receive or give love and care. You need to strengthen ties with others. Sour milk means you feel deprived of nurturing, or you experience problems instead of successes. Choking on milk means you feel overprotected. <u>Mental-Spiritual</u>: Warm milk means you are relaxing and centering yourself.

mine: <u>Physical</u>: Entering or being inside a mine indicates you are penetrating to the core of an issue, looking for deeply buried riches, resources, and secrets. You are focusing on the inner workings of your body. <u>Emotional</u>: A collapsed mine shaft means you need to work harder to free emotional issues that are blocked. You may be claiming what is "mine." <u>Mental-Spiritual</u>: Bringing the contents of a mine to the surface means that issues from your subconscious are becoming conscious. If you are buried by a cave-in, you need to be quiet and grounded, absorb wisdom from the earth, and attune to the divine feminine awareness. *(see cave)*

minister *(see priest)*

mirror: <u>Physical</u>: You are examining yourself and your image. The way you appear indicates the way you think you look to others, or something you need to admit to yourself. The image in the mirror represents your secret, inner self. <u>Emotional</u>: A fogged mirror means a hazy self-concept and questions about goals, identity, and purpose. A cracked or broken mirror means a fragmented personality, a disturbed and distorted sense of self. Breaking a mirror means you are shattering an old image of yourself or ending an old habit. If you're being watched by others through a two-way mirror, you feel criticized or scrutinized unfairly, or you are highlighting a behavior in yourself that you want to change. <u>Mental-Spiritual</u>: You're focusing on your imagination and the link between your conscious mind and subconscious. Seeing images reflected in a mirror is a safe way to work with information from your subconscious. If you're looking through a two-way mirror, you're seeing the hidden dynamics of an issue that concerns you.

money: <u>Physical</u>: You're focusing on your intrinsic value, inner abundance, confidence, self-worth, and success. You're looking at your energy level. Winning money means that success and prosperity can easily manifest for you. Losing money indicates depleted inner resources, temporary setbacks, or the need to be more detached concerning outcomes. Investing money in the stock market means you have faith in your own talent and potential. <u>Emotional</u>: Having inadequate money denotes fear of losing status, or being unprepared, weak, passive, out of control, and powerless. To be underpaid or not rewarded monetarily means you feel ignored, neglected, undervalued, and unloved. Hoarding money means you're focusing on what you don't have; you are worrying about debt, unemployment, or negative cash flow in waking life. Stealing money or having money stolen, means you need to let go and trust that you'll have what you need. You feel envy toward fortunate people, as though you are being unfairly deprived. You need to reach toward the things you value and feel entitled. <u>Mental-Spiritual</u>: You're experiencing inner richness and values concerning provision, deservedness, and influence. You're looking at attitudes about love and matters of the heart. Giving money away means you're giving love and support to yourself and others. Finding money means you need to express gratitude for what you have and expect improved circumstances.

monitor: *(see screen)*

monkey: <u>Physical</u>: You need to be more playful, humorous, mischievous, or even silly. You are acting immature or playing tricks on other people, who don't appreciate it. You need to develop greater agility and flexibility. You need to develop better communication skills. You're dealing with repressed sexuality. <u>Emotional</u>: You don't want to be controlled, or are trying to control someone else. You're experiencing deceit or are deceiving others. You want more companionship and community. <u>Mental-Spiritual</u>: You need to develop a more serious, focused attitude and stop "monkeying around," jumping from thing to thing. You need to be more ingenious and inventive. You are giving in to worry, doubt, fear, excuses, distractions, the chattering "monkey mind," and need to find stillness through meditation.

monster: <u>Physical</u>: You need to acknowledge your untapped power and capacity to have a positive impact in the world. Slaying monsters means you successfully deal with rivals and advance to a higher position. <u>Emotional</u>: You are afraid of inner rage, hatred, hungers, or desire for control. You feel threatened or are plagued by negative or obsessive thoughts. You're facing repressed fears, a trauma, or qualities you've judged negatively and haven't accepted in yourself. <u>Mental-Spiritual</u>: Killing a monster means you are absorbing the power of that particular thought form into your totality, thus achieving psychological completion and wholeness.

moon: <u>Physical</u>: You are interested in traveling, cycles of growth and self-expression, and anything that fluctuates constantly. You're focusing on feminine energy and what is hidden. A new moon means new beginnings, potential, gestation, waiting, and resting.

Emotional: You're focusing on your changeable emotional or irrational nature, feelings of lunacy, drama, and manic-depressive self-expression. A full moon shows a need for full self-expression, magic, romance, nurturing, reaping rewards, and completion. Mental-Spiritual: Your thoughts need to be more mystical, intuitive, and fluid. A lunar eclipse signifies that your feminine side is being overshadowed or blocked temporarily.

mother: Physical: You're focusing on unconditional love, shelter, comfort, life, guidance, and protection. You are caretaking others or part of yourself. Emotional: You need nurturing and to feel your own caring, receptivity, sexuality, pleasure, seduction, attractiveness, and fertility. You are working out unfinished business with your mother, and whether you feel abandoned or smothered. Mental-Spiritual: A generous, nurturing mother figure represents creativity, growth, and abundance. Mothers are wise guardians and guides, who bring important messages, So if you hear your mother call you, listen well.

mountain: Physical: You are facing obstacles, challenges, and the desire to reach a difficult goal or decision. Climbing a mountain means you need to develop ambition, determination, and stamina. How you climb depicts your inner and outer process of achievement. Reaching the summit means you've accomplished your goals, are successful, and now have a new view of your life. Emotional: You are avoiding hard work and want to take the easy way and escape from demanding situations. Mental-Spiritual: Being on a mountaintop means you are actively pursuing spiritual evolution, involvement with a sacred process, or a higher realm of consciousness, knowledge, and truth. If you fall off a mountain, you are in a hurry to succeed without thoroughly thinking about or honoring your path.

mouse: Physical: You are experiencing minor irritations and annoyances, or problems with insincere, sneaky friends. Something is pestering you, gnawing away at you, or something you value is being eroded slowly through other people's jealousy or greed. If you kill a mouse, you're overcoming disturbances and petty problems. Emotional: You're focusing on your lack of assertiveness, fear, meekness, and feelings of inadequacy. Mental-Spiritual: You're curious, looking into everything, hungry for answers. Focusing on small ideas and details can bring rewards.

mouth: Physical: You are focusing on physical and nonphysical hunger and self-nurturing through eating. Emotional: You're looking at tendencies toward gluttony, greed, and sexual desire, as well as emotions like disgust, approval, awe, generosity, or stinginess. Mental-Spiritual: You need to communicate, to talk about an issue that's bothering you or share ideas. Perhaps you've said too much and need to keep your mouth shut. *(see lips)*

movie: Physical: You are observing your own life to understand it, or are watching life pass you by, living vicariously through others. Starring in a movie means you need more attention, to express yourself more colorfully, or have a greater impact. The role you play or character you're drawn to represents an element of life you are preparing to embody. Emotional: You want to escape from the reality of your own life or protect yourself from painful emotions. Mental-Spiritual: Movies often symbolize the process of dreaming itself. Being in a movie and watching it simultaneously can provide the trigger for a lucid dream. You're looking at your life purpose and plan. *(see DVD)*

mud: <u>Physical</u>: You are involved in a messy, confusing situation, problem, or relationship. You need to cleanse your body internally. If your face or clothes are muddy, your reputation is being questioned or damaged by too much "mudslinging." <u>Emotional</u>: Mud is water (emotion) and earth (the physical), and symbolizes stirred-up emotions that affect your success. You feel weighed down or depressed. You are too perfectionistic and need to be more uninhibited and down to earth. <u>Mental-Spiritual</u>: If you're stuck in the mud, there is difficulty making progress due to mental resistance, negative thinking, and unconscious habits. A mudslide means a sudden release of negative beliefs and ideas of failure.

museum: <u>Physical</u>: You are looking for artifacts and treasures (memories, talents, skills, creations) you have stored away from the past. You're reviewing and reflecting on the things you value. You need a breath of fresh air, more movement, and vitality. <u>Emotional</u>: You need to break free of tradition and old habits and take some risks. Memories bring emotional issues you have to deal with. You feel removed from the experiences of your life. <u>Mental-Spiritual</u>: You are visiting the higher dimensions looking at the records of your past and the planetary history.

music/musical instruments: <u>Physical</u>: Hearing harmonious, soothing music means you are focusing on balance, beauty, high-level self-expression, pleasure, and healing. You are removing blocks to better energy flow. If you're playing or composing music, you're expressing your creative talents, communicating effectively, and engaging with the flow of life. Musical instruments represent different parts of your nature, from your sexuality to spirituality. <u>Emotional</u>: Hearing discordant or sad music links to painful inner issues, while wild, erratic music connects to your animal nature. You are accessing memories. <u>Mental-Spiritual</u>: Hearing or composing music means you are moving through the higher mental and spiritual realms, reorganizing patterns in your awareness to incorporate increased harmony, joy, and sensitivity. You're using your intuition.

mustache: *(see beard)*

N

naked: <u>Physical</u>: You are awkward or out of place in your social setting. If you are uninhibited being nude, you feel comfortable in your own skin, and are entitling yourself to full, carefree self-expression, and to be seen for who you really are. You're tired of maintaining a facade. You're trying to be something you're not. <u>Emotional</u>: If you're uncomfortable being nude or in a state of undress in public, you feel ridiculed, disgraced, caught off guard, unprepared, exposed, or anxious about how others see you. You feel shame or guilt about your shortcomings being shown to the world. <u>Mental-Spiritual</u>: You are examining your inner truth and bringing forth new aspects of your character you've been unaware of, or hiding. You are defenseless, focusing on your innocence.

navel: <u>Physical</u>: You're focusing on your originality, your connection to your mother and nurturing, or to your birth or rebirth. You need to center and find middle ground. <u>Emotional</u>: You are too self-absorbed.

You are looking at unconscious codependency issues or how you feel drained by people who want to control you by taking care of you. If you pierce your navel, you're asserting your need to feel unique. Mental-Spiritual: You're connecting with universal divine feminine energy. If you're contemplating your navel, you're reaching down into the unknown, focusing on your divine origin, remembering your soul.

neck/throat: Physical: You're focusing on how you connect your mind and body, head and heart, or any two significant things. You're experiencing a slowdown or bottleneck. You're examining how confidently you express yourself and how willful you are. Emotional: You feel vulnerable about speaking your truth and sharing your ideas, or are restricting your feelings. You're afraid to "stick your neck out" and put yourself at risk. A thick or stiff neck means a stubborn, prideful, quarrelsome nature. A beautiful neck indicates a graceful, sensitive nature. Mental-Spiritual: You're focusing on finding your voice, communicating easily, and having faith in yourself and others. You're looking at your capacity for inspired creativity, so if this area is constricted or strangled, you feel stifled about using imagination, or your intuition is cut off. Having your throat cut means you are surrendering personal will to divine will.

net: Physical: You need to expand out into the world and gather in greater resources. You need to follow leads to meet new, helpful people. Emotional: You feel caught in a net of confusion, intrigue, or limitation. You are entangled in a complicated life situation. Mental-Spiritual: You're focusing on the global grid of energy, the internet of information, or your network of personal contacts.

newspaper: <u>Physical</u>: You are focusing on current or breaking information you need to operate effectively. You feel out of touch or behind and are trying to bring yourself up to speed. You're looking at promoting yourself or your business, or "spreading the news" about something. You're focusing on the power of media and a need to communicate effectively or see through biased reports. <u>Emotional</u>: You feel other people know too much, or not enough, about you, or they are misunderstanding or slandering you. You are shocked by upsetting, sudden news. <u>Mental-Spiritual</u>: You are receiving precognitive information or knowledge from other dimensions. You are becoming aware of something important.

night: <u>Physical</u>: A nighttime dream setting indicates something is still unconscious and seeking to be known. You are focusing on discovering secrets or mysteries. <u>Emotional</u>: You are dealing with subjects about which you feel fearful, uncertain, or directionless. You feel anxiety about being in the dark or alone. You're experiencing stealthy motives, sneakiness, or feelings of a dark or questionable nature. You're hiding something. <u>Mental-Spiritual</u>: You are introverted and contemplative. You're relaxing into a softer, intimate awareness that isn't action-oriented, where you feel freedom from social conventions.

north: <u>Physical</u>: You are seeking to correct your life direction. You are attuning to ancient wisdom, the elders, and a neutral point of view. You are experiencing frozen conditions and lack of momentum. <u>Emotional</u>: You feel coldness and lack of intimacy. <u>Mental-Spiritual</u>: You are aligning to "true north" or magnetic north, where you will find universal truth and clear inner guidance.

nose: <u>Physical</u>: You are being curious or perhaps too "nosy," meddlesome, interfering, or pushy. <u>Emotional</u>: If your nose is stuffed up, broken, out of joint, or bleeding, you have invaded someone else's reality and been rebuffed, or you haven't been trusting your intuition and higher sensitivity. <u>Mental-Spiritual</u>: You need to "follow your nose," and pay attention to intuition and instinct to avoid danger and find your way. You need to "sniff out" or detect new or hidden information, or learn more about a situation at hand.

numbers/mathematics: <u>Physical</u>: You are evaluating in great detail a situation in your waking life. You are solving a problem, finding a new approach. You are focusing on multiplicity, relative size, or a multifaceted process. Specific numbers represent different aspects of your personality, ways of doing things, stages of your growth process and the creation cycle, and time periods. You're giving yourself coded guidance about how to proceed. A date on a calendar, street address, phone number, number of objects, or a number superimposed over a scene, all indicate important clues. <u>Emotional</u>: You need to be careful about being overly emotional, or conversely, too rational. You have emotional associations with the numbers you see: a year of your life, date of an important event, how many children you have, or a lucky number. <u>Mental-Spiritual</u>: You're attuning to spiritual understanding, large patterns of consciousness, and archetypal human qualities. In complex numbers, examine each of the single digits, add them together until you have one digit. This core number reveals a deeper meaning. Look for the qualities of the numbers as listed below to find hidden meanings:

✔ **(1)** Individuality, authenticity, autonomy, personal will, courage, assertiveness, self-determination, self-reliance, inner strength, leadership, dictatorship, pioneering spirit, impulsiveness, impatience, beginnings, entrepreneurial ability, originality, independence, risk-taking behavior, authority, self-absorption, ego lessons, definition of personality

✔ **(2)** Cooperation, harmony, balance, receptivity, giving, mirroring, diplomacy, peacemaking, comparison, merging and dissolving boundaries, sharing, co-creation, relationships, partners, approval, agreements, linking and bridging, teaching, counseling, negotiating, indecision, oscillation, conflict, sensitivity, empathy, patience, female energy, marriage/divorce

✔ **(3)** Self-expression, creativity, open-mindedness, drama, social activity, popularity, communication, release, ease, flow, humor, outgoingness, spontaneity, imagination, verbal skill, promotion, sales, public speaking, singing, teaching, writing, performing, indecision, naturalness

✔ **(4)** Structure, personal discipline, work, effort, tangible results, responsibility, tradition, construction/building, the body, methodical, patience, determination, practical action, endurance, loyalty, limitation, attachments, business skill, three-dimensional design and art, seriousness, stubbornness, real estate/housing, focus, commitment, karma, overcoming obstacles, strength

✔ **(5)** Freedom, movement, change, travel, new experience and ideas, sensory stimulation, curiosity, restlessness, versatility, flexibility, cleverness, agility, mathematical and verbal ability, impatience, dancing, adventure, superficiality, temptation, communication, creativity, foreign cultures and languages, creativity, promotion, confusion, lack of security, paralysis

✔ **(6)** Service, nurturing, balance, adjustment, creation of divine harmony, beauty, settling down, idealism, romance, healing, wellness, art, counseling, teaching, events and gatherings, nutrition and food, cosmic parent, home and family, intimate groups, centers, openheartedness, sympathy, martyrdom

✔ **(7)** Truth, universal laws and metaphysics, love of knowledge, study, academia, research, perfectionism, privacy, introspection, objectivity, abstract/conceptual thinking, analysis, refinement, precision, silence, meditation, music, investigation, behind the scenes, mathematics, science, technology and computers, alignment of personal and divine will, aloofness, planning, retreats, spiritual pilgrimages, ego death, revelation of the spiritual

✔ **(8)** Manifestation, authority, power, competence, business and executive ability, organization, administration/management, systems, strategy, money, success, achievement, drive, ambition, materialism, professionalism, value system, superstructures, justice, the higher order of things

✔ **(9)** Universal awareness, compassion, altruism, humanitarian service, collective consciousness, idealism, romance, dreams/visions, big thinking, social and political action, personal loss or disappointment, invisibility, nonphysicality, mysticism, impersonalness, inspiration, generosity, completion, surrender, philosophy, imagination, sympathy, broad outlook, feeling overwhelmed, spaciousness, death and the other side

nurse: *(see doctor)*

nut: <u>Physical</u>: You are looking for the core, meat, or kernel of truth inside an idea, person, situation, or yourself. If you consider nuts as a pun for testicles, you are focusing on the physical health of this body part, or on sexuality. If you are eating nuts, you feel prosperous and confident about attaining your desires. <u>Emotional</u>: You're focusing on craziness, confusion, or "nutty" behavior. You feel "nuts" for someone or something, or someone is "driving you nuts." <u>Mental-Spiritual</u>: You are focusing on valuable ideas, latent talents that can be developed, or other seeds of new creativity and growth. *(see acorn, seed)*

0

oar: <u>Physical</u>: You are focusing on your ability to move yourself forward, steer a steady course, or change directions on a dime. You are struggling against circumstances. If you are paddling with one oar, you need to work with others to stabilize your momentum. A broken oar means a handicap or setback. <u>Emotional</u>: You are exerting control over your emotions. You feel a lack of support. If you've lost your oars, you feel powerless and at the affect of circumstances. <u>Mental-Spiritual</u>: If you're rowing with a team of people, in unison, you are focusing on ideas of collaboration, cocreation, and are moving through the collective consciousness.

ocean: <u>Physical</u>: You are looking at deeper patterns concerning creativity, fertility, birth and death, and human origins. You are contemplating how unlimited you are and how much you're capable of expressing. You're harmonizing yourself with the tides and currents of life. <u>Emotional</u>: You're examining deep emotions (oceanic grief or terror), secrets, and fears of vastness or nature's annihilating power. If you're in stormy seas, you probably have chaos in your life. If you are being pulled under or facing a tsunami, you're struggling against overwhelming conditions in waking life. <u>Mental-Spiritual</u>: You are focusing on reaching limitless mind, the source of life, the collective consciousness, and the deep history of the planet, exploring issues shared by your culture or humanity. Swimming deep in the ocean means you're traveling in the spiritual realms, free from limitations, in touch with ancient wisdom. A calm ocean means inner peace and spiritual revelation.

octopus: <u>Physical</u>: You are involved with many different things, or are changing your self-expression, or colors like a chameleon. You are successful at getting what you want. <u>Emotional</u>: You feel clingy or possessive, or emotionally engrossed and smothered by entanglements. You fear being dragged down by your desires or other people's emotional needs. You've experienced or perpetrated sexual harassment. You're tuning in to spirits of the underworld. <u>Mental-Spiritual</u>: You have a brilliant intelligence, many ideas simultaneously, a rich imagination, a hunger for life, and the capacity to take in and synthesize huge amounts of information.

old age: <u>Physical</u>: You're focusing on your life experience and internal ageless wisdom that may have been written off by others or by part of your own mind.

You're entering a pleasurable stage of life. <u>Emotional</u>: You are afraid of the aging process, frailty, or of letting go and allowing yourself to be cared for. You have ambivalent feelings about your lineage and ancestors. You're afraid you'll be seen as old-fashioned and ineffective. You need to be flexible and open-minded. <u>Mental-Spiritual</u>: You need to honor maturity. An old lesson has a new application. You're learning to be more philosophical, forgiving, innocent, and at peace. You need to review and reconcile your life. *(see grandparent)*

onion: <u>Physical</u>: You're examining your personal growth process, or you need to see how a situation in your life is multilayered. You are peeling back the layers of yourself to get to the root of a problem. <u>Emotional</u>: You feel sad or need to cry about something. You are warding off an evil influence or something you sense is detrimental to you. <u>Mental-Spiritual</u>: You are expanding your wisdom, growing in stages, patiently. You are full of an almost magical power to protect what's good.

orange: <u>Physical</u>: You need to be more stimulated, invigorated, enthusiastic, expansive, happy, determined, encouraged, and assertive. Orange represents purification, creative urges, ambition, appetites, and boldness. You like getting attention and being visible. <u>Emotional</u>: Rusty orange is linked to autumn and an experience of harvest, winding down, and giving a last show of lively color before deeply resting. You feel warm, sunny, sociable, excited, but not overly passionate or aggressive. <u>Mental-Spiritual</u>: You are stimulated mentally. Orange monks' robes mean purification of negative desires and release of clinging tendencies.

orphan: <u>Physical</u>: You are focusing on being independent and successful on your own, as well as looking for where and with whom you truly belong. <u>Emotional</u>: You feel unloved, rejected, lonely, unwanted, invisible, needy, insecure, or misunderstood. You fear abandonment or isolation, or can't find your place. <u>Mental-Spiritual</u>: You're looking at the importance of your parents, what you need to receive from parents, how to be a good parent, and what family means in the broader sense. If you're helping orphans, you are opening your heart to serve in some way.

ostrich: <u>Physical</u>: You are in your own private world not facing reality, are unwilling to accept the truth, or are avoiding or denying responsibility or uncomfortable experiences. You need to be more practical, alert, and courageous. <u>Emotional</u>: You are avoiding repressed emotions, or are caught in delusions. You feel you don't fit with your peers, like this largest bird that cannot fly. <u>Mental-Spiritual</u>: You need to hone your perceptual skills, handle problems immediately, and discover something that's right in front of you. Ostriches represent people who appear religious but don't act holy.

otter: <u>Physical</u>: You need to develop greater playfulness, lightheartedness, and joy. You're focusing on happiness, good fortune, cleverness, fluidity of motion, and cleanliness. <u>Emotional</u>: You're making friends with your emotions, learning to swim through tough spots, let go of resistance, and be more flexible in your habits. You need to express tenderness with friends and loved ones. <u>Mental-Spiritual</u>: You have the skill to intuitively see what's below the surface of things, and the ability to find nourishment in the hidden depths of spirit. The otter is particularly connected with women and precognition.

outlaw: *(see criminal)*

owl: <u>Physical</u>: You're about to experience change or an important transition, or you're practicing shape-shifting. You need more, or less, solitude. You need to move swiftly, purposefully, and silently. <u>Emotional</u>: You are afraid of the dark, death, or your subconscious mind. Owls bring messages and secrets from the other side or the unconscious, which may trigger anxiety or growth. You are caught in deception or illusion. You are brooding or too introspective. You are comfortable with your shadow self. <u>Mental-Spiritual</u>: You are considering higher education, or increasing your intellectual knowledge. You need to use better judgment. You need to hone your intuition and keen observational skills. You can penetrate into the darkness to see what others can't. You have the potential to be clairvoyant, see behind masks into the soul. You are ready to experience a death and rebirth or spiritual initiation to a new level of awareness. Owls are particularly connected to the moon and magic.

oyster: <u>Physical</u>: You are looking for the prize pearl, the experience of being rewarded handsomely for your efforts. You are working hard to make something beautiful from humble beginnings. You feel lucky, as though "the world is my oyster." You want more sexual activity and eroticism. <u>Emotional</u>: You are shutting others out with a defensive attitude, or you feel enclosed in a hard, protective shell. You feel others want to take advantage of your natural gifts and beauty. You're afraid of new experiences. <u>Mental-Spiritual</u>: You are focusing on thoughts of beauty, ripening and growing yourself spiritually gradually over time, transforming from a grain of sand to a precious jewel. You're creating a fertile, safe environment or context in which you can develop optimally.

p

pain: <u>Physical</u>: Experiencing pain in a dream can link to real pain, or memory of pain from the near or distant past. It can be a warning to pay attention to a specific area of the body, and can mean you are tired. Someone in your life is acting as a pain in the neck or causing you pain. <u>Emotional</u>: You are experiencing emotional pain that is connected to the meaning of the body part where you experienced the physical pain. You feel loss, humiliation, or rejection. <u>Mental-Spiritual</u>: You are experiencing an empathic connection to another person's, or society's, pain.

painting/photograph/portrait: <u>Physical</u>: You are looking at visions you hold about life, how a process will unfold, or what you can become. You're focusing on beauty, inside and out. Take your artistic abilities more seriously. <u>Emotional</u>: The mood of the image, its color, crispness, realism, size, and texture all give clues about how you feel about yourself and your future. You're picturing the worst, or seeing how you want things to turn out. <u>Mental-Spiritual</u>: You're becoming aware of false images, ideas, or hopes. You are using your imagination to create your reality. You are showing yourself a snapshot of something important that requires attention.

parachute: <u>Physical</u>: You are focusing on taking a great risk or on escaping from a situation in which you feel trapped. You are coming down to earth to face reality. <u>Emotional</u>: You are concerned about survival, and the fear of being out of control or crashing and failing. You have protection and security during a time of turmoil. If your parachute doesn't open, you feel abandoned or betrayed by supporters. <u>Mental-Spiritual</u>: You're designing an escape plan. You're encouraging yourself to have faith and let go.

parade: <u>Physical</u>: You want to publicly display your various talents and character traits in a celebratory, upbeat way. You need more variety, color, music, social activity, and cooperation with others. <u>Emotional</u>: Watching a parade means you need to get more involved in life and not just look on shyly from the sidelines. You feel blocked about showing your true colors. <u>Mental-Spiritual</u>: You are going through a specific rite of passage, or remembering one from your past. You're aligning your ideas and life direction with the people around you.

paralysis: <u>Physical</u>: You feel helpless about a situation in your life, you need to be totally still and attend to something, or just do nothing for awhile. You feel frozen and unable to act. You are experiencing part of the dream cycle itself, where during REM, rapid eye movement, sleep the body becomes "paralyzed" and doesn't move. <u>Emotional</u>: You feel dominated, power-less, depressed, unable to express yourself freely or make your own decisions, possibly due to uncon-scious fear. If you associate paralysis with aliens or evil forces from the underworld, it means you feel vul-nerable and need to strengthen your core sense of self and your boundaries. <u>Mental-Spiritual</u>: You've reached an impasse where your beliefs and world view no longer serve your growth. You need to attune to the still, small voice within to find new direction.

paramedics: *(see ambulance)*

parrot: <u>Physical</u>: You are speaking without understanding what you're talking about. You need to pay attention to what you really mean, to using the right words, and being original, not just "parroting" what other people say. <u>Emotional</u>: You're upset by others gossiping or not understanding you. <u>Mental-Spiritual</u>: You are reminding yourself about your core intelligence and cleverness. You are learning to be more fluid in your communication skills.

party: <u>Physical</u>: You need more social activity, celebration, relaxation, and exchange with others. <u>Emotional</u>: A birthday or surprise party means you need recognition, to feel greater self-worth, and to be grateful for your life. A dinner party means you are focusing on the nurturing, support, and love you give and receive with a close circle of friends or colleagues. <u>Mental-Spiritual</u>: You are processing a recent interaction with others. You need to develop greater comfort with shallow conversation, or you need more introversion or extraversion.

passport: <u>Physical</u>: You are focusing on your identity and ability to make transitions between phases and situations. You need freedom of movement and to be welcome in new groups, associations, endeavors, or places. You need to have permission from an authority figure to do something. <u>Emotional</u>: If you lose your passport, you feel like an outsider, that you are trapped, or have anxiety about authorities. <u>Mental-Spiritual</u>: You are in a process of finding yourself and discovering who you are. You're preparing to explore many parts of your identity and knowledge or embark on a spiritual quest.

peacock: <u>Physical</u>: You want to express yourself more dramatically, without reservation. You are looking for greater prestige, confidence, pride, or the ability to celebrate. <u>Emotional</u>: You are covering over feelings of being plain or shy with color, showiness, vanity, bragging, or an attitude of superiority. <u>Mental-Spiritual</u>: Peacocks are connected to the phoenix and represent the soul. You see with the many eyes contained in the peacock's plumes, or you are shedding your plumage, identity, and growing it anew. You are transforming from plain to magnificent.

pelican: <u>Physical</u>: You are taking on and carrying more than you need or is healthy for you. You have a greater capacity than you think. <u>Emotional</u>: You need, or want to give, nurturing and care. You need to focus on your selfless, charitable nature. <u>Mental-Spiritual</u>: You are full of knowledge and resources. The pelican symbolizes piety and Jesus in Christian legend.

penguin: <u>Physical</u>: You are focusing on qualities of hardiness, endurance, humor, playfulness, and quirkiness. Your problems aren't overly serious; you need to be steady and coolheaded. <u>Emotional</u>: You are looking at how couples work patiently together to support each other, how nurturing fathers can be, how loyal and protective parents need to be. You are focusing on fluid movement through difficult emotional times. <u>Mental-Spiritual</u>: You are attuning to survival of the spirit amidst dire circumstances, the power of great love, intuition, and the group mind. You are aware of polarized, black-and-white perception.

periscope: <u>Physical</u>: You have a problem related to your neck or eyes. You need to stretch out and rise above a current situation to find a clear view.

<u>Emotional</u>: You are moving past emotional confusion and murkiness by finding a more neutral point of view. <u>Mental-Spiritual</u>: You are maintaining contact with the collective consciousness and your feelings while ascending to a higher level to gather important data and perspective.

pets: <u>Physical</u>: You're focusing on an aspect of yourself that you need to love, especially if the symbol is a personal pet. The pet is teaching you a lesson, like being more compassionate, trusting, playful, or independent. You're dealing with a person similar to the animal. <u>Emotional</u>: You need to develop more vulnerability, loyalty, and responsibility for others. You want more attention, affection, and unconditional love, and to be able to demonstrate your own love more openly. You want a better home and family life. <u>Mental-Spiritual</u>: You are focusing on informal, personal connections to others and the world, and on opening your heart.

phoenix: <u>Physical</u>: You are ready for a new phase of life, dramatic change, and deep renewal. You are releasing something that is holding you back, perhaps an old definition of yourself. <u>Emotional</u>: You are experiencing anxiety about loss and change. You feel like destroying part of a life you've built without understanding why. <u>Mental-Spiritual</u>: You want to believe that anything is possible, and you have the power to change things for the better. It is time to have faith in your soul so you can transform into your most radiant self. You can regenerate, no matter how bad things look.

pig: <u>Physical</u>: You are experiencing your various appetites. You are hoarding or "hogging" something, the limelight, someone's time, or money. You are too messy, dirty, smelly, fat, or unkempt. <u>Emotional</u>: You're focusing on gluttony, greed, stubbornness, or feeling dirty, especially concerning sexual desires. You need to clean up your act and express your sweet nature. <u>Mental-Spiritual</u>: You are focusing on being intelligent, clever, instinctual, and prosperous.

pill: *(see medicine)*

pocket: <u>Physical</u>: You're focusing on a part of yourself you're not aware of, or a place inside where you hide precious parts of yourself: memories, secrets, or inner resources. You have a physical problem where too much or too little energy is collecting. You're focusing on female reproductive organs. Putting something in a pocket means you want to possess, protect, or personally use what the item represents. Pockets sewn shut mean you must use your valuables or give them away. <u>Emotional</u>: You are concealing something, indicated by the hidden object. Pockets turned inside out mean openness and sincerity. Hands in pockets mean you are waiting for the right time to act, are showing others you aren't aggressive or interfering, or you feel helpless. <u>Mental-Spiritual</u>: Finding something in a pocket indicates an ability or new knowledge coming to light, or aid coming to you. A hole in your pocket means you're unconsciously leaking energy or resources.

poison: <u>Physical</u>: There is a condition in your life that is physically or emotionally toxic to your well-being. Something is weakening your life force. <u>Emotional</u>: You have bitter feelings or are trying to free yourself from a hurtful condition or emotionally toxic atmosphere. Someone is secretly sabotaging you, or you are in pain due to bad chemistry with someone. <u>Mental-Spiritual</u>:

You are operating from a world view that doesn't fit your character and life purpose. You must rid yourself of negativity.

polar bear: <u>Physical</u>: You're focusing on being powerful and resourceful in spite of difficult conditions. You blend in with your surroundings. You need more solitude. <u>Emotional</u>: You feel isolated and want affectionate companions who understand you. You feel highly protective of family and friends. You are trying to be warmhearted in the midst of fearful people. You are breaking through emotional barriers and frozen feelings. <u>Mental-Spiritual</u>: What you have is precious. You have a connection to higher dimensions and deep space.

police: <u>Physical</u>: You are exploring issues of authority and control (external and internal), reminding yourself to be conscientious, keep your word, live a balanced life, or avoid reckless behavior. You're looking at the value of conventionality, rules, social mores, and order in your life. <u>Emotional</u>: You feel chaotic and full of commotion, and need to settle down. You feel violated, powerless, and need rescue, protection, and security. You feel threatened by an authority, or guilty. <u>Mental-Spiritual</u>: You are breaking rules, crossing boundaries into forbidden territory, creating disorder in your mind, and you need to live in alignment with universal laws. Your spiritual guides are directing you.

pool: <u>Physical</u>: You are focusing on a need to relax, have some recreation, exercise, and a greater energy flow. Floating or swimming in a pool means you seek peace, a feeling of luxury, or a release of daily worries and responsibilities. You want greater freedom, fluidity, and magical movement. <u>Emotional</u>: You're becoming comfortable with your emotions. Being pulled under the water represents overwhelming circumstances in your waking life. Other people in the pool indicate social relationships and how you join in or miss out on nurturing experiences. <u>Mental-Spiritual</u>: You're developing intuition and empathy. Being in the deep end means you are entering the collective consciousness and exploring your spiritual origins. *(see swim)*

postcard: *(see letter)*

pregnancy: <u>Physical</u>: You are exploring the idea of becoming pregnant, or are pregnant. You are taking responsibility for another person or animal. Something new is gestating and about to emerge in your life. Miscarriages and aborted pregnancies mean you aren't ready for a new phase of creativity or lack the energy to complete a project. You are ready for an increase in your income. <u>Emotional</u>: You feel anxiety about being alone, or about being crowded and responsible for others. You feel stuck and impatient, waiting for something to happen. <u>Mental-Spiritual</u>: You are focusing on what's original about yourself, what you want to create, and what ideas are becoming interesting to you. *(see baby, birth)*

priest/minister/guru: <u>Physical</u>: You are examining your experience with religion and religious leaders, and how you connect with the spiritual part of yourself and life. You're looking at how you give your power away to experts. <u>Emotional</u>: You feel confused or lost and need inner guidance, comfort, and reassurance. You are relieving a guilty conscience. <u>Mental-Spiritual</u>: You are connecting with spiritual teachings, developing greater virtue in yourself, and revealing your own spiritual qualities, strengths, and abilities.

You are moving beyond your personal self and ego into higher dimensions.

prison: <u>Physical</u>: You're looking at the limits you impose on yourself or allow others to impose on you, and the way you stifle your creativity. You can't escape from rules, restrictions, and responsibilities. <u>Emotional</u>: There are parts of yourself, or subconscious fears, you have locked away and want to examine and release. You are dealing with authority problems, feelings of guilt, punishment, being trapped or restrained, or excluded or shut out. <u>Mental-Spiritual</u>: You are living inside a box of limited thinking and fixed beliefs, narrowing your possibilities. You need to be still, remove distractions, and focus on your core self.

psychic: *(see fortuneteller)*

public speaking: <u>Physical</u>: You're focusing on your ability to speak your truth, convey your message, and express yourself confidently and joyfully. <u>Emotional</u>: You're examining feelings of being scrutinized or judged by others, weighing the quality of what you offer, and assessing your comfort level with being visible. You are exposing your own weaknesses. <u>Mental-Spiritual</u>: The topic of your talk shows what issues you are concerned about and what your message is, while the setting for the talk shows where you feel people are receptive or not receptive to you.

purple: <u>Physical</u>: You need to experience more richness in life, a greater feeling of royalty, rank, and deservedness, as well as distinction and dignity. You have mixed feelings about the church, priesthoods, and pomp and ceremony. <u>Emotional</u>: You need to surrender, have faith, let go of negative emotions, and feel protected by unseen forces. You are feeling romantic or nostalgic. <u>Mental-Spiritual</u>: You are stimulating your spiritual life and universal understanding, your awareness of unity, spiritual healing, miracles, mystery, magic, transformation, and transmutation.

purse: *(see wallet)*

pyramid: <u>Physical</u>: You're focusing on your largest, highest goals and deepest yearnings. You've accomplished a goal, especially if your dream includes the apex. You need to visit a holy place. <u>Emotional</u>: You are finding insight and understanding about your deepest feelings, experiencing a release from suffering and pain by bringing the hidden into the light. You feel anxiety about an ordeal you must go through to prove yourself. <u>Mental-Spiritual</u>: You are searching for ancient wisdom, esoteric knowledge, secrets, and higher energy. You need to remember that life is sacred. You are transforming your personal, materialistic, human experience into its spiritual counterpart. *(see mountain)*

Q

quicksand: <u>Physical</u>: Your energy is being drained. You are on unstable ground, or have been tricked or trapped by something that at first seemed solid and safe. You need to be patient, change your tactics and perspective, (such as, lying on your back in quicksand will free you), and call on inner resources or outside help to unstick yourself. <u>Emotional</u>: You feel overwhelmed and dragged down into your subconscious by heavy emotional issues. The more you struggle, the more exhausted you become. You feel unsupported and powerless. <u>Mental-Spiritual</u>: You are out of touch with your true self, caught in too much materialism and resistance. You need to stop fighting, strip yourself of excess weight and baggage, and work with the universal forces. You need to remember you're lighter than the entrapping situation and by filling with your own essence, and taking it easy, you will rise to freedom. *(see paralysis)*

quilt: <u>Physical</u>: A patchwork quilt represents many aspects of yourself and your life that you are seeing as interrelated and forming a beautiful, harmonious pattern. You are recycling old experiences into new endeavors. <u>Emotional</u>: You want a warm, comforting, protective, emotional environment. <u>Mental-Spiritual</u>: You want to know and use all of yourself. You are integrating many ideas and experiences into yourself, allowing yourself to be complex and colorful, yet orderly. *(see blanket)*

R

rabbit: <u>Physical</u>: You are focusing on fertility, sexuality, the proliferation of work or self-expression, or increasing your abundance. A rabbit in the garden means you're experiencing the subtle destruction of your efforts and resources, or a setback in personal growth. You are running from problems. <u>Emotional</u>: You need to be less soft and docile, passive, and naive. You need greater humility and vulnerability. You feel you are the victim of predators, or have been wounded by life's basic insensitivity. You feel criticized, hunted down, or hounded. You want to be petted or cared for. <u>Mental-Spiritual</u>: You are unwisely idealistic. You believe in luck. You are sacrificing yourself or something precious for the good of others. Going down the rabbit hole means you are looking inside to find your deepest self and the origins of the universe. A white rabbit means magic and spiritual awakening.

rain: <u>Physical</u>: You are washing away old structures, cleansing yourself, fertilizing, replenishing, and nurturing a new period of growth and expansion. If the rain is gentle, you're about to experience a peaceful, productive time. If the rain is heavy, you can expect an increase in opportunities and abundance. <u>Emotional</u>: A heavy rain means feeling overwhelmed by dark, gloomy, depressing emotions, often accompanied by tears. Subconscious issues and emotions are entering your conscious mind. Too much unwanted rain means you feel you have bad luck or are being punished. <u>Mental-Spiritual</u>: You need to trust in providence. You are looking for the silver lining inside the dark clouds, attuning to the heart, the feminine, and nurturing.

rainbow: <u>Physical</u>: You have weathered difficulties and better, happier times are on the horizon. <u>Emotional</u>: You need to feel more optimistic and lucky. <u>Mental-Spiritual</u>: You are dreaming of better things, getting in touch with your destiny. You are bridging worlds, connecting your earthly experience to the divine. You are reminding yourself to be joyful, imaginative, and even magical. The pot of gold at the end of the rainbow means the revelation of your soul and your true nature as light and spirit.

ram: *(see sheep)*

rat: <u>Physical</u>: You are worried about contamination, germs, filth, physical sickness or disease; you're feeling ratty and rundown. You "smell a rat," or discover people acting in underhanded, stealthy, thieving, or sabotaging ways. Someone has "ratted" on you, betrayed, or lied about you. You need to stop, rest, and get out of the "rat race." You are an adaptable survivor, though perhaps without morals. <u>Emotional</u>: You feel apprehensive, worried, disgusted, or repulsed. Something is gnawing at you, undermining your peace of mind or confidence. You're experiencing frightening instincts, urges, or distasteful parts of yourself. Someone is using sex for material gain, or is deserting ship when difficulties arise. <u>Mental-Spiritual</u>: You are inquisitive, sniffing out answers and new experiences. You are clever, resourceful, and instinctive. White rats mean protection from beneficent forces.

red: <u>Physical</u>: You are focusing on your physical vitality and energy, heart, blood, blood pressure, metabolism, respiration rate, a birth or breakthrough, or survival. You are involved in something dangerous, exciting, impulsive, passionate, intense, willful, violent, or explosive. You need to develop more courage, high visibility, and leadership skills. You're warning yourself to be careful about accidents, to slow down or stop, or deal with an emergency. <u>Emotional</u>: You feel hot, frustrated, angry, warlike, and vengeful. You need greater stimulation, eroticism, and romantic love. <u>Mental-Spiritual</u>: You are focused on beginnings, basic life force, the power of the deep earth, and making quick decisions. You need to find balance between passion and safety. You need to pay attention.

refrigerator: <u>Physical</u>: You need plenty of resources and provisions on hand to accomplish what you want to do. <u>Emotional</u>: You are hoarding something, afraid you won't have enough. You've put your ignored feelings on ice. You need nurturing or are responsible for caretaking others. You want to feel abundant. <u>Mental-Spiritual</u>: You are preserving important thoughts or secrets for use later, or keeping yourself fresh, pure, and ready for action. *(see food)*

renovation: <u>Physical</u>: Renovating a house or building means you are reorganizing and reinventing yourself and your life. <u>Emotional</u>: You feel old or outdated and are afraid you'll lose value to others. <u>Mental-Spiritual</u>: You are changing the way you see and act in the world. You're replacing old ideas with a new world view and new knowledge.

resort/spa: *(see vacation)*

restaurant: <u>Physical</u>: You need physical nourishment. A fast food restaurant means you're not letting yourself integrate the full value of what you receive, or are ignoring your social needs. The restaurant's ambiance symbolizes how close you'd like to be in your relationships with other people. <u>Emotional</u>: You want greater emotional intimacy, or a more romantic or colorful mood. A bad meal or poor service means you don't feel important or worthy, or you aren't giving others enough value. <u>Mental-Spiritual</u>: You need intellectual stimulation and exchange of ideas with others. Cafeterias mean abundant variety and a wealth of ideas. You are ready to receive nurturing in an "all you can eat" fashion.

rhinoceros: <u>Physical</u>: You have great determination and follow-through. You need to work toward your goals, and not let anything get in your way or side-track you. You are focusing on male sexuality.

<u>Emotional</u>: You are provoked easily and react with forcefulness and blind rage. You are protected, shielded, and thick-skinned, avoiding your feelings. You need to develop greater vulnerability and tone down your warlike nature. <u>Mental-Spiritual</u>: You are developing instinct and intuition, opening your third eye. You are maintaining clear boundaries concerning your identity.

ride: <u>Physical</u>: Riding in a vehicle means you are seeking a new destination, letting someone else help you get there. You are resting for awhile from being responsible. Riding a horse or other animal means you're accessing your instinctual nature to help you move forward. <u>Emotional</u>: Someone else is controlling you, and you feel helpless, passive, or that you are "just along for the ride," with no say in things. <u>Mental-Spiritual</u>: You are contemplating, observing, and gestating, waiting for the right vision, enthusiasm, and moment to guide your life in a new direction.

right: <u>Physical</u>: The right side of the body, and anything to the right, symbolizes action, forward motion, personal power to accomplish, masculine or yang energy, and cultural standards. <u>Emotional</u>: You are afraid to vary from the norm, be out of control, or to be wrong. You need to break some habits and be open to your feelings. <u>Mental-Spiritual</u>: You're focusing on logic, analysis, goals, will, and movement toward the conscious, outer-directed part of yourself. If you are left-handed, your meanings for left and right may be reversed.

ring: <u>Physical</u>: You're focusing on commitment, belonging, completion, and wholeness. You are contemplating marriage, or divorce. You are part of a group or cause to which you've pledged loyalty. <u>Emotional</u>: Losing a ring means you are looking at your commitment or love for the person, group, or ideals it stands for. <u>Mental-Spiritual</u>: Rings connect you to universal knowledge. Receiving a ring means you are connecting to specific qualities and ideas represented by the giver of the ring, your grandmother's courage, your father's love. Or, you are taking on an identity, the prestige of your alma mater.

river: <u>Physical</u>: You're looking at the flow of your energy, your life path, or the passage of time. Crossing a river means you're intentionally entering a new phase, facing emotional issues to do it. Watching a river from its banks means you need to be more involved in creating your life. <u>Emotional</u>: You're focusing on your emotional processes, and whether they are peaceful and progressing slowly, or flooded and in turmoil, with rapids and snagged debris, complex emotional issues. Being in a boat or swimming in a river means you're immediately involved in an emotional process. How much you steer or guide yourself shows how proactive you are in your life. The condition of the water — clear, muddy, turbulent, stagnant — shows the state of your emotions. <u>Mental-Spiritual</u>: Flowing with the river represents peace or surrender to a higher power. You are linking yourself to, and moving toward, a greater source of inspiration and wisdom. Trying to go upstream means you're out of harmony with your purpose.

road: <u>Physical</u>: You're focusing on the journey of life, your direction, and how you reach your goals. The kind of road indicates your current process. A straight, flat, well-marked road means you're going in the right direction, moving directly to your goals.

A twisty, bumpy, muddy, unpaved, impassable, or steep road means you are struggling or uncertain. If you're on a superhighway, you are going fast, or too fast. <u>Emotional</u>: A roadblock means you feel stuck, held back, or checked up on by someone in authority. Being stranded means you feel unsupported and isolated. Running off the road means you must pay attention and be more responsible for your success. <u>Mental-Spiritual</u>: You are focusing on your destination or life purpose, and on how you make the journey. You need to pay attention to the quality and details of the process as well as end results.

robin: <u>Physical</u>: You are focusing on the coming of spring, a new beginning, opportunity, or birth. You are starting first and can expect success. "The early bird gets the worm." <u>Emotional</u>: You feel fresh and ready to tackle any emotional challenge. <u>Mental-Spiritual</u>: You're experiencing a burst of new ideas, optimism, and spiritual renewal.

roof: <u>Physical</u>: You need protection, shelter, and material comforts. <u>Emotional</u>: You feel vulnerable in the world at large and want a smaller focus to operate within. You are afraid of being exposed. <u>Mental-Spiritual</u>: There is a barrier between your daily awareness and the higher realms, which can be your ideology, philosophy, ideals, and world view. A leaky roof means new information, or spiritual awareness is becoming conscious. If the roof is caving in, you must recommit to your ideals, or you can't live up to your own high expectations. *(see ceiling)*

room: <u>Physical</u>: You are looking at your various talents, aspects, and life activities. Discovering rooms you didn't know were there means you are discovering new capacities or roles. Moving from one room to another means you're changing focus and shifting your mode of self-expression. <u>Emotional</u>: A basement or attic space indicates you are contacting your sub-conscious mind and fears, blockages, or old memories. The décor and mood of the room indicate emotional issues. <u>Mental-Spiritual</u>: You are focusing on a specific set of ideas, or entering a specific reality to explore an aspect of yourself.

rooster: *(see chicken)*

roots: <u>Physical</u>: You need to be grounded, or committed to a place, activity, or person. You are exploring the origins of your life and family. You need to get back to basics. <u>Emotional</u>: You've been too wishy-washy or flighty, and need to "set down some roots" and stop avoiding uncomfortable feelings. <u>Mental-Spiritual</u>: Roots symbolize the need to connect deeply with the collective consciousness or subconscious mind. You are on the verge of a revelation. Roots growing into your house or water pipes indicate deep wisdom surfacing for you.

rope: <u>Physical</u>: You are examining how you connect to things you see as separate from you, what you are grasping at, how you secure things, and how entangled or tied up you are by situations in your life. Uncoiling a rope means the beginning of a new phase, while coiling a rope means a successful completion of a difficult task. Someone throwing you a rope is a promise of assistance and rescue. Climbing a rope means you are determined to succeed and overcome adversity. <u>Emotional</u>: Being tied up means you feel criticized, restricted, and helpless in your self-expression. Climbing down a rope means you feel disappointed, incapable, and have given up, or you are coming back to earth safely without falling or failing. <u>Mental-Spiritual</u>: Walking a tightrope means you are concentrating on your path, paying attention to the nuances of what keeps you safe and on purpose.

rose: <u>Physical</u>: You're focusing on love, romance, respect, honor, beauty, innocence, and appreciation for a great performance or job well done. You're looking at femininity and female sexuality. <u>Emotional</u>: You want to feel sweet, beautiful, and loved. The openness of the flower indicates your level of emotional openness and self-expression. A bud means you're closed and afraid, while a wide-open, flat, spent rose means you're exhausted. A single rose means gratitude. <u>Mental-Spiritual</u>: You have a complex, elegant self-expression and spiritual awareness. You are unfolding gracefully. Note the color of the rose: white, innocence/purity; pink, romance/love; red, passion; yellow, friendship and caring; black, illness or death.

ruins: <u>Physical</u>: You are focusing on the possible destruction or failure of a project in your life. You are aware a phase is coming to an end and offers no more benefit. Your life is in ruins, or your security has collapsed. <u>Emotional</u>: You feel the loss of a relationship, a part of your identity, or a goal. You feel depressed and defeated. <u>Mental-Spiritual</u>: You are about to begin again, to experience rebirth. Ancient ruins indicate you are discovering or remembering deep parts of yourself and secrets from your distant past. You are uncovering the ancient wisdom of the collective consciousness, or piecing together your history throughout time.

running: <u>Physical</u>: Running for exercise means you're looking at your energy level, strength, exuberance, discipline, and the force you have to move through life. You need to speed up, slow down, or pace yourself. <u>Emotional</u>: Running away from something means you need to face an issue, you feel trapped or pressured, or you're not taking responsibility for your actions. Running in slow motion or where your feet won't move as you intend them to means you lack confidence, self-esteem, or are ambivalent about a goal. <u>Mental-Spiritual</u>: Competitive running means you're focusing on how to achieve your purpose, how much you need to use personal will, why you feel ambitious and motivated, and what's behind your current challenges and rivalries. *(see competition)*

S

saint/spiritual guide: <u>Physical</u>: You are focusing on the amount of good you contribute to the world, whether it be through actions or philanthropy. You are experiencing difficulties and must not lose heart; you can make it through. You need to shift your focus from material concerns to the quality of your inner life. <u>Emotional</u>: You feel uneasy or guilty about current choices and behaviors. You need to make amends for something you did. You are sacrificing yourself for others or are suffering. <u>Mental-Spiritual</u>: You are focusing on a high ideal. You're questioning your spiritual path or considering another that may result in others disapproving of you. You are receiving spiritual guidance from a higher level of your own self. *(see angel, animals)*

school: <u>Physical</u>: You're focusing on what you can learn from your circumstances. You need to pay attention to new information or points of view. You're learning about yourself and improving your life. You're learning the hard way. <u>Emotional</u>: You're remembering your school years, especially the time when you went to the kind of school in the dream, when you felt insecure about making the grade, were unpopular, had authority problems, or surprising success. You have performance anxiety and are afraid of failing. <u>Mental-Spiritual</u>: You are examining how you learn. You are exploring higher realms, bringing knowledge back to your daily life from the collective consciousness. You are learning a spiritual lesson. *(see test)*

scientist: <u>Physical</u>: You need to be more careful about details and proof. You need to experiment more, and focus on invention and practicality. <u>Emotional</u>: You feel that people are judging you for being too eccentric or mental; you need to feel more and allow emotions to enrich your life. You need to celebrate. <u>Mental-Spiritual</u>: You need to be inspired and remember your higher purpose. You need to be guided by intuition and beauty. You are focusing on patterns of mathematics and knowledge in higher dimensions.

scissors: <u>Physical</u>: You need to take control or get rid of something in your life. You need to cut away excess that's weighing you down. <u>Emotional</u>: You feel cut off from others, or cut out of or denied opportunities. You are angry and tempted to attack someone. You dread a coming separation or loss of a loved one. Men may fear emotional castration. <u>Mental-Spiritual</u>: You need to cut through to the heart of the matter, or be decisive. You're experiencing sarcasm or criticism from others. Cutting something out of paper or fabric means you are carefully defining an idea or plan. *(see cut, knife)*

search: <u>Physical</u>: You are looking for something that is missing or needed in your life, possibly a part of yourself, or you are becoming aware that you need more than you have. <u>Emotional</u>: You are trying to remember something from your subconscious that is blocked. Your identity is threatened by the loss of something; the object gives clues to the characteristic you need to re-own and integrate. <u>Mental-Spiritual</u>: You are working out a solution to a problem. If you are searching the internet, you are moving through the collective consciousness aligning with your higher purpose.

seed: <u>Physical</u>: You are focusing on the beginning of something, creating the first steps carefully so the end result will unfold well. You need "seed money" to start a new venture. You're looking at concepts like vitality, fertilization, germination, and the continuity of life. You've "gone to seed," or stopped taking care of yourself. <u>Emotional</u>: You feel anxious about your potential and ability to initiate new things. <u>Mental-Spiritual</u>: You're focusing on your heritage, the human psyche, and soul. Seeds of new ideas have been sown in your mind and you're helping new experiences develop from them. *(see acorn, nut)*

sex/sex organs: <u>Physical</u>: You want more physical intimacy, sexual relations, or emotional love. You are activating or merging with new aspects of yourself and life represented by your dream partner. You're focusing on your balance of yin and yang energy. <u>Emotional</u>: If your partner is famous, you are telling yourself you are as good or talented as he or she is. You're examining vulnerability and intimacy issues, sexual problems, and past abuse experiences. You are anxious about being alone, want someone to rescue you, or want to be distracted from problems. You're looking at how receptive and aggressive you are. <u>Mental-Spiritual</u>: You're experiencing longings of a spiritual nature, a desire for communion.

shadow: <u>Physical</u>: You're focusing on parts of yourself you've rejected, hidden, or defined as weak, evil, or ugly. You are tired, weak, or out of practice, "a shadow of your former self." <u>Emotional</u>: You are dealing with uncomfortable negative emotions like jealousy, rage, greed, shame, or panic. You feel insecure, passive, depressed, or paranoid because you're "living in someone's shadow" or in the shadow of an event you can't forget. You are nervous and jumpy, "afraid of your own shadow." <u>Mental-Spiritual</u>: You have doubts based on your insecurities, or you are certain, knowing something "beyond the shadow of a doubt."

shark: <u>Physical</u>: You're focusing on a person who is greedy, unscrupulous, selfish, and aggressive, with no regard for others. You have legal or money problems and are dealing with lawyers and creditors. You need to be more direct in pursuing a goal, or have more stamina. <u>Emotional</u>: You're focusing on frightening emotions you believe can destroy or devour you. Sharks in a feeding frenzy means you're looking at collective negative emotions like violence or hatred. You feel threatened by something you can't reason with or control. <u>Mental-Spiritual</u>: You need to be less distracted by superficial ideas and focus on what is most important. You are accessing ancient wisdom about how to survive.

sheep: <u>Physical</u>: You are focusing on developing self-confidence, individuality, and initiative, especially if you dream of a ram. <u>Emotional</u>: You are easygoing and readily influenced by others. You feel like one of the flock, without personal power or influence, conforming or going along with the flow. You feel like an outcast, "the black sheep of the family." You feel panic and skittishness about some issue in your life. You are rushing headlong into situations, being hotheaded. Mental-Spiritual: You hesitate to express your ideas openly, or are shy, apologetic, or sheepish about being yourself.

shoes: Physical: You're looking at the way you connect to reality and live your life. Changing your shoes means you're changing roles, taking a new approach, or evaluating your goals. Worn, tattered shoes mean you need to focus on being grounded and in touch with details. High heels mean you want to accentuate your sexuality. Boots mean you are working seriously or dealing with trying conditions where you need a good footing. Emotional: You need to feel protected as you move forward. Slippers mean you need to relax and feel comforted and homey. Mental-Spiritual: Ill-fitting shoes that hurt your feet mean you lack energy or confidence in your path and purpose. Losing a heel means your basic assumptions about life are incorrect or unstable. Outdated shoes mean your convictions and ideas need updating.

silver: Physical: You're focusing on wealth, what you receive and give, your investments, or savings. Emotional: You need to feel soothed, cooled, more feminine, or introverted. You're focusing on an emotional or sentimental treasure. Mental-Spiritual: You need to have a neutral attitude. You're connecting with the moon, the silver lining inside dark clouds, positive thinking, intuition and psychic ability, and magic.

size: <u>Physical</u>: You're looking at the importance you attach to people or things, or the power and authority others have over you. <u>Emotional</u>: You feel dwarfed by someone's dramatic or dominant self-expression, or you are belittling others. A towering object means you want to feel invulnerable and strong. <u>Mental-Spiritual</u>: Tiny objects mean you need to pay attention in a much closer way.

skeleton/spine: *(see bones)*

skin: <u>Physical</u>: You are looking at how sensitive you are to the environment or others, and how you represent yourself to the world. You need to penetrate further into an issue or situation. <u>Emotional</u>: Skin problems or rashes mean you feel irritated, self-conscious, self-critical, ashamed, too visible, or uncomfortable about how you appear to others. You are being too superficial or shallow. Covering your skin with clothes means you feel vulnerable and are shielding your inner self. "Baring lots of skin" means you invite intimacy. Being "thick-skinned" means you are unaffected by criticism. <u>Mental-Spiritual</u>: You are focusing on your personal self, as separate from the unified field of energy in the universe. You are looking at beauty that is not only skin deep.

skunk: <u>Physical</u>: You are driving people away with a negative attitude or repellent language, or there is someone who is fouling your environment with bad behavior. "Something stinks" in your life. You are leaking vital energy or sexual energy, dumping woes and responsibilities onto others. <u>Emotional</u>: You have suppressed anger that is on the verge of exploding. You feel defensive. You've been walked on and want some respect. You need to assert yourself and dare to be outrageous. <u>Mental-Spiritual</u>: You need to examine the kind of people who are attracted to you, and why. Look at the kind of reputation you have, and what you contribute to the world.

sky: *(see air)*

slow motion/speeding: <u>Physical</u>: You are giving yourself important feedback about your pace in waking reality. Moving in slow motion, like wading through deep water, snow, or mud, is akin to paralysis; you are experiencing stress, frustration, and obstacles in a real situation. You also may be experiencing part of the natural dreamstate where the body stops moving. You are moving too fast in a relationship or project. <u>Emotional</u>: You feel anxious about meeting a deadline, driven to complete a goal, and are pushing yourself or others too hard. <u>Mental-Spiritual</u>: You are experiencing the different frequency rates connected to various dimensions and states of awareness. *(see paralysis)*

snake: <u>Physical</u>: You are focusing on life force energy (kundalini) and sexuality, instinctive drives, feminine energy and power, healing, and regeneration. You are entering a time of change and renewal. You need to have a healthy mistrust for someone. <u>Emotional</u>: If you personally fear snakes, the symbol serves as a warning of potential danger concerning something in your life. You feel tempted by someone who may be sly, as "a snake in the grass." <u>Mental-Spiritual</u>: You're focusing on connecting with the underworld, the subconscious, goddess power, psychic energy, or the ancient wisdom of the earth. Certain snakes, like cobras, symbolize shrewdness and unwavering truth. Serpents awaken unconscious urges and increase your knowledge.

snow: <u>Physical</u>: You're focusing on qualities like still-ness, purity, innocence, peace, and tranquility. You're making a clean start with a fresh perspective.
<u>Emotional</u>: You feel indifferent, isolated, shocked, restricted, or neglected. Snow and sleet mean frozen or unexpressed emotions, while hail relates to feeling battered. Being snowed in means you must deal with a backlog of suppressed emotion before you can reen-gage with the world. Melting snow means you're facing, understanding, and releasing frozen emotions and inhibitions. <u>Mental-Spiritual</u>: Newly fallen snow means you're seeing the world with fresh eyes and a sense of wonder. A snowflake represents your soul's unique expression, complexity, and beauty. Your thoughts come from a quiet, neutral place.

south: <u>Physical</u>: You need to be more physical, pas-sionate, fiery, and sensual. You need movement and dancing. You can endure difficulties without com-plaint, and bring projects to culmination. <u>Emotional</u>: You are opening your heart and warm feelings, healing emotional wounds through joy, generosity, and humor. <u>Mental-Spiritual</u>: You're focusing on the spirit of the earth, the power of the sun's life-giving rays. You can receive revelations and understand that what seemed secret is actually obvious through open-mindedness.

spaceship: *(see UFO)*

spider: <u>Physical</u>: You are caught in an entanglement by someone who is trying to trap you. You need to stay away from an alluring situation. You are focusing on feminine power, the calculating nature of some women, a devouring mother, or female seductions. You are entering a highly creative, productive phase where you'll be rewarded for your hard work. You need to pay attention to your "web," the Internet, your network of contacts, or your family connections. You know how to attract the resources you need. <u>Emotional</u>: You feel someone is sucking the life out of you. You feel trapped in a sticky or clingy relationship. A painful spider bite means you are externalizing a subliminal emotional wound. <u>Mental-Spiritual</u>: You are attuning to high levels of knowledge, mathematics, the neural net, and world energy grid. You are focusing on how you are creating your destiny. Spiders are considered power animal totems, spiritual guides, and protectors.

squirrel: <u>Physical</u>: You need to reserve supplies for a future time or are retaining too much and need to let go. You need to store your energy for times of need. You are entering a planning and gathering phase. You need to clear away clutter. You're overactive and need to calm down. <u>Emotional</u>: You're afraid of not having enough, expect the worst, or are feeling hypernervous about danger. Your behavior is erratic, or you are dodging traps. You need to let go of the superficial things that won't sustain you over time. <u>Mental-Spiritual</u>: You are clever, adaptable, and can access anything you need. You understand safety and safe places. You take no more than you need. You need to discard outmoded thought patterns, worries, and stress.

stage/theater: <u>Physical</u>: You're looking at your life and how you live it. Performing on stage shows roles you are playing, your current behavior, how you present yourself to the world, and how you interact with society. Being in the wings means you're observant, preparing to take action. You are learning to work with a team. <u>Emotional</u>: You want to be the center of attention, or receive recognition. Forgetting your lines indicates you feel unprepared or inadequate where you must perform to attain success. You are putting on a false act and need to be honest. <u>Mental-Spiritual</u>: You're focusing on how extensive you want your reality to be; "All the world is a stage." You're practicing how to let your self-expression be inspired. *(see acting)*

stairs: <u>Physical</u>: You are planning the steps you need to take to accomplish a goal. Walking upstairs means material and insights are surfacing and coming to you. Walking downstairs means you are accessing deeper reserves inside yourself, you're about to experience some setbacks, or you're rejoining the world after a hiatus. <u>Emotional</u>: Going downstairs means there is something from your past you need to acknowledge, you're dipping into your subconscious to access repressed fears, or you're retrieving useful lessons. <u>Mental-Spiritual</u>: You are moving between levels of yourself, or contemplating a process of either focusing, descending, or expanding — ascending your awareness and understanding. You are in a process of change and transformation. Each step is a lesson on your path. Spiral stairs signify growth or rebirth.

star/shooting star: <u>Physical</u>: You desire self-fulfillment, fame, and fortune. You are about to experience a new birth or changes in your life. You are entering a lucky phase. Your hopes, dreams, and wishes can come true. An opportunity is being pointed out to you; pay attention. <u>Emotional</u>: You need recognition and greater self-esteem. Being "star-crossed" means frustration because your desires don't line up with your destiny. <u>Mental-Spiritual</u>: You're focusing on high ideals, spirit, and your destiny. "It's in the stars" or "My stars" means your life is guided by higher forces; stars represent high states of consciousness and were considered by the ancients to be gods and goddesses who died and now guide us.

steal: *(see thief, criminal, cheat)*

stomach: Physical: You need to pay attention to what you eat, and how you assimilate your food. Similarly, you need to be careful about the people you bring close to you and the kind of support you give yourself. Emotional: You're receiving emotional, instinctual information. A knot in the stomach means you sense something is wrong or false about a situation. Not being able to "stomach something" means you are disgusted, afraid, or threatened to the point of physical nausea and vomiting. Mental-Spiritual: You are digesting new ideas, attitudes, and nourishing resource materials.

storm: *(see hurricane)*

stranger: Physical: A new part of your self is emerging, and you need to get to know it to see what it has to offer. You will receive news from afar. Emotional: Repressed, unfamiliar emotions are surfacing, and you are wary about your safety. You're focusing on a general threat or fear. Kissing a stranger means you long for a new relationship. Mental-Spiritual: You're experiencing a visitation from a being or spiritual guide from another realm, perhaps a deceased loved one. You are receiving guidance from a deep part of yourself.

strangle/suffocate: Physical: You are experiencing a situation or relationship that smothers you or doesn't give you enough space. Something or someone is holding you back. You're repressing or denying a vital aspect of your self-expression, your truth, or are hesitating to share your message. <u>Emotional</u>: Choking indicates an inability to swallow something, like a lie or an idea that is inappropriate for you. Someone is forcing you to behave in a certain way, and you feel revulsion. <u>Mental-Spiritual</u>: You need to reconnect with your inspiration, the source of life, faith, trust, and the present moment. You are focusing on expressing your true nature without restriction. *(see neck)*

subway: <u>Physical</u>: You are moving through life and reaching your goals via subliminal methods. You are exploring hidden aspects of yourself. <u>Emotional</u>: You feel claustrophobic or trapped, or lost amidst a maze of confusing feelings that never seem to become conscious. <u>Mental-Spiritual</u>: You're activating your intuition and instinctual knowing, exploring the collective subconscious mind. *(see tunnel)*

sun: <u>Physical</u>: You need to be outdoors more often. You're focusing on your vitality, radiance, and what creates good health. You want strong, positive relationships where things are obvious and on the up and up. You are lucky and inclined to be productive, hardworking, and enjoy what you do. <u>Emotional</u>: You feel positive and encouraged, especially about dealing with difficulties and healing emotional wounds. You feel good will toward all. <u>Mental-Spiritual</u>: You are focusing on creativity, intellectual brilliance, enlightenment, and insight. Two suns in the sky mean a fortunate event on your horizon.

surgery: <u>Physical</u>: You are concerned about an upcoming surgery. You are removing or cutting away old issues from your life and personality. You need to eliminate something or someone from your life that is not positive. <u>Emotional</u>: You are facing and healing deep emotional wounds. <u>Mental-Spiritual</u>: You are opening yourself up to grow in new ways. You are working at higher levels with spiritual guides to repattern your energy body, streamline your spiritual growth process, and remove karma. *(see cut, doctor)*

swamp: <u>Physical</u>: You are living through a period of struggle, challenges, setbacks, and slow progress. You are "swamped" with work, demands on your time, and responsibilities. You feel stuck and lack motivation but must keep on. You will experience success through dangerous and intriguing means. Your sexuality is super-charged. <u>Emotional</u>: You feel anxious about mysterious dangers that can emerge suddenly and threaten your safety. You are facing unruly or depressing emotions. <u>Mental-Spiritual</u>: You have an abundant imagination. You are passing through a test of character on your hero's journey. *(see hero)*

swan: <u>Physical</u>: You are focusing on qualities like grace, beauty, elegance, dignity, fluid movement, stateliness, and balance. The swan's long phallic neck links to male sexuality. You want to be prosperous, with greater prestige and wealth. You're singing your "swan song," preparing to let go of something important, or leave a period of your life behind. <u>Emotional</u>: You are looking at your own inner beauty, ease of being yourself, and presence under pressure. Someone is being mean to you under the guise of beauty. <u>Mental-Spiritual</u>: You're focusing on intuition, transformation, ugly duckling to swan, and knowledge of the future.

swim: <u>Physical</u>: You want greater fluidity and less resistance in the way you move through life.

Emotional: You are involved in a psychological growth process or therapy. You need emotional support. Swimming underwater easily means you are submerged in your feelings, processing deep issues you haven't been willing to face. Drowning means you feel overwhelmed by repressed emotions. Mental-Spiritual: Swimming represents movement of your awareness between realms as you explore unconscious and subconscious issues. Ecstatic feelings while swimming indicate you are flowing through higher spiritual realms. *(see pool, ocean)*

sword: *(see knife, cut)*

T

tail: Physical: You are focusing on maintaining balance, remembering something from your past, or you're waiting for someone or something to catch up with you. You're looking at basic vitality, male sexuality, and sexual needs. A situation is dragging out, taking too long. Emotional: A wagging tail means happiness and excitement. A curly tail means mischievous, sometimes lustful, feelings. A switching tail means you feel annoyance, irritation, or occasionally, pleasure. "Hightailing it" means you're moving rapidly, suddenly, or high-spiritedly. To "turn tail" or leave with your "tail between your legs" means you are humiliated, defeated, or frightened and want to flee from difficulty. Mental-Spiritual: You're focusing on instinct and urges. Holding the tail of an animal means you're following your gut instinct. Cutting off a tail "curtails" access to the wisdom of the body and earth.

taxes: <u>Physical</u>: You're balancing out what you give and what you receive, looking at the price you pay for your lifestyle, or acknowledging that you must pay for past actions. <u>Emotional</u>: You feel guilty, or you owe a debt to someone or society. You feel unfairly dominated by an all-powerful authority, or have lost your self-directedness. <u>Mental-Spiritual</u>: Refusing to pay taxes means you are a nonconformist or are rebelling against societal mores and collective beliefs. You're examining your karma.

teacher: *(see authority)*

teeth: <u>Physical</u>: You are grinding your teeth, or there is a potential tooth problem. You are examining the subtle balances in your body and life that maintain health. You are focusing on confidence, competence, assertiveness, aggression, and your ability to cut through or bite through tough or confusing situations. You are looking at your ability to engage and accomplish things: "I can sink my teeth into it," or I've "bitten off more than I can chew." Loose teeth or losing your teeth indicates you're losing power, courage, your grasp on a situation, or the ability to succeed. A gleaming white movie-star smile indicates you are putting on a show, or someone is too seductive. <u>Emotional</u>: You're self-conscious about your appearance and self-worth. Losing teeth means you fear looking foolish, being embarrassed, unattractive, getting older or impotent, or you refuse to face reality and are retreating to infancy. You've lost self-respect. Biting or being bitten means you feel angry and defensive. <u>Mental-Spiritual</u>: You are looking at how you articulate and express yourself. Rotten, yellow, or decaying teeth link to lies, insincerity, lack of character, and untrustworthiness. Swallowing a tooth means you may have to "eat your words."

telephone call/voicemail/text message: <u>Physical</u>:
You're focusing on how you communicate, what you
want to communicate, and difficulties communicating.
Wrong numbers, disconnected calls, bad connections,
lost numbers or addresses, and unanswered calls
mean you are conflicted about saying or hearing something, or that you have trouble making connections in
life. A conversation with a specific person means you
have an issue that needs to be discussed, or you need
to understand that person. <u>Emotional</u>: Not answering
a call or returning a message means you want to keep
an emotional issue at a distance, you feel overwhelmed and unable to communicate, you feel unsupported, or you're involved in a relationship problem.
Calling 911 means you urgently need support from
yourself or others. Leaving a message means you need
to be heard or need help. <u>Mental-Spiritual</u>: You are
connecting telepathically with your higher self or
others. You're receiving guidance, "getting the message." *(see cellular phone)*

telescope: <u>Physical</u>: You need to take a closer look at
some situation or bring an aspect of your life into
focus. <u>Emotional</u>: You feel anxious about the future
and the potentially dangerous or negative outcome of
a situation. <u>Mental-Spiritual</u>: You need to see things
that are far off or understand the specifics of a coming
process or event. Looking into space at stars and planets means you are developing intuition, clairvoyance,
and precognitive abilities, as well as exploring higher
realities. Your focus is too narrow; you're missing the
big picture.

television/monitor: <u>Physical</u>: You're focusing on your
inner process, the way your energy flows, and your
self-image. Seeing yourself onscreen means you need

to be more objective about yourself. <u>Emotional</u>: A monitor that freezes or blacks out means you need to drop into your feelings and break addictions to visual stimulation. <u>Mental-Spiritual</u>: You're examining your mind, thoughts, logic, and intuition, and how you receive, integrate, and express your ideas. You're looking at your attention span and how distracted you are. You need to concentrate on one thing. You're receiving a message.

tests: <u>Physical</u>: Taking a test or exam means you're entering a new level of expertise, responsibility, and authority. You are ready for something new, to advance in your life. <u>Emotional</u>: You are focusing on anxiety about measuring up, meeting expectations, being worthy, dealing with the unknown, and succeeding. <u>Mental-Spiritual</u>: You are measuring your current level of expertise so you can plan your life. You are involved in a spiritual initiation, entering a new level of consciousness.

theater: *(see stage, acting)*

thief: <u>Physical</u>: Someone, something, or an aspect of your own mind is stealing or wasting your energy, time, or resources. Life is too demanding. <u>Emotional</u>: You feel vulnerable about your boundaries and need to take a stronger stand for yourself, or you're overstepping others' boundaries. You are too isolated and self-protective. You don't feel entitled to abundance. You're afraid of losing what you have. You feel limited or unworthy, or that there is an unfair distribution of benefits. You feel envious of others' good fortune. You feel disrespected, manipulated, violated, invalidated, taken advantage of, and undervalued. <u>Mental-Spiritual</u>: An idea or issue in your subconscious is pushing into your awareness. You must re-own a part of yourself you've judged as negative. *(see cheat, criminal)*

throat: *(see neck, strangle)*

ticket: <u>Physical</u>: You are focusing on new goals or a new beginning or direction. Whether it's a ticket for a movie, concert, plane, train, bus, lottery, or raffle, you have permission to enter a new place or experience, travel wherever you want, see what you need to see, or win a prize. You're looking at the price you pay to get ahead and what you've earned. <u>Emotional</u>: A lost ticket means you feel like an outsider, or that you won't be able to have or experience something you want. You feel confused or frustrated about making progress. <u>Mental-Spiritual</u>: You're examining your beliefs about what you deserve and are entitled to. You are about to experience a higher level of awareness. *(see keys)*

tongue: <u>Physical</u>: You're hungry or sexual. Whether you are speaking with a "forked tongue," lying, "tongue in cheek," joking, a "silver tongue" charming, or giving someone a "tongue-lashing" criticizing, you're focusing on how you communicate and use speech. A wagging, loose tongue means you're gossiping, talking too much, or being talked about. <u>Emotional</u>: Having to bite or hold your tongue means you feel silenced, judged, and limited in your self-expression. Ripping someone's tongue out means you are extremely angry with something the person has said. <u>Mental-Spiritual</u>: Having your tongue cut out indicates you need to be silent and listen, watch what thoughts you've been voicing, and find new ways to express yourself. *(see mouth)*

tornado: *(see hurricane)*

tower: <u>Physical</u>: You're focusing on individuality and the need to isolate yourself to discover who you are. Being in an ivory tower means you are separated or insulated from ordinary life and its problems. Coming down from a tower means you are rejoining the world and becoming accessible. You're focusing on male sexuality. <u>Emotional</u>: You need to be a tower of strength for someone, or need unconditional support yourself. You feel you are being punished and ostracized. <u>Mental-Spiritual</u>: You are too aloof and cerebral and need to balance yourself with more sensitivity. You have high hopes or you feel superior to others. You need to obtain a higher world view or broader perspective about a situation.

traffic: <u>Physical</u>: Traffic on streets, at airports, in hallways, or on sidewalks means you are crowded, overwhelmed, and confused and need time and space to yourself. <u>Emotional</u>: A traffic jam means you feel blocked and frustrated at not being able to move as fast as you want. You need to develop patience and tolerance for people's differences. You feel minimized, unimportant, and helpless. <u>Mental-Spiritual</u>: You are mindless and need to be more conscious. You're part of a collective consciousness going the same direction, or in many directions simultaneously. You need to be in the moment, have faith that everything is in order, and that you'll reach your destination just when you need to be there.

train: <u>Physical</u>: You are focusing on "staying on track" in your life. You are headed in a specific direction toward goals, social and work-related, shared with others. Missing a train means a missed opportunity. A train wreck means you're encountering an unexpected obstacle that seriously disrupts your progress and throws your life into chaos. <u>Emotional</u>: You feel you're conforming and not being original enough. A train going through a tunnel indicates you're experiencing a life lesson you can't avoid. A freight train means you're carrying burdens and problems. <u>Mental-Spiritual</u>: You need to think in an orderly, sequential way with a clear "train of thought." You're focusing on the momentum and speed of your life's evolution. A derailed train means you've gotten off track and need to realign with your life purpose.

treasure/inheritance: <u>Physical</u>: Finding treasure or a treasure chest means you are discovering hidden skills, talents, and opportunities, or that help is coming. You are entering a period of materialistic gain and are bound for success. Receiving an inheritance means you are integrating all your past talents, experiences, and luck so you feel empowered to create and do more in your life. <u>Emotional</u>: You need to feel more worthy and gifted. You're avoiding applying yourself and want rewards without having earned them. Losing treasure means a downturn in your luck, a loss of friends, or a period of introspection. <u>Mental-Spiritual</u>: An inheritance indicates you're making a leap in your spiritual growth, and you benefit from the work and experience of your family lineage. Life has more meaning and is richer.

tree: <u>Physical</u>: You're focusing on the power of your personal growth, individuality, and stability. A tall, healthy tree means a flourishing, vibrant life. A newly leafing or blossoming tree means your self-expression is entering a new creative phase. A thick trunk means you are strong and rugged, while a thin, narrow trunk means you are more sensitive and flexible. Climbing a tree means you are achieving your goals and reaching

higher positions at work and in society. <u>Emotional</u>:
Trees with many connecting branches mean you want
to know your family lineage, or have a family of your
own. A withered tree means you need to activate your
feelings and loosen up. A diseased tree means you are
out of balance and need nurturing and healing. Cutting
down a tree means you are sabotaging your own life,
and in effect, killing yourself. A fallen tree means a sacrifice. <u>Mental-Spiritual</u>: Magnificent old grandfather
and grandmother trees mean you're attuning to
ancient wisdom, the divine, and the "tree of life."

trial: *(see judge)*

trumpet: <u>Physical</u>: You are announcing your intentions:
to achieve something, to be interested in something, to
move forward, or to change. You are spreading the
news, teaching, promoting, or you need to send your
messages and creations into the world. You're preparing
to lead a charge and are rallying people to your cause.
<u>Emotional</u>: You want people to know you've arrived. You
want to get attention and be recognized. <u>Mental-Spiritual</u>:
Hearing a trumpet indicates you need to pay attention
to something coming from your subconscious mind or
soul, or from life.

tunnel: <u>Physical</u>: You are making a transition from one
phase of life to another, involving a period of restriction from which you cannot escape. The period of concentration or difficulty must be lived through and
learned from until you naturally come out the other
side. You're focusing on female sexuality and birth.
<u>Emotional</u>: You need security and nurturing. You feel
anxiety about being in limbo, where unknown, clan-
destine things can happen. Exiting a tunnel means
you're coming out of depression or a time of anxiety.

You feel blind and punished. <u>Mental-Spiritual</u>: You have a limited perspective, and are exploring and living out issues in your subconscious. Seeing light at the end of a tunnel means hope, and a new phase of life with new awareness is just ahead.

turkey: <u>Physical</u>: You are focusing on the cycle of giving and receiving, being generous, sharing yourself with others, and counting your blessings. You are looking at the ideals of family, tradition, or sacrificing your time or part of yourself for someone else. A flock of turkeys means recognition, honor, or a rise to prominence. Shooting a turkey means you are trying to acquire wealth in an underhanded way. Hearing gobbling means you are gossiping or are being talked about by insincere friends. <u>Emotional</u>: You need to be more humble, and not so prideful, or you need more self-esteem. <u>Mental-Spiritual</u>: You are being silly or are not thinking clearly. Native Americans connect turkeys with luck, wisdom, and spiritual vision, and use turkey feathers in cleansing rituals.

turtle: <u>Physical</u>: You have been indoors too long. You are focusing on feminine energy, the womb, fertility, conception, and pregnancy. You want good luck, good health, and longevity. You need to learn to be at home anywhere and find new opportunities wherever you are. You need to reconnect to center, be grounded, and balance the physical, emotional, and spiritual energies in yourself. You're going through a slow phase, need to slow down, or resist change just because you're bored. <u>Emotional</u>: You need to be patient, persistent, have good personal boundaries, respect others' boundaries, and be more self-reliant and nonviolent. You can be too sensitive, withdrawn, uncomfortable in insecure settings, or perceive danger too quickly. You need to come out of your shell, stop hiding, show your true self, and be more involved and vulnerable with others. You need to go inside yourself and honor your feelings. <u>Mental-Spiritual</u>: You are focusing on Mother Earth, the divine feminine and goddess energy, and ancient wisdom. You need mental and psychic protection by being centered and fully present, by focusing and meditating on what's true and real.

U

UFO/spaceship: <u>Physical</u>: You're focusing on the sudden appearance of something or someone. You need to change direction suddenly and have no limits on what you consider possible. You're exploring a new situation that is unlike anything you've ever seen before. There are more advanced possibilities for you. <u>Emotional</u>: You feel alienated from others. You are too "spacey" and need to come back down to earth. You're involved in a relationship with someone you think is out of this world. You want to be whisked away from suffering or the mundane, or to feel special. <u>Mental-Spiritual</u>: You are an independent, imaginative, and creative thinker. You need a different, perhaps unusual, perspective to transcend circumstances and explore new, creative solutions. You want to connect with other worlds, find higher knowledge, and spiritual purpose. Your consciousness is moving up into the highest realms of the collective consciousness, contacting spiritual guides. *(see aliens)*

umbrella: <u>Physical</u>: You need to protect your finances, and save for a rainy day. If you're carrying an umbrella, you are focusing on being prepared, safe, and lucky. <u>Emotional</u>: You are putting up a shield against worries and negative emotions, or developing strategies to avoid upsets. Closing an umbrella means you're ready to face emotional issues and needs. A broken umbrella, one that won't open, or one that's turned inside out, means you feel overexposed to the world and unprepared to face your problems. Inviting someone to walk under an umbrella with you means you want greater generosity, intimacy, and trust in relationships. <u>Mental-Spiritual</u>: There is a barrier between you and higher information. You are unifying ideas or components of yourself or your work under a common theme.

underground: <u>Physical</u>: You need to focus on your body's inner dynamics. You are working with your deeper senses like hearing, touch, and smell. <u>Emotional</u>: You are dealing with subconscious issues or painful emotions that are hidden or repressed. You want greater security, inner peace, and quiet. <u>Mental-Spiritual</u>: You are discovering ancient secrets and knowledge, especially pertaining to feminine energy. *(see cave, subway, tunnel)*

underwear: <u>Physical</u>: Something you normally keep hidden is being revealed, or layers are being peeled away concerning some person or issue so you can see what's true. You're focusing on privacy, modesty, honesty, or being exposed. You are experiencing a loss of respect or reputation. You're exploring erotic images and memories. <u>Emotional</u>: Being in your underwear in public indicates you feel vulnerable, embarrassed, or ashamed, or you're hesitating to reveal true feelings, attitudes, actions, or habits. You're taking an emotional risk. You are experiencing unwanted intimacy or emotional neediness. <u>Mental-Spiritual</u>: You're getting down to the essence of an issue, overcoming distractions and illusions.

unicorn: <u>Physical</u>: You want to experience more magic in life. You are focusing on the qualities of solitude, privacy, beauty, that which is unattainable, purity, healing, wisdom, and renewal. You are looking at being able to fight fiercely while also maintaining harmony and gentleness. <u>Emotional</u>: You need to let loose and welcome synchronicity and miracles. You need to focus on innocence, sweetness, and your right to freedom. <u>Mental-Spiritual</u>: You are linking the physical and spiritual realms. You have high ideals, hope, and insight into a current situation. You are opening your imagination, intuition, and clairvoyance. The horn means you are safe from all incurable diseases and poisons.

urinate: <u>Physical</u>: You are releasing energy, toxins, and impurities. You are getting rid of an unwanted situation. You are involved in a territorial dispute or need to assert dominance. <u>Emotional</u>: You're afraid of an uncontrolled release of emotion that might prove embarrassing. You are angry, "pissed off," or want someone to go away, "piss off." Someone urinating in your space means you feel invaded, intimidated, violated, or even threatened sexually if there is exposure of the genitals. You feel put down or fouled, as though someone is "pissing on" your work or character. <u>Mental-Spiritual</u>: You're experiencing a release of tension and worry. Ideas that have served their purpose need to be eliminated.

V

vacation/resort/spa: <u>Physical</u>: You need a break from your daily routine to do something different and recharge yourself. You need to acknowledge the good work you've done and reward yourself. You need to lose weight, get some bodywork, and improve your diet. <u>Emotional</u>: You need to feel there is joy to be had in all things. You're being too dutiful or too escapist, feeling you must please others or rebelling against authority. <u>Mental-Spiritual</u>: You're examining how you lose energy and enthusiasm. You are focusing on how relaxing the present moment is, that resting in your true self is the best vacation of all.

vacuum: <u>Physical</u>: Vacuuming a room means you are cleansing your body of impurities. You are too over-whelmed and need to be empty and still, as though in a vacuum, to regather your energy. You're experienc-ing a void, waiting for the next phase of life to unfold. <u>Emotional</u>: You feel isolated, empty, depressed, or in panic. You need to clean up your act and rid yourself of negative emotions and habits. You feel sucked in by, or helpless to resist, someone's drama and neediness. <u>Mental-Spiritual</u>: You need to suspend your inner chat-ter, enter a deep meditative state, and experience what's beyond form and the mind. A higher part of you is calling you out and up to receive guidance.

valley: <u>Physical</u>: You've finished a cycle of creativity and you are preparing for a new one. You're exploring the highs and lows in life. Being in a valley means you're at a low point, which can be a peaceful, restful, regenerating paradise or intimidating as you look for a pathway out. You are focusing on female sexuality.

Emotional: You want to feel sheltered and protected. Entering a valley that connects to ideas of dying, or an end to something, brings up anxiety and sorrow. You feel gloomy and troubled about problems, losses, setbacks, or disappointments. You feel blind. Mental-Spiritual: You're focusing on being in your lifetime, versus being in spirit, and the containment of being physical. You need to relax and allow yourself to be taken care of by higher forces.

vampire: Physical: You are drained and exhausted by events or people. Others are taking from you without giving back, or you aren't noticing what you're receiving. Someone is invading your space or trying to make you do something against your better judgment. Emotional: You are acting like a victim, are giving your power away to charming seducers, or are dealing with people who feel victimized, or who are addicts. You're obsessing about something. You greedily want someone else's energy or success. You feel anxious about being sexually pressured, losing your virginity, or making an unhealthy commitment that traps you. You're facing dark, repressed emotions and desires. Mental-Spiritual: You're looking at the contrast between being civilized and noble and being ferocious and without morals.

vehicle: Physical: You're examining how you focus yourself in, and move through, different realms of consciousness. A car, bicycle, motorcycle, or train symbolizes your physical body, personality, or life. Elevators and stairs symbolize moving between realms. Driving the vehicle means you're controlling your journey and choosing your direction. Emotional: Boats or other water vehicles symbolize how you traverse the emotional realm. Being a rider in a vehicle means you've given your power to another and are being passive. <u>Mental-Spiritual</u>: Airplanes, hang gliders, rockets, or UFOs symbolize how you move through the mental and spiritual realms. Co-travelers mean you are part of a group consciousness where people share a similar path and life lesson. A stolen vehicle means you've lost your connection to a particular reality or focus and need to put attention on recreating it.

veil: *(see hood)*

vein: *(see artery)*

visitor/visitation: <u>Physical</u>: To have a visitor means that news or information is coming to you. You are focusing on beginning a new relationship. You are accessing parts of yourself that haven't become normal yet. <u>Emotional</u>: Being a visitor means you need to feel that you are welcome and belong. You want to feel like family with others and integrate the moods and feelings of different places into your makeup. <u>Mental-Spiritual</u>: You are connecting with nonphysical beings, like people who have died or spiritual guides. You are receiving an important message from higher dimensions. If you know the visitor, you are focusing on integrating the quality you associate with him or her into yourself. *(see stranger)*

voice/voices: <u>Physical</u>: You need to speak your truth. You are focusing on how you express yourself and what your message is. <u>Emotional</u>: Your subconscious is contacting you, bringing forth important feelings, or you feel fragmented, neurotic, and paranoid. You need to pay attention to inner needs. <u>Mental-Spiritual</u>:

Hearing a literal voice speaking to you means an important message is coming from your soul or spiritual guides. You might hear a single word, a phrase, an entire message, or even detailed instructions. If the voice belongs to someone you know, you may be receiving a telepathic call for help or important information you should act on in waking life.

voice mail: *(see telephone calls)*

volcano/lava: <u>Physical</u>: You're focusing on tension in yourself or in a relationship that has built to the breaking point. You need to relax and let off steam. You're experiencing pressure or an unavoidable crisis or challenge. <u>Emotional</u>: You feel extremely frustrated or angry, and need to be careful not to explode violently. You're dealing with someone who has an explosive temper. Lava means you need to express your pent-up feelings. <u>Mental-Spiritual</u>: Your mind is inspired and intensely creative, spewing forth ideas rapidly and in no particular order. New ideas from the depths of your soul and subconscious are surfacing.

vomit: <u>Physical</u>: You need to purge yourself of something that is toxic or unhealthy for you. There is a person or situation you can't stomach, that is not nurturing. <u>Emotional</u>: You need to reject or discard an aspect of your life that is revolting. You refuse to accept a situation, change, or relationship. <u>Mental-Spiritual</u>: You recognize and reject what is untrue or doesn't align with your life purpose.

vote: <u>Physical</u>: You need to speak your mind, express yourself authentically, and share yourself with others. Voting for an unpopular choice where others know your position means you need to stand up to judgment. <u>Emotional</u>: You are too passive and apathetic. You want to belong to and contribute to the functioning of a group. You need recognition, conviction, courage, and passion. <u>Mental-Spiritual</u>: You are too opinionated, or you need to examine issues open-mindedly, clarify your positions, and take a stand for what you believe. You are highlighting what you want in your life.

vow: <u>Physical</u>: You are focusing on keeping your word and following through. You need to make a commitment. <u>Emotional</u>: You're afraid of letting others down or being weak and unprincipled. <u>Mental-Spiritual</u>: You are examining your behavior and habits, and where you fall short of doing your best. You are realigning with your destiny and intending to live as your soul.

vulture: <u>Physical</u>: You are focusing on the approaching death of a part of your life, the need to eliminate dead or unwanted parts of your personality, or to recycle old aspects of yourself for new uses. Aggressive, opportunistic people are hanging around waiting to feed off your creations, and you must vigilantly chase them away. You need to be a hardy survivor. <u>Emotional</u>: You feel lonely, ugly, unloved, discriminated against, and misunderstood. You need to watch your tendency to be greedy or gluttonous. You feel you are getting the dregs and leftovers, scrounging for nourishment and recognition. You need to face something in your own underworld. <u>Mental-Spiritual</u>: You are disrespecting or judging others to feed your ego. You are receiving a warning about the death of someone, the failure of something, or a disaster.

W

waiter/waitress: <u>Physical</u>: You are focusing on catering to the demands of others. You need to notice the people who are helping and serving you. <u>Emotional</u>: You need to develop more gratitude, humility, patience, and tolerance. A surly, unconscious, inattentive waiter means you feel unsupported by friends or colleagues. You feel used and unappreciated. <u>Mental-Spiritual</u>: You need to focus on the true purpose of service, and how you receive as you give. You are overcoming your ego, practicing the Golden Rule.

wall: <u>Physical</u>: You are encountering obstacles, barriers, and boundaries to your progress. Jumping over or breaking down a wall means you can overcome difficulties and succeed. You need to stop, pay attention to your path, and possibly shift your direction. <u>Emotional</u>: Building a wall means you need more privacy and introspection, or you are protecting yourself from danger or from people you don't like. You are stubbornly refusing to move forward or express your feelings. <u>Mental-Spiritual</u>: A hole in a wall means you can see through a limited way of thinking, old habits, and resistance. You are becoming aware of the boundaries and transitions between possible realities. Walking through a wall means you can use your intuition, faith, and positive attitude to turn obstacles into opportunities.

wallet/purse: <u>Physical</u>: You are focusing on your personal identity, financial resources, and the things you consider necessary for survival in the world. <u>Emotional</u>: Losing a purse or wallet means you aren't paying attention to what's valuable, or you are too attached to security, definitions, and habits. <u>Mental-Spiritual</u>: Losing your wallet means you need to let go of an aspect of your identity and refocus on who you really are underneath.

wash: <u>Physical</u>: You're cleansing and purifying part of yourself. Washing your hands means you're releasing yourself from a relationship. Washing anything, a car, clothes, vegetables, or face, means you want that thing, and what it represents, to function optimally, like new. <u>Emotional</u>: You are tending to your ordinary world with kindness and respect. Trying to get a stain out means you feel guilt or shame. <u>Mental-Spiritual</u>: Washing yourself ritually, as in a river or fountain, means you're cleansing yourself of sin, inviting forgiveness.

watch: *(see clock)*

water: <u>Physical</u>: You need to cleanse yourself. You're focusing on sexuality and letting go. "Getting your feet wet" means you are willing to try something new. <u>Emotional</u>: You're focusing on emotions and the subconscious mind. Cloudy, murky water means emotional confusion. Floods, tidal waves, and turbulent water mean you feel overwhelmed, threatened, and chaotic, while drought indicates being out of touch with inner juiciness and feelings. Frozen or evaporating water indicates emotional paralysis or volatility. The power to control water means you are working on controlling emotional outbursts. <u>Mental-Spiritual</u>: Clean water means good sense and clarity. Smoothly flowing water means contentment and peace of mind. Diving into deep water means you're exploring unknown areas of the self. Wading in shallow water indicates a cautious attitude. Breathing underwater means you are open to the collective consciousness and intuitive awareness. Walking on water means you have control over emotions and doubt through faith in yourself and the divine.

weave: <u>Physical</u>: You are making something out of nothing. You are integrating diverse elements to produce beautiful and useful results. You are creating greater strength from the marrying of weaker elements. <u>Emotional</u>: You feel you are coming apart or unraveling. You need to be patient throughout a growth process or transition. You're becoming comfortable with diverse aspects of yourself. <u>Mental-Spiritual</u>: You are exploring ideas like the whole is greater than the sum of its parts, it's important to see the big picture, and complexity contains components that work together in harmony. You are piecing together information or an explanation.

wedding: <u>Physical</u>: You are thinking about marriage, or divorce. You're at a new beginning or transition. You are unifying or balancing two parts of yourself, like the anima and animus, the physical and spiritual, or the internal and external. <u>Emotional</u>: You are examining your anxiety about commitment and independence, loneliness and loss of self-expression. Being at a friend's wedding means you feel left out, left behind, or need to commit to something in your own life. <u>Mental-Spiritual</u>: You are giving yourself important data about how you connect with people and examining the meaning of ceremony. You are opening and expanding your heart. *(see marriage)*

weeds: <u>Physical</u>: You are crowded with clutter and distracted by activities that are not on purpose. You are hardy and can flourish anywhere. <u>Emotional</u>: You feel underappreciated, straggly, disordered, and ugly. You are neglecting part of yourself. Pulling weeds means you need to rid yourself of negativity, grudges, and relationships that have gone awry so you have space to grow. <u>Mental-Spiritual</u>: You are rooting out and clearing old ideas and negative thoughts from your mind. There are attitudes and beliefs that are interfering with your personal growth. You are finding beauty in the mundane.

well: <u>Physical</u>: You are digging down, seeking a source of energy and motivation deep within. <u>Emotional</u>: You are dealing with your deepest emotional patterns, and source of love. The well that never runs dry indicates your inner wealth is inexhaustible. A dry well means you feel exhausted. You need to offer nurturing to others and let people gather around you and see you as a blessing. <u>Mental-Spiritual</u>: You are accessing the deepest recesses of the collective consciousness, from which you are drawing up knowledge, wisdom, your divine nature, and unlimited resourcefulness.

west: <u>Physical</u>: You are focusing on the end of a cycle or phase, on the positive side of surrender, rest, silence, darkness, and death. It's time to stop, let go, pause a moment, or complete a project you've been involved with too long. You are concerned with finality. If something "goes west," it is destroyed or lost. <u>Emotional</u>: You're anxious about growing old, facing things you consider evil or bad, entering the unknown, or changing. You need to be fluid, adaptable, and able to "shape-shift" easily. <u>Mental-Spiritual</u>: You seek self-understanding through introversion, dreams, intuition, faith, and trust. You are focusing on reaching into other dimensions, contacting nonphysical beings and spirits of the dead. You are concerned with healing the earth. You point out truths by doing things in a contrary, humorous manner.

whale: *(see dolphin)*

wheel: <u>Physical</u>: You are looking at cycles of growth, the "wheel of life," or the completion of a phase or a project. Your daily routine is too repetitive; you need variety and spontaneity. A turning wheel means you are progressing steadily, or you're looking at the ups and downs of life. <u>Emotional</u>: You feel frustrated and anxious because you're caught in a repetitive cycle going nowhere. You need to be less serious and more "freewheeling." <u>Mental-Spiritual</u>: You are looking at karma, reincarnation, the wheel of rebirth, and the long-term evolution of the soul. Seeing "wheels within wheels" means you're contemplating something that cannot be understood superficially. You are focusing on parallels through the microcosm and macrocosm.

whip: <u>Physical</u>: You are contemplating being controlled or controlling something through threats, domination, or punishment. You need discipline and control in your life. You need to "crack the whip," "whip up some enthusiasm," and be more motivated to produce results. You are "whipped," or exhausted. <u>Emotional</u>: You're lashing out at others with hurtful remarks and accusations. You feel punished or attacked. You are dealing with issues of physical, sexual, or emotional abuse. You're focusing on issues of sexual submission and having to be obedient to others. <u>Mental-Spiritual</u>: You are making a point, critiquing something, or developing mental prowess; being "smart as a whip."

white: <u>Physical</u>: You are focusing on purity, perfection, goodness, innocence, simplicity, virginity, sterility, and cleanliness. You're beginning something. You feel complete and whole. You're stuck with something that cost a lot but has no useful purpose, like a white elephant. <u>Emotional</u>: Being "white as a sheet" means you feel frightened or are ill. You are protecting yourself by "telling a white lie" so you don't upset someone. <u>Mental-Spiritual</u>: You're attuning to spiritual light, the sacred, joy, transcendence, radiance, spiritual birth, enlightenment, ecstasy, faith, and the yang side of the divine.

window: <u>Physical</u>: You're focusing on your world view, your outlook on life, looking outside to external things, or inside to your inner self. You're looking at how much of the outer world you let in. The type of scene you see gives an indication of what's coming in your life, or what you expect. <u>Emotional</u>: Being outside looking in can mean you feel excluded from belonging, or you're in an introverted period. Curtains that are drawn indicate a refusal to see clearly because you are withdrawing. A broken window means greater vulnerability and contact with the world. <u>Mental-Spiritual</u>: Washing windows means you are clearing your perception and intuition. You need to pay attention to the moment and "a window of opportunity."

witch: <u>Physical</u>: You are focusing on something that might be an ill omen or superstition. You're looking at negative ideas about women. <u>Emotional</u>: You're dealing with a suppressed aspect of your feminine energy that you have judged negatively, which needs to be understood. You want more magic and ease. <u>Mental-Spiritual</u>: You're focusing on the destructive aspect of the subconscious. You're aware of "the witching hour" when the magical reality shifts back to the mundane. Since witches' original roles were as priestesses and representatives of inner wisdom, you're focusing on intuition and healing, and connecting to a deep understanding of the universal laws. *(see monster)*

wolf: <u>Physical</u>: You're focusing on healthy family values and loyalty. A ravenous part of yourself or a life situation is devouring your energy or creativity. Something threatening is at the door. You are being too much of a "lone wolf," and need more nurturing social activity. <u>Emotional</u>: An innocent part of you has been seduced. You are afraid of aggressive, lustful, male sexual energy. You are afraid of your own tendencies toward self-destruction, aggression, rage, or uncontrolled sexual desire. You've been "crying wolf," and no one will help you. <u>Mental-Spiritual</u>: You are learning about your instinctual wildness, intuition, the seasons of life and death, and the deep wisdom of group relations. You are connecting with a spiritual guide and protective companion on your life journey.

women: <u>Physical</u>: Any female figure represents your anima or the way you use and understand feminine energy. You need to express more, or less, receptivity, unconditional love, appreciation, and presence. <u>Emotional</u>: You are facing unresolved issues with your mother or female relatives. <u>Mental-Spiritual</u>: How the women are dressed provides a clue about the area of your life that needs more yin energy. You are focusing on intuition, empathy, faith, and inspiration.

worm: <u>Physical</u>: You're focusing on sneakiness, or something entering your life by covert, even cowardly, means. You need to be practical, down to earth, and humble. Something is decaying and on its way out of your life. You're focusing on male sexuality. <u>Emotional</u>: You feel low-down, dirty, and disgusting, or downtrodden and oppressed. You've felt weak and passive, but sense that it's time for "the worm to turn," for you to take control of your life. <u>Mental-Spiritual</u>: If you have a "worm's eye view," you know or understand a small, often lowly, part of a situation. You are creating pathways through fixed beliefs systems and a dense world view.

write: <u>Physical</u>: You are communicating to yourself about a situation in waking life. You are out of touch with a loved one and need to make contact. If "the writing is on the wall," it's evident that something is not going to succeed. <u>Emotional</u>: You are expressing or clarifying and defining your feelings and creativity. <u>Mental-Spiritual</u>: A deep part of you is sending you important guidance about life direction and personal growth. If someone else is writing, this shows an aspect of you that is seeking to express itself. *(see letter)*

X-rays/X-ray vision: <u>Physical</u>: You are focusing on the inner workings of your body, scanning for things that might be out of harmony. You're penetrating into the hidden problems in your current life situations. <u>Emotional</u>: You need to look more deeply at the cause of emotional upsets. If you are being X-rayed or viewed by someone with X-ray vision, you feel vulnerable and exposed, as though your secrets are being revealed to the public. You are worried that a deception will be discovered. It is advisable to stop defending yourself. <u>Mental-Spiritual</u>: You desire greater inner knowledge, to see past surface appearances to the true nature of things. You have penetrating insight into relationships, problem-solving, and diagnosis.

Y

yardstick: <u>Physical</u>: You are focusing on how well you're performing, comparing yourself against your own or other people's standards. <u>Emotional</u>: You feel anxiety about measuring up or being exactly right. <u>Mental-Spiritual</u>: You need to soften any rigidity or unyielding qualities in yourself. You are looking for a new way to understand yourself, wanting to dissolve the usual constraints society imposes.

yellow: <u>Physical</u>: You need energy, especially the vigor of muscle energy. You want to attract attention or pro-mote yourself. <u>Emotional</u>: You need to cheer yourself up and develop warmer feelings toward yourself and others. Yellow promotes happiness, spontaneity, humor, naturalness, and enthusiasm. You need to develop greater courage and decisiveness. <u>Mental-Spiritual</u>: You are actively and open-mindedly working with your intellect, creativity, imagination, memory, and communication.

yoga: <u>Physical</u>: You are focusing on developing self-discipline and physical precision in your performance, either in a physical practice, like athletics, or in your work. A particularly convoluted or difficult posture means you feel you must play an unnatural and uncomfortable role in waking life. <u>Emotional</u>: You're focusing on calmness and being centered. You need to feel the subtleties of your own emotions and how they affect your body. <u>Mental-Spiritual</u>: You are learning to control your mind and body, finding the balance and integration of the parts of yourself, and thus, harmony with the universe.

Z

zebra: <u>Physical</u>: You are focusing on how to camouflage yourself in an environment where you stand out too much because of polarized beliefs or actions. <u>Emotional</u>: You feel too exposed when out in the open. You feel too caught in conflict or struggle. A zebra, or any black and white animal, symbolizes the need for integration of the dark and light, good and evil. <u>Mental-Spiritual</u>: You are focusing on ideas of right and wrong, the attraction of opposites, or two distinctly different roles in yourself. You are seeking balance, unity, and harmony.

zipper: <u>Physical</u>: You are focusing on quick action, closure to a situation, or the need to be quiet, "zip your lip." A stuck zipper indicates a frustrating situation that must be untangled. <u>Emotional</u>: If clothes are unzipped, you are experiencing a loss of control or feeling of exposure in your life. <u>Mental-Spiritual</u>: You are focusing on ideas that are sexually exciting, or that connect two separate realms of thought. You are in a process of deconstructing ideas or creating new understanding.

zoo: <u>Physical</u>: You're involved in a situation that is chaotic and wild. You need to create more order and neatness in your life. <u>Emotional</u>: You feel a loss of freedom, that your talents are unnoticed, or that you are on display or being caged in an artificially tame world. <u>Mental-Spiritual</u>: You are looking at ways to find harmony among diverse people or are integrating unusual ideas.

Part III

The Part of Tens

The 5th Wave   By Rich Tennant

"I'm writing in my dream journal. Does it count
if the meaning of a dream is revealed to you
in another dream?"

In this part . . .

*p*art III provides a little "dream dessert." In these pages, you can find ten useful techniques for exploring dream messages and ten of the most common dreams and their meanings.

Chapter 6

Ten Techniques for Exploring Dream Messages

• •

*D*reams are little realities that are entirely fluid, intu-itive, and responsive to a change of thought or intent. This means you can play with their form to dis-cover insights, and not feel as locked in or helpless as you might in everyday life. You can expand the scope of a dream, change the action, bring in imaginary helpers, talk to an imaginary dream expert, or use a creative process to find hidden connections between symbols. In this chapter, you can explore ten helpful methods for finding the messages in your dreams.

Back Up and Extend a Dream

1. **Pick a dream with clear images, where you remember the beginning, middle, and end.** In your imagination, run through the dream. Familiarize yourself with the symbols, feelings, actions, and characters.

2. **Return to the beginning and instead of run-ning it as is a second time, imagine you're backing it up so you can see what happened**

just before the dream began. Make a note of the predream activity. Replay it from the new starting point to where it stopped before.

3. **Keep playing the dream past its normal end-point.** See what happens next. Use the new insights about causes and outcomes to help you find the deeper messages in your dream.

Add an Extra Character

1. **Pick any dream, but a frustrating or frightening one works especially well.** Review the beginning, middle, and end, remembering the feelings, symbols, and actions.

2. **Just at the point where you get frustrated or terrified, introduce a new character into the dream.** Let your imagination invent someone, and continue the dream with the intervention and help of the new person, entity, or animal. What happens next? How does the dream resolve?

3. **How does the new character represent a new part of you that might want to be activated?** What is the lesson your soul is trying to teach you?

Expand the Scope of the Dream Environment

1. **Enter your dream and review it from beginning to end.** Then go back to any point where

you are centered in a location, inside or outside. Slow the speed way down or freeze-frame the action. Now look around. What direction are you facing: east, south, west, or north? What's to the left, right, and behind you? Where's the light coming from? Are there other people nearby you didn't notice before? If you're inside, go outside. If you're outside and there's a house or vehicle, go in. Try zooming up in the air and see the lay of the land. What's just beyond the horizon?

2. **Notice what extra information you receive.** How does that data help you understand the dream process and message? You can repeat the process with other dream locations within the same dream and see how the expanded knowledge helps the pieces fit together.

Dialogue with Symbols or Dream Characters

1. **Create an imaginary dialogue with a dream character.** The conversation can be between you and the character, or between two characters. Have the characters ask each other questions. Why are you here? What's your complaint or biggest problem? What are you good at doing? How are you supposed to help me? How can I help you? What do you want to do next?

2. **Create an imaginary dialogue with a dream symbol.** Focus attention on a symbol, give your energy to it, and let it give its energy to

you. Enter and merge with the symbol, become it, then speak directly in first person about what you represent, what your expertise is, and why you appeared at this time. Describe how you feel and why. What do you need help with? What is your message?

Face Your Monsters and Take Your Power Back

1. **If you're being chased or threatened by a dream monster, wild animal, serial killer, science fiction character, or violent family member or ex-spouse, you can turn things around quickly.** Review the dream later in a meditation, moving to the point where the anxiety reaches its crescendo, and you feel the most helpless and panic-stricken. In the meditation, stop running or acting like a victim. Turn and face your pursuer. Pull out an imaginary weapon that is more powerful than your opponent. Ask: Why are you chasing me? What do you want from me? What do you need to tell me? See what the character says. If the scene wants to progress into a dialogue, let it. You might demand of it: Give me a present!

2. **Once the tension resolves and you find understanding, let the image of the "opponent" melt and dissolve.** As it does, the energy that was in it flows back into you and you become stronger, more confident, and full of yourself.

Make Quick Associations

1. **For each symbol, write a string of associated words, as fast as you can, without reading back over the list.** For instance, if the symbol were camera, you might write: lens, shutter, film, eye, click, blink, view, zoom, look, pictures, color, format.

2. **Then write a series of words or phrases that convey emotions or a feeling-state you associate with that symbol, such as, private view, enjoy, preserving a moment, being close to people and landscapes, magical images, loving details, perfect framing.**

3. **From the new associations and meanings, see what insights are freed from your subconscious, and what feels real and useful when connected to a process in your waking life.**

Redream and Change Your Dream's Outcome

1. **If you have a troubling dream (someone steals your car, you plant a garden and it dies, you flub a speech in front of a thousand people), you can go back later in a meditation and re-dream it.** Simply sit quietly and bring the dream to mind, review it, and reenter it. At the point where things start to go awry, shift the plot. The thief is about to hotwire your car and a loud squealing alarm goes off,

attracting the attention of neighbors or passersby, scaring the thief away. Your garden is planted, and just as it begins to wilt, you spray magic fairy dust over the whole thing, and it starts to glow with extra light. You are struggling with your speech and you see the Dalai Lama sitting in the front row, smiling and nodding encouragement, and you immediately relax and become eloquent and funny.

2. **After changing your dream so it flows to a new conclusion, which may surprise you, notice what you've been trying to show yourself about a real issue in your life and what you're capable of doing.**

Invite a Hero or Expert to Give You Insights

1. **Imagine yourself sitting casually at a sidewalk cafe.** Get the feeling that you'd really like to talk to an "expert" about what your dream means. Suddenly, someone slips from the crowd and sits down at your table. He or she says, "I'm sorry I'm late for our appointment. I got word you wanted to talk to me. I'm _____. How can I help you?"

2. **Notice his or her face, eyes, clothes, the energy of his body, the feel of his maturity, the light coming from him.** Explain your dream and let him tell you what the parts of the dream mean, what's going on inside you,

and what you need to do next. Allow the experience to unfold spontaneously. When it's finished, thank him, come back, and record what happened.

3. **Why did that particular person appear to you?** Is there a symbolic meaning? Does he or she have a quality you want to activate in yourself?

Write a Story, Fable, or Poem from a Dream

1. **Write a children's story or fable based on your dream.** This is especially fun to do with a child or a friend. Or, role-play your own inner five-year-old, or 100-year-old self, and alternate between yourself and your role. First tell your dream or a single dream scene. Then let the other person or your pretend self add a made-up scene. Then you add more. Keep going this way until it comes to a natural end. If you get stuck, ask yourself, What else could have happened at this point? The next day you might take the dream you had that night, add it to the end of the storyline, and continue the process. You might actually make a blank book by folding sheets of paper and stapling them together. Then write and illustrate the dream story, and finally, create a title for it.

2. **Every dream can be written as a poem.** You can excerpt powerful pieces of the dream and turn them into three-line haikus. Write a poem

around a list of words from your dream, or draw a picture of your dream. Then make lists of word pairs from the dream (red mountain, spiral cloud, rushing mud) and write a poem using those phrases tied together in a meaningful way. Your intuitive poetic voice often interprets the symbols naturally as you write. You might try writing your dreams in both narrative form and poetic form side by side in your dream diary.

Make a Dream Collage

1. **Cut up old magazines and save pictures of wild animals, cars, airplanes, monsters, flowers, trees, toys, dolls, dogs, cats, birds, fish, foods, kids doing different things, old people, adults in sunglasses, mountains, lakes, backyards, bedrooms, shoes, and sky.** Paste images that connect to your dream on a big sheet of paper, overlapping them or making connections between images, perhaps doing some pencil drawings of the dream alongside. You'll find the dream expands as you add related images and meanings. As the dream collage grows in complexity, tell yourself the new story that's taking shape.

2. **When you're finished, write the complete story from beginning to end on the back of the collage or in your dream diary.** What is the hidden message? What guidance do you receive from your inner voice?

There are 700 references to dreams in the Bible. The longest recorded dream is three hours and eight minutes. The tune for "Yesterday" came to Paul McCartney in a dream. He heard a classical string ensemble playing, and said: "I woke up with a lovely tune in my head." Golfer Jack Nicklaus found a new way to hold his golf club in a dream, which he credits with improving his golf game.

Chapter 7

Ten Common Dreams and Their Meanings

● ●

*Y*ou've probably experienced one of these ten common types of dreams in your life; they focus on themes universal to most of us. Under these dreams are emotions we all share that preoccupy us, but that we don't especially like to deal with consciously. By working with the inner messages in common dreams, you can maximize your confidence, creativity, and effectiveness in waking life.

My Teeth Are Falling Out!

It's especially popular now to have gleaming white, movie-star teeth, so if your teeth are dirty, diseased, disintegrating, or falling out in your dreams, you're probably worrying about how pleasing and attractive you are to others and to sexual and romantic partners. You may be afraid of getting old. Teeth also relate to self-expression and effective communication, so losing teeth can mean you're embarrassed about something you've said, or you're having trouble saying what you really mean. The real essence of teeth is their ability to bite through, to cut, tear, and grind. As human animals, you retain a vestige of snarling — showing teeth as a "stay back" warning — in our disarming smile. If your teeth fall out, you lose personal power and your ability to be assertive, decisive, and self-protective.

You might ask yourself: Where do I lack confidence or feel powerless? With whom do I feel self-conscious or insecure? How am I angry or frustrated? Where should I take action to "bite through" something, or chew something thoroughly so I understand it?

I'm Naked in Public!

You're going about your business and suddenly realize you're naked or in your underwear at work or at the grocery store. Exposure dreams bring to light the things you don't want others to know about you and places where you feel vulnerable. Suddenly everyone sees through you. Being naked in front of others also implies being caught off guard or being unprepared, uninformed, uneducated, or unpracticed.

Try asking yourself: What have I been hiding? Where do I feel like a phony? What's wrong with being seen for whom I *really* am? Where do I feel invisible? Can I tolerate, or even love, my imperfections? Who am I afraid will reject me? What am I telling myself I need to be prepared for — for my *own* sake?

A Monster Is Chasing Me!

You're running, trying to outpace or outwit your pursuer, and he/she/it's gaining on you! Suddenly your legs are paralyzed! Chase dreams often represent fears of facing up to something you've judged negatively, like your own rage, shame, or irresponsibility, for example. Or, you may feel threatened by someone or by a possible failure. If you become paralyzed, you probably need to stand still and meet your pursuer to receive an important message. Or, you may be experiencing the normal "paralysis" that occurs in the REM (rapid eye movement) sleep state.

Try asking yourself: What do I feel threatened by? What am I avoiding? Who have I given my power to? Where have I surrendered my right to "take up space"? Where do I feel helpless or unsupported? How do I deal with conflict?

I'm in My Childhood Home; It Has New Rooms!

Houses are symbols of the self, so returning to an old house means you are looking back at an old way of being, past habits, identities you've held, and outdated concepts you've been operating from. Perhaps you need to bring repressed memories to the surface to be healed. Trying to live in an old house that might be too small for you now, or seeing things that need repair, means you're becoming conscious of how much you've grown and what you're renovating in yourself. When your old house has new rooms, you've added new talents, experiences, people, and components to your life.

You might ask yourself: What parts of my house need refurbishing? Am I comfortable in this space? Which room is my favorite? What do the new rooms symbolize?

I'm Making Love with a Movie Star!

Sex dreams are often about merging several aspects of yourself together, or loving a part of yourself you've judged or rejected. Sex with a celebrity can mean you want more visibility, self-worth, and recognition, or you are activating qualities in yourself represented by the famous person. Sex with an authority figure like a professor, doctor, or boss, can show how it feels to have greater power and knowledge so you can be more effective in the world. Sex with a foreigner or someone of another race might mean you are integrating the character traits of that culture or racial consciousness into your personality. Sex with someone of your own gender may simply show you how to better accept and love yourself.

You might ask yourself: What quality or experience am I activating in myself? What do I admire about this lover that is a key to a new ability of mine?

I Lost My Wallet and Keys!

Dreams of loss point to areas where you are too attached to something; you are telling yourself, "Let go and see what comes next when you don't have it all locked down." Losing your wallet can indicate it's time to reexamine your identity. Losing your car may mean you need to look at your need for movement, freedom, and independence as you've defined it. Losing keys points to a fear of losing authority or access to an opportunity. Losing money can mean you're letting go of what's been valuable to you so you can revalue your core self.

Ask yourself: How have I outgrown ideas of who I am? Where do I need to let go and trust the unknown part of myself to provide for me? Where do I need to experience space and emptiness instead of clutter?

I'm Taking a Test and Didn't Study!

You have an exam and can't find the room, you are late, or haven't studied. You're in a play and forgot your lines. Performance anxiety dreams point to areas in your life where you feel judged by others or unprepared for a challenge. You fear if you don't do well, you'll be rejected and ridiculed. If the setting is academic, you probably need to pay attention to new knowledge or to a lesson that's part of your personal growth process. If it's a play or a keynote lecture, you may be ready to express yourself more fully, to be more articulate and confident in the world.

You might ask yourself: What new opportunity do I want but don't feel ready for? How could I feel adequately prepared? How do I feel I might let others down? Who has expectations of me and who am I afraid of not pleasing?

1 Found Money or Jewels!

Dreams about finding valuables operate on several levels. You may be awash in debt, fear that you'll never have enough, or that you'll lose what you have. You want to feel lucky, abundant, influential, and rich, so you try it out in your dreams. Under these worries often lurks a deeper fear — that you don't deserve to be loved, supported, or cared for. Your deep self is showing you what it feels like to be blessed. Gaining money or valuables really means you're gaining in emotional well-being, confidence, and power. You may be preparing to increase your creativity and abundance level, to feel that having more is normal.

Try asking yourself: Who gave me the money or valuables? What or who does this person represent to me? Where did I find the valuables and what do the place and kind of item represent to me? What's my attitude as I receive: greedy, worried, egocentric? How do I act after I've received: powerful, generous, relaxed?

I'm Having Surgery on My Eyes, Brain, Heart, or . . . !

Hospital and surgery dreams are often symbolic of a fundamental change you're making in the way you live, the way you work with energy and run your body, and how you construct your identity and world view. On rare occasions, they are warnings about actual health problems, or they indicate you're exhausted and need to rest and be cared for so you can shift to a new phase of self-expression. You may need to get something out of your system, change your habits, move to a new location, or release a person from your life. You may need to open yourself to emotional healing and new experiences. If you experience anesthesia in the dream, you're probably avoiding your feelings, worries, or responsibilities. If you're bleeding profusely in the dream or feel actual pain, you are telling your conscious mind that part of you feels out of control, severely drained, and mortally wounded by trauma or cruelty.

Try asking yourself: What or who has caused me to feel so wounded and helpless? Why am I focusing on this particular area of my body? What are the surgeons doing to help me? Is there a change occurring in my subtle energy body? After I heal, what will I be capable of doing? How is the pattern of my awareness changing?

My Car Won't Stop or Go!

"Difficulty with your vehicle" dreams usually arise when events in your waking life seem out of control, you feel powerless over something, or are afraid you're about to fail or "crash." Your car is rolling backwards, the brakes won't work, you're trying to steer from the back seat, the tires are flat, the ignition doesn't catch. Vehicles are symbols for the way you move through experiences in your life. Cars, motorcycles, bicycles, buses, or trains represent physical experience and your body; boats signify emotional experience; planes connect you to mental experience; and rockets and UFOs represent spiritual levels.

Once you see what level of yourself you're focusing on, determine whether you are the driver or passenger. This shows how you feel about being able to direct your own life. Driving from the back seat means you need to step up and be more responsible. Someone else driving means you've given your authority away. Next, look at how the vehicle is functioning. Problems indicate problems you may have in real life. The steering or brakes don't work: you're going too fast and are about to make a big mistake. The tires on the right side are flat: you're afraid to move forward and take new actions. The starter won't work: you need to renew your motivation and passion.

Try asking yourself: In what area do I feel disabled or powerless? Who did I give power to? How am I out of control? What in my life needs to work properly? What can I do to move freely?

Appendix

Dream Diary Writing Prompts

• •

*A*s an extension of your dream diary practice, I want to give you some additional writing ideas to prompt informative, insightful responses from your deeper self. Asking the right questions can be very powerful, especially if you remain neutral and receptive and allow your intuitive voice to answer spontaneously. The responses you receive can open and refine your dreamwork process and intuition.

Motivating Yourself

1. **Start with the following phrases and write several paragraphs on each until you feel finished.** You might want to repeat the phrase several times as you write to maintain a fresh connection with your source.

    If I could remember what I do in my dreams, I'd . . .

    If I knew my dream activities were real, it would change my experience of myself because . . .

> If I knew I could try anything in my dreams and not get hurt, it would encourage me to . . .

2. **Write from your body's point of view, in first person (starting with "I . . ."), about why you're not remembering your dreams as well as you might.** What are your body's recommendations for increasing your dream life?

3. **Answer the following statements, repeating each one ten times:**

> If I could know anything in my dreams, I'd like to know . . .

> If I could go anywhere in my dreams, I'd like to visit . . .

> If I could meet anyone in my dreams, I'd like to get to know . . .

> If I could create or invent anything in my dreams I'd like to create . . .

> If I could avoid dreaming about a particular subject, it would be . . .

4. **On a scale from 1 to 10, with 10 being the highest or best, rate the following abilities:**

> Your ability to be consistently enthusiastic

> Your ability to be calm and centered

> Your stress and anxiety level

> Your level of depression or apathy

> Your energy level in the early morning,
> the late morning, the early afternoon, the
> late afternoon, the early evening, the late
> evening

Afterward, write about how these factors
affect your attitude about dreams and your
ability to dream.

5. **Write about your specific dream goals for the
   week.** As you write, notice which one or two
   appeal to you the most.

6. **Write about your "innocent expectations"
   in life.** What do you assume will come to you
   effortlessly? What do you expect you will
   never attain, and what do you expect to be
   difficult? How might these expectations affect
   your dream life?

7. **Describe your ideal bedroom in detail.** What
   would you do in your ideal bedroom? How
   would it feel to dream there?

Remembering Your Dreams

1. **Write about the animals you consider to be
   your allies, especially those you could imagine helping you remember your dreams.**
   What is each animal's specialty and how would
   each animal guide you?

2. **Describe in detail a dream recall ritual that
   comes to you from your inner self; one that
   will work specifically for you.**

3. **Meditate for ten minutes and write about the process you experience.** The process could be anything and different each time you do it. How did it feel to your body? What happened to your emotions? What images did you notice? How long could you maintain it? How did you feel afterward? Could you recall any fleeting dream images?

4. **Pick three well-known people or characters from books, from any time in history, who you think could help you with your dreams.** Write about what each person would do for you and how they'd do it.

Energizing Your Dream Diary

1. **Describe a collage of images you might assemble to decorate the cover of your dream diary.** What goes next to what?

2. **List ten reasons why you can't possibly do a daily writing practice — then list ten ways you could.**

3. **Write a paragraph completing each of the following:**

   If I were Picasso, my dream journal would be filled with dreams about and would look like . . .

   If I were Mother Teresa, my dream journal would be filled with dreams about and would look like . . .

If I were George Burns, my dream journal would be filled with dreams about and would look like . . .

If I were Amelia Earhardt, my dream journal would be filled with dreams about and would look like . . .

Enhancing Your 24-hour Awareness

1. **Write about your process of falling asleep.** Describe the bodily sensations you experience. Do you have sleep disturbances during the night? What happens to your body then? Describe your experience of waking up and how you could refine the process.

2. **Write a pre-sleep prayer asking for help remembering and recording your dreams and aligning with your own higher dimensions, your soul, and the divine.** Then write a blessing to say after your prayer, one that addresses your desire to help those you love, or people who are in need in the world.

3. **If I were fully conscious 24 hours a day, I'd feel capable of . . .** (repeat ten times)

4. **Write an imaginary account of your journey into dreamland.** Pretend that you can remember every detail of what you're doing from the moment you close your eyes until you open them again. Don't allow any blank spots.

5. **Write about how some of the themes from your daily life may have carried over into your dreams.** Look for parallel themes, repeating symbols.

6. **Write about how some of the themes from your dreams may have carried over and affected what you subsequently did in your daily life.**

7. **Write about what you observed by being mindful of a mundane task.**

8. **Write about why you forgot to pay attention to something.** What are your justifications? What do you lose by skimming across the surface?

9. **Write about a time when activity in another dimension (such as, someone's death) interrupted your ability to concentrate while you were awake.**

10. **Notice the times today or recently that you "left your body" and blanked out.** Write about what triggered you to leave.

Sorting through Love and Fear

1. **Make notes next to all the dreams you've remembered this week.** How many are primarily love-based? How many primarily fear-based?

2. **Using stream of consciousness — writing whatever comes into your mind — make up**

three superconscious or love-based dreams, writing nonstop without rereading. Take five minutes to do each.

3. **Using stream of consciousness, make up three subconscious or fear-based dreams, writing nonstop without rereading.** Take five minutes to do each.

4. **Make a list of the subconscious and superconscious symbols and actions in your dreams from the past week.** What might each signify? Write about how each might relate to your daily life.

5. **Write about what you label this week as "good," desirable, or pleasing — write about what you label this week as "bad," undesirable, or upsetting.** Why do you hold these judgments?

6. **Pick a "bad" dream, think back through your life to earlier similar episodes, and write about as many as you can, and then pick a "good" dream, think back through your life to earlier similar episodes, and write about as many as you can.**

7. **Transform a nightmare into a useful dream and write about what you needed to do to shift the outcome and the insights that came as a result.**

8. **Looking back at your dreams and waking experiences for the past few weeks, write about what your soul is trying to do to help you.**

9. **List five "shoulds" that affect**

   The way you act with other people.

   How you progress in life and attain success.

   How you view yourself.

   Write about the negative consequences that your subconscious thinks underlie each of your "shoulds." For example: I should be quiet. If I'm too loud, people will think I'm selfish and reject me.

Programming Your Dreams

1. **Make a list of five problems you'd like to solve, or questions you'd like insight about.** Pick the most important one and program a dream to help you with it. Write about the response you get. If you don't receive a dream, make one up with stream of consciousness writing.

2. **Loosen your "question-answer" imagination by pretending to be your body giving you advice.** Write spontaneously about:

   If I were my body, giving me a dream about how to heal my (backache, carpal tunnel syndrome, insomnia, and so on), I'd project the following images . . .

   If I were my body, giving me a dream about what I want to eat and don't want to eat, I'd project the following images . . .

If I were my body, giving me a dream about how to improve my energy level and regulate the flow of my energy, I'd project the following scenarios . . .

3. **Write out a detailed description of how you see yourself optimally expressing a new skill, and program a dream to practice the skill.**

4. **Imagine you're a famous (painter, sculptor, dancer, architect, musician) with no creative blocks, and write a stream of consciousness dream sequence involving your creative genius as if you are them.** What do you learn about the creative process?

Interpreting Waking Dreams

1. **Make a list of ten images from daily life that stand out to you.** What might each of them mean if they occurred in a dream?

2. **Make a list of the signs or waking dreams you notice for one week, and write about the underlying themes and the connecting threads.** Now relate those themes to the themes you notice in your sleep dreams for the same period of time.

3. **Make a list of the subtle signs or signals you notice in one day, and write about the underlying messages.**

4. **Write several paragraphs describing a time your body acted directly from instinct and led you to discover something interesting.**

5. **Write several paragraphs about a time a sign or waking dream connected meaningfully to your future.**

6. **Write about how you are either ahead of yourself (in the future) or running behind (in the past).** What prompts you to go forward or backward in time? Write about what you might be avoiding, the seeming benefits of being elsewhere, and what happens when you bring your entire awareness into the present moment.

7. **Write several paragraphs about your recent experiences of synchronicity.** What were you bringing to your attention?

8. **Try to catch as many of your daydreams, fantasies, preoccupations, and flashes of insight today as possible, and record them in your diary, writing about what conversation is going on inside yourself under the surface.**

Interpreting Sleep Dreams

1. **Scan through your dreams and make a list of scenes where you experienced fear, worry, or anxiety, and then list scenes where you felt uplifted, excited, or inspired.** Write in first person as your soul about each scene, such as, "I caused myself to experience this so that . . ."

2. **Pick a dream, center yourself, and ask your body to write about what it knows about the core purpose of the dream.** Let yourself write in a stream of consciousness, without editing or rereading. Begin by writing: The core

purpose of this dream is to show myself . . . . I chose the symbol of the <blank> because to me it represents <blank>. Let yourself write, word by word, until you feel complete.

3. **Examine your recent dreams and notice their structure.** Have you dreamed predominantly in fragments? Have they been epic movies? Were they composed of two, three, or four scenes? Write about why you like the style of your dreams. What does one powerful fragment give you that a longer dream might not? Why does your subconscious like to have a beginning, middle, and end?

4. **Write about what one of your dreams means, as though you are (Sigmund Freud, Carl Jung, Buddha, Jesus, your grandmother, your inner five year old, whoever).**

5. **Pick a dream, go back through it in your imagination and while you're in it, look to the left, to the right, look behind you, and write about what you see.**

6. **Pick a dream where you woke before the action was complete, or where an action taken by a character was ineffectual, and write about why your subconscious caused the flow to be interrupted.**

7. **Review your dreams and make a list of all the statements, directives, specific questions, or literal words or phrases you saw or heard in the dreams.** As you see them now, grouped together, out of context, write about the impressions you have about what you're really telling yourself.

8. **Examine your recent dreams for puns, exaggerations, and opposite meanings, and write about the hidden meanings you find.**

9. **Go through your dream diary and pick three dreams, and then write your opinions and judgments about what occurs in each.** See how those statements show you about your deeper self.

Working with Symbols

1. **Make a list of the symbols in your dreams from the past week, and write about how each might relate to your physical and emotional life right now.**

2. **List five symbols from your dreams this week.** Write out the vertical path of their essential meaning; then the horizontal path of their associative meanings.

3. **Pick five colors, other than the seven standard rainbow colors (pick, for example, turquoise, chartreuse, olive green), and enter the experience of what each one represents.** Write about your body's primal responses. What emotions do you feel? What impressions do you receive? What happens to your mental clarity with each? What does each color "know about"?

4. **If the numbers of your home address appeared on a house in your dream, what would they mean?** Write about the qualities

your home is activating in you based on the archetypal meanings of the numerals.

5. **List the people in your nuclear family, including grandparents, aunts and uncles, and cousins.** For each one, decide: What color would symbolize them? What kind of food would symbolize them? What other odd symbol pops to mind for each?

6. **Draw a symbol that represents**

   The essence of your creativity.

   Your future success.

   Your personal truth.

   Your current health.

   Something from your shadow self.

7. **Write a paragraph about what your full name means.** What characteristics, sensations, and emotions does it elicit? What impressions might it give others?

8. **Pick three to five symbols from one dream and write directly as each one, then write directly about their interrelationships with each other.**

9. **Pick three dream fragments and write out an interview with your dream self about each one.**

10. **Pay attention to the cliches and puns you hear this week, and write them in your diary, exploring the underlying meaning of each.**

Empowering Your "Life Dream"

1. **Pick three dreams from your diary and write about what has happened to you since you dreamed each one, placing special emphasis on insights, ideas, experiences, and even other dreams that tie in thematically.** How has your understanding of the dream meaning deepened over time?

2. **Pick three dreams and determine the message, and then decide what actions you are going to take to integrate the dream's advice — then, act!** Write about what happens.

3. **Go through your dream diary with an eye to finding the life lessons peppered through your recent dreams.** Make a list of the themes and specific issues you're working on.

4. **Examine your dreams for the personality traits of the various dream characters.** If each trait is something you might want to activate or balance within yourself, how would doing this help you learn a life lesson?

5. **Make up a life-work vision for yourself that has the elements of a mission or a calling.** Totally blue-sky it and don't listen to your inner skeptic. How much do you think you're capable of doing?

6. **Examine your dreams to see what they are telling you about your life dream.** Have they been indicating a new direction, or new goals?

7. **Scan through your diary and write about the types of decision-making dreams you've had.** How have they given you direction, and about what issues?

8. **Write about your life dream as extensively as you can.** Then write about your desires and things you want to do after you've felt the reality of your life dream. List the actions you could take to bring that reality closer to you physically.

9. **Look through your dream diary and make a list of ten dream characters you had relationships with.** For each, write about what your dream self was showing you concerning how to relate more successfully.

10. **List ten people or animals you have relationships with in your daily life.** Then write about what character traits each represents to you and why it's important to you to develop or fully understand these traits.

Improving Relationships

1. **Think of one of your friends who seems to be troubled or in need of help right now.** Ask for a dream to shed light on their problem, and to show you how you might counsel them. Incubate a dream and when you receive one that seems like the answer to your request, call your friend and tell them about it. See if together, the two of you can interpret it.

2. **Finish the following sentences with as many answers as you can:**

   If I could know anything about my relationship with <blank>, I'd like to understand . . .

   If I could help <blank>, the most appropriate thing to do or say would be . . .

   If I could find true forgiveness for <blank>I'd need to let go of/understand . . .

   If I could begin a new relationship with someone, I'd like them to have these qualities . . .

3. **Go through your dream diary and list the romance or sex dreams you've had.** What, besides wishful thinking, might have been the purpose of these dreams?

4. **Write several paragraphs about the taboos you've broken in your dreams.** How did it feel? What did you learn? Why did your dream self want to open that particular area? Did you receive increased energy as a result?

5. **Write about the times you've experienced telepathy, in ordinary reality and in dreams, with someone else.** How did it feel? How did the communication occur? Was it in a visitation from someone far away, or on the other side?

Enhancing Healing

1. **Scan through your dream diary, noting any dreams that might be about your health**

or body. Write about each: If this were a forecasting dream, what would my dream self be trying to tell me?

2. **Scan through your dream diary, noting any dreams that might be about your health or body.** Write about each: If this were a therapeutic or healing dream, what would my dream self be trying to tell me?

3. **Write about three possible scenarios that would put you in a state of deep peacefulness.** Write about the sensory detail, how your body responds to being there, and how you would use each setting for maximum benefit.

4. **Make up three dream scenarios where you are healed of some problem you currently have — mental, emotional, energetic, or physical.** How does it happen? Who helps you? Where are you when it happens? What advice do your helpers have for you?

5. **Write out three dream scenarios depicting yourself in optimum health.** How do you look? What are you doing? How are you interacting with others? How do you remain healthy?

6. **Let yourself fantasize and write about how you would help heal a friend, relative, or even a public figure who suffers from an injury or illness.** Imagine that anything is possible, and you can use any technique that comes to mind.

7. **Examine your dreams and write about symbols and imagery pertaining to possible imbalances in your system, illnesses, accidents,**

parts of the body, or problems other people might be having. Are you dreaming about your own health, or the health of another? Is it literal or symbolic?

Index

USINESS, CAREERS & ERSONAL FINANCE

Fundraising DUMMIES
0-7645-9847-3

Investing DUMMIES
0-7645-2431-3

Also available:
- Business Plans Kit For Dummies 0-7645-9794-9
- Economics For Dummies 0-7645-5726-2
- Grant Writing For Dummies 0-7645-8416-2
- Home Buying For Dummies 0-7645-5331-3
- Managing For Dummies 0-7645-1771-6
- Marketing For Dummies 0-7645-5600-2

- Personal Finance For Dummies 0-7645-2590-5*
- Resumes For Dummies 0-7645-5471-9
- Selling For Dummies 0-7645-5363-1
- Six Sigma For Dummies 0-7645-6798-5
- Small Business Kit For Dummies 0-7645-5984-2
- Starting an eBay Business For Dummies 0-7645-6924-4
- Your Dream Career For Dummies 0-7645-9795-7

OME & BUSINESS COMPUTER ASICS

Laptops DUMMIES
0-470-05432-8

Windows Vista DUMMIES
0-471-75421-8

Also available:
- Cleaning Windows Vista For Dummies 0-471-78293-9
- Excel 2007 For Dummies 0-470-03737-7
- Mac OS X Tiger For Dummies 0-7645-7675-5
- MacBook For Dummies 0-470-04859-X
- Macs For Dummies 0-470-04849-2
- Office 2007 For Dummies 0-470-00923-3

- Outlook 2007 For Dummies 0-470-03830-6
- PCs For Dummies 0-7645-8958-X
- Salesforce.com For Dummies 0-470-04893-X
- Upgrading & Fixing Laptops For Dummies 0-7645-8959-8
- Word 2007 For Dummies 0-470-03658-3
- Quicken 2007 For Dummies 0-470-04600-7

OOD, HOME, GARDEN, HOBBIES, MUSIC & PETS

Chess DUMMIES
0-7645-8404-9

Guitar DUMMIES
0-7645-9904-6

Also available:
- Candy Making For Dummies 0-7645-9734-5
- Card Games For Dummies 0-7645-9910-0
- Crocheting For Dummies 0-7645-4151-X
- Dog Training For Dummies 0-7645-8418-9
- Healthy Carb Cookbook For Dummies 0-7645-8476-6

- Home Maintenance For Dummies 0-7645-5215-5
- Horses For Dummies 0-7645-9797-3
- Jewelry Making & Beading For Dummies 0-7645-2571-9
- Orchids For Dummies 0-7645-6759-4
- Puppies For Dummies 0-7645-5255-4
- Rock Guitar For Dummies 0-7645-5356-9
- Sewing For Dummies 0-7645-6847-7
- Singing For Dummies 0-7645-2475-5

NTERNET & DIGITAL MEDIA

eBay DUMMIES
0-470-04529-9

iPod & iTunes DUMMIES
0-470-04894-8

Also available:
- Blogging For Dummies 0-471-77084-1
- Digital Photography For Dummies 0-7645-9802-3
- Digital Photography All-in-One Desk Reference For Dummies 0-470-03743-1
- Digital SLR Cameras and Photography For Dummies 0-7645-9803-1
- eBay Business All-in-One Desk Reference For Dummies 0-7645-8438-3

- HDTV For Dummies 0-470-09673-X
- Home Entertainment PCs For Dummies 0-470-05523-5
- MySpace For Dummies 0-470-09529-6
- Search Engine Optimization For Dummies 0-471-97998-8
- Skype For Dummies 0-470-04891-3
- The Internet For Dummies 0-7645-8996-2
- Wiring Your Digital Home For Dummies 0-471-91830-X

WILEY

SPORTS, FITNESS, PARENTING, RELIGION & SPIRITUALITY

0-471-76871-5   0-7645-7841-3

Also available:
- Catholicism For Dummies 0-7645-5391-7
- Exercise Balls For Dummies 0-7645-5623-1
- Fitness For Dummies 0-7645-7851-0
- Football For Dummies 0-7645-3936-1
- Judaism For Dummies 0-7645-5299-6
- Potty Training For Dummies 0-7645-5417-4

- Buddhism For Dummies 0-7645-5359-3
- Pregnancy For Dummies 0-7645-4483-7 †
- Ten Minute Tone-Ups For Dummies 0-7645-7207-5
- NASCAR For Dummies 0-7645-768
- Religion For Dummies 0-7645-526
- Soccer For Dummies 0-7645-5229-
- Women in the Bible For Dummies 0-7645-8475-8

TRAVEL

0-7645-7749-2   0-7645-6945-7

Also available:
- Alaska For Dummies 0-7645-7746-8
- Cruise Vacations For Dummies 0-7645-6941-4
- England For Dummies 0-7645-4276-1
- Europe For Dummies 0-7645-7529-5
- Germany For Dummies 0-7645-7823-5
- Hawaii For Dummies 0-7645-7402-7

- Italy For Dummies 0-7645-7386-1
- Las Vegas For Dummies 0-7645-7382-9
- London For Dummies 0-7645-4277
- Paris For Dummies 0-7645-7630-5
- RV Vacations For Dummies 0-7645-4442-X
- Walt Disney World & Orlando For Dummies 0-7645-9660-8

GRAPHICS, DESIGN & WEB DEVELOPMENT

0-7645-8815-X   0-7645-9571-7

Also available:
- 3D Game Animation For Dummies 0-7645-8789-7
- AutoCAD 2006 For Dummies 0-7645-8925-3
- Building a Web Site For Dummies 0-7645-7144-3
- Creating Web Pages For Dummies 0-470-08030-2
- Creating Web Pages All-in-One Desk Reference For Dummies 0-7645-4345-8
- Dreamweaver 8 For Dummies 0-7645-9649-7

- InDesign CS2 For Dummies 0-7645-9572-5
- Macromedia Flash 8 For Dummies 0-7645-9691-8
- Photoshop CS2 and Digital Photography For Dummies 0-7645-9580-6
- Photoshop Elements 4 For Dummies 0-471-77483-9
- Syndicating Web Sites with RSS Feeds For Dummies 0-7645-8848-6
- Yahoo! SiteBuilder For Dummies 0-7645-9800-7

NETWORKING, SECURITY, PROGRAMMING & DATABASES

0-7645-7728-X   0-471-74940-0

Also available:
- Access 2007 For Dummies 0-470-04612-0
- ASP.NET 2 For Dummies 0-7645-7907-X
- C# 2005 For Dummies 0-7645-9704-3
- Hacking For Dummies 0-470-05235-X
- Hacking Wireless Networks For Dummies 0-7645-9730-2
- Java For Dummies 0-470-08716-1

- Microsoft SQL Server 2005 For Dummies 0-7645-7755-7
- Networking All-in-One Desk Reference For Dummies 0-7645-9939-9
- Preventing Identity Theft For Dummies 0-7645-7336-5
- Telecom For Dummies 0-471-77085-X
- Visual Studio 2005 All-in-One Desk Reference For Dummies 0-7645-9775-2
- XML For Dummies 0-7645-8845-1